"Happy in the
Service of the Lord"

"Happy in the Service of the Lord"

African-American Sacred Vocal Harmony Quartets in Memphis

Second Edition

Kip Lornell

The University of Tennessee Press / Knoxville

Second Edition.
Originally published in 1988 by the University of Illinois Press.

The paper in this book meets the minimum requirements of the American
National Standard for Permanence of Paper for Printed Library Materials.
∞ The binding materials have been chosen for strength and durability.

Library of Congress Cataloging-in-Publication Data

Lornell, Kip, 1953–
    Happy in the service of the Lord: African-American sacred vocal
harmony quartets in Memphis / Kip Lornell. — 2nd ed.
        p.   cm.
    Includes bibliographical references and index.
    ISBN 0-87049-877-0 (pbk.: alk. paper)
    1. Gospel music—Tennessee—Memphis—History and criticism.
I. Title.
ML3187.L67   1995
782.25'4'08996073076819—dc20   94-18735
                                                              CIP
                                                              MN

This book is dedicated to Kim & Cady, aka Babe 1 and Babe A

Contents

Preface to the Second Edition   ix

Acknowledgments   xix

Chapter 1. *"One Hundred Years of Singing in Harmony"*   1

Chapter 2. *"We Are the Spirit of Memphis"*   42

Chapter 3. *"I've Got on My Traveling Shoes"*   78

Chapter 4. *"A Family of Singers"*   109

Chapter 5. *"The Forces That Shape Spiritual Quartet Singing"*   134

Chapter 6. *"On Records and over the Airwaves"*   166

Finale: *"Blessed Are the Dead"*   188

Appendix I. *Memphis Quartet Listing*   201

Appendix II. *Jethroe Bledsoe's 1952 Travel Diary for the Spirit of Memphis*   203

Comprehensive Memphis Gospel Quartet Audiography   205

Selected Gospel Quartet Audiography   227

Sources and Resources   231

Interviews   235

Bibliography   237

Index   245

Preface to the Second Edition

I completed work on the first edition of this book, *"Happy in the Service of the Lord": Afro-American Gospel Quartets in Memphis,* during the fall of 1987. Based on my doctoral dissertation, it was the first book to examine the development and importance of black American gospel quartet singing. Specifically, I described the musical culture of black gospel quartets in Memphis, Tennessee, from the late 1920s through the early 1980s. My intent, both then and now, has been to place this important and influential genre of African-American music within its historical and cultural framework—an approach that could be called "the study of musical culture."

The great majority of the information and basic data contained in *"Happy in the Service of the Lord"* comes from my fieldwork and research in Memphis over a four-year period beginning in 1979. In addition to numerous informal conversations and formal interviews, I sometimes observed quartet singing in performance at local churches. More often I attended quartet rehearsals, which proved to be more interesting and rewarding than the actual programs themselves. When the singers got together in their homes, they often remembered a story or some long-forgotten incident, and I was able to ask specific questions about aesthetics or how a particular song was arranged.

As I gradually became more immersed in this special world, the complexities of this musical genre became apparent. Tracing group histories and their myriad changes in personnel proved particularly challenging and required great care and patience. Simply dealing with dozens of individuals, many of whom moved within very constricted and intertwined circles, provided another interesting puzzle as I learned who was still speaking with whom, why certain people changed group alliances so often, or how specific people rose to positions of prominence within this tightly knit community. I also had to untangle not only the threads of years of personal relationships but also the language of the quartet culture. What, for example, was a "trainer" and how did he work with singers? For that matter, what did "unions" have to do with this music?

This study represents a multifaceted account of religious musical expression in a city that is world renowned for its blues and soul music. African-American music in Memphis is most often equated with Frank Stokes, Booker T. and the MGs, Will Shade, Rufus Thomas, Sam and Dave, B. B. King, or Al Green. However, gospel quartet singers have created yet another vital form of black vernacular music in Memphis—one with its own unique musical heritage, spatial patterns, aesthetics, and history. Perhaps more than any of the other musical communities with which I have worked, quartet singers in Memphis integrate their music into everyday life; indeed, many of them try to live the life about which they sing. *"Happy in the Service of the Lord": Afro-American Gospel Quartets in Memphis* paid them a small tribute, which they earned many times over and so richly deserve.

Exactly six years after completing the first edition of this book the brightly hued leaves are slowly turning brown, the hours of bright daylight continue to diminish, our baby Cady is standing up on her own, and I am once again at work on this topic. Its present title, *"Happy in the Service of the Lord": African-American Sacred Vocal Harmony Quartets in Memphis,* underscores the fact that this is not the same book published by the University of Illinois Press, but a true second edition. And I am heartened to note that a few positive strides forward have occurred in black American gospel quartet research since *"Happy in the Service of the Lord": Afro-American Gospel Quartets in Memphis* first appeared in 1988. Its "Finale" suggested numerous topics worthy of investigation, and they remain largely untouched. Thankfully, a handful of scholars have stepped forth in answer to this call—unfortunately their efforts remain gen-

erally unavailable in the form of dissertations or other lengthy unpublished studies of quartets.

Doug Seroff, for example, has nearly completed his book-length
study of the Fisk University Jubilee Singers, a fascinating topic so
complex and complicated that his lengthy manuscript covers only
their first thirty or so years! Already the need looms large for a volume on this group's considerable twentieth-century activities. Lynn
Abbott's careful and insightful article—"'Play That Barber Shop
Chord': A Case for the African-American Origin of Barbershop Harmony" appeared in the fall 1992 issue of *American Music;* his book
about the New Orleans quartet scene, which is the product of more
than ten years of research, remains in draft form. However, the manuscript is tantalizingly close to being completed, and Abbott has se-
cured a contract with the Smithsonian Institution Press. Ray Funk
continues his research on quartets, which usually appears in the
form of liner notes and other brief essays. Most recently he has been
looking at the recorded performances of compositions written by
W. Herbert Brewster and Lucie Campbell—two Memphians who
play an important role in this book.

Three other academic studies of black American sacred quartets
followed my own efforts by about four years. In 1987 Ray Allen
completed a thorough examination of quartets in New York City
and received his Ph.D. from the University of Pennsylvania. Another study of quartet singing in Louisiana—Joyce Jackson's solid
dissertation from Indiana University—examines the cultural and
musical nature of groups in Baton Rouge, Louisiana. Samuel
Buchannan's rather hasty and derivative overview of the history of
quartets focuses upon the Norfolk Jubilee Quartet, the Golden
Gate Quartet, Mitchell's Christian Singers, and the Selah Jubilee
Singers, and forms the core of his doctoral research at New York
University. One hopes that other students are waiting in the wings,
inspired by the good works of those who preceded them and the
doors they cracked open.

More good news comes from discographers, who have been hard
at work on updating our factual knowledge of the recording end of
black gospel music. Many group discographies have appeared in
Blues & Rhythm: The Gospel Truth and other specialized magazines. But except for updates and corrections, two essential books
have superseded these more ephemeral publications. Cedrick

Hayes and Bob Laughton's long-awaited postwar gospel discography, which circulated on computer disks for several years in anticipation of its hard-copy publication, finally saw the light of day late in 1992 as *Gospel Records, 1943-1969: A Black Music Discography*. And the fourth edition of *Blues and Gospel Records 1902-1943* will be more inclusive, encompassing not only the seminal and vitally important Fisk University Quartet, but many other previously excluded groups.

Of the commercially published works related specifically to quartets, Ray Allen's *"Singing in the Spirit"—African American Sacred Quartets in New York City* remains the only book published since *"Happy in the Service of the Lord";* fortunately it's both provocative and a valuable contribution to scholarship. Based on his dissertation, Allen looks not only at the local history of gospel quartet singing (his brevity on this subject is the book's only important shortcoming), but at the context for quartet singing.

Coming from an academic background that encompassed training in both folklore and anthropology, Allen focuses on quartet singing as an "event" within black Christian culture and as a fervent expression that often releases the Holy Spirit. Issues related to urbanization and the constant mediation between down-home values and the realities found in their current New York City home not only permeate the book, but are the subject of an important chapter, "Back Home: Southern Identity in the Urban North." Finally, *Singing in the Spirit* examines the performance styles of several gospel quartets, including the tensions between what Allen characterizes as "sacred folk music and popular culture," which have helped to shape the very nature of contemporary performance practices.

Not surprisingly, the wider field of African-American gospel music has received greater attention. Most notable are Michael Harris's study of Thomas A. Dorsey, and *We'll Understand It Better By and By*, edited by Bernice Johnson Reagon. Both are quite worthwhile additions to the canon, though Reagon's volume has a broader agenda. In her introductory essay, the editor characterizes this volume as a look "not only at specific practices taking place over a two hundred year period within organized religious service but also at the role of sacred music and worship in shaping the sound and rhythm of African American culture as a whole." The essays about gospel composers Charles Albert Tindley, Lucie Campbell, Thomas Dorsey, W. Herbert Brewster, and Kenneth Morris form the essence of *We'll Understand It Better By and By*. Horace Boyer contributes a series of essays that focus on the musical aspects and a list of the specific works by each composer, while a variety of other black American music scholars have written separate articles about their social, historical, and spiritual importance. The critical issues of performance and the commercialization of black gospel music are not overlooked, especially in the three pieces about Roberta Martin, and in Portia Maultsby's interesting survey "The Impact of Gospel Music on the Secular Music Industry." The work of scholar Irene V. Jackson, who wrote an important 1974 dissertation about Roberta Martin and other works about black American gospel music, is strangely absent from this volume.

Michael Harris wrote an absorbing essay, "Conflict and Resolution in the Life of Thomas Andrew Dorsey," for Reagon's anthology, but his major contribution is an important book *The Rise of Gospel Blues: The Music of Thomas Andrew Dorsey in the Urban Church*. More than a critical biography of Dorsey, Harris has written about the tensions and conflicts within black sacred music. Dorsey was well known as the composer of "Take My Hand, Precious Lord" (1932), "Hide Me in Thy Bosom" (1939), and "Search Me, Lord" (1948), among others. However, his importance as a gospel music publisher and innovator in the performance of gospel music is perhaps as critical as his composing. Thomas A. Dorsey stood at the core of this major revolution, which essentially began within the black community by Charles A. Tindley at the turn of the century and was propelled into the mainstream by Dorsey during the 1930s and 1940s.

The Rise of Gospel Blues explores some of the conflicts that arose during Dorsey's life and extends them to larger issues within black American culture. The duality felt by many African Americans— their search for nation and racial identity—was keenly felt by Thomas Dorsey, as was the tension between his life as a secular and sacred performer. Harris also examines the balance between the old ways of the South with the newly emerging gospel sound that appeared in churches in Chicago, as well as the conflicts between the lower economic classes with the emerging middle class that came with urbanization. The slowly evolving spirituality that pervaded Dorsey's life, the commercial success that it ultimately inspired, and the conflicts caused by these two factors stand at the core of Harris's complex and influential study.

In addition to these lengthy scholarly studies are numerous articles about the history of black American gospel quartet singing. A few have been published in an academic journal *Theomusicology: A Journal of Black Sacred Music,* which came into existence about the time I completed the first edition of this book. This provocative journal, edited by Jon Michael Spencer, delves not only into contemporary articles and the relationship between the sacred and secular, but also into valuable history reprints. Most of these pieces are not the product of the academy, appearing instead in popular and fan magazines such as *Blues & Rhythm: The Gospel Truth, Rejoice!, Juke Blues,* and others. A great deal of new information has also been disseminated by way of extensive liner notes and short monographs that accompany reissues of gospel quartet material from the golden age of the 1920s through the 1950s. Unfortunately, most of these reissues either remain all but obtainable in the United States or very quickly go out of print.

In fact, the steady stream of LPs, cassettes, and CDs of reissued quartet recordings from as early as the 1890s, as well as a handful of contemporary performances, remains the most important public display of interest in this music. Much of the early material has been reissued in Europe, partly because of copyright laws that decree that aural material older than fifty years is in the public domain. Such copyright laws encourage small independent companies to issue older performances that are ignored by Sony (CBS) and BMG (RCA) because they sell hundreds of copies instead of the tens of thousands of units required by the corporate bottom line. Thus a handful of miniature companies based throughout Europe have reissued many of the recordings by the Norfolk Jubilee/Jazz Quartet, the Birmingham Jubilee Quartet, the Heavenly Gospel Singers, and other quartets whose recordings fall within the time frame allowed by the more lenient copyright laws that rule these countries. Despite such high expectations and a relatively small audience, these reissues have slipped past the corporate number crunchers into the hands of a growing number of fans and scholars. Even new material has gotten to the marketplace: among the best and most exciting contemporary recordings are the Global Village cassettes by the Gospel Harmonetts of Demopolis, Alabama, and their anthology of New York City community-based quartets.

The work of these selfless researchers is reflected in, and at times incorporated into, the second edition of this book. *"Happy in the Service of the Lord": African-American Sacred Vocal Harmony Quartets in Memphis* also expands its own scope and updates several sections into the middle 1990s. For example, I have revised and thoroughly updated my historical overview of gospel quartets "One Hundred Years of Singing in Harmony" into a longer, more comprehensive study. A fresh, deeper look at the spiritual and Christian basis for sacred music and the importance of performance and performance practices forms the foundation for a new chapter, "The Forces That Shape Sacred Quartet Singing." The bibliography has been expanded to include not only the recent work about quartets, but the significant books and articles on black gospel music in general. Finally, the discography has been rechristened an "audiography," a name that reflects the fact that these recordings now appear in three media: cassette, compact discs, and long-playing albums. Not only has the name changed, but the audiography has been updated to reflect up-to-the-minute research available as of November 1994. A second section, "Selected Gospel Quartet Audiography," which includes provocative performances by such outstanding national or regional groups as the Soul Stirrers, Norfolk Jubilee Quartets, and the Pilgrim Travelers, has been added.

Despite its sharp geographical focus on Memphis, Tennessee, this second edition holds larger implications for scholars of African-American music in particular and American music in general. I am not suggesting that it be *the* model that all scholars should follow, but *"Happy in the Service of the Lord": African-American Sacred Vocal Harmony Quartets in Memphis* stands as one attempt to study, dissect, and describe a community of black religious singers. Several factors regarding its broader implications became clearer to me as I reread the published reviews of the first edition, thought about revisions, reshaped sections of the original book, updated the appendixes, and wrote a new chapter.

First, the book underscores the importance of oral histories in research about American vernacular music. Interviews constitute the overwhelming majority of the primary sources for this book, as they have for the other scholars of black quartet singing. This bald fact emphasizes how much of our musical history has not been written down, but the results of dogged fieldwork reemphasize another fact: much of twentieth-century American music history remains within our grasp. But such research must be timely. Because of the recent deaths of such important Memphis figures as Elijah Ruffin, Jethroe Bledsoe, and Reverend Brewster, you would be hard-pressed to complete this type of book if you'd begun your research in 1995. At the least it would be a very different study. Now is the time for other focused studies in other geographically distinct sections of the United States and in other related genres, such as the mass choirs found in Pentecostal church, soloists in the gospel tradition, and the role of shape-note singing in black communities in the deep Mid-South.

Second, this book points to the need for a multidisciplinary approach to the study of music. Purely musical matters are discussed in sections of several chapters, but I also draw upon my background in cultural geography, folklore, and anthropology as well as American music history. The result is a more well-rounded approach to the study of music in culture than one finds among scholars who are trained in a single discipline. Research into the twentieth-century American vernacular music must be undertaken from a variety of perspectives because it provides us with a perspective that transcends a purely historical/musicological study. Unlike the music investigated by most traditional historical musicologists, twentieth-century American music remains vital, alive, and has not yet been relegated to a musty archive in Stuttgart or Vienna.

Third, the role and importance of the mass electronic media must be taken into account when studying black American gospel music. Largely a phenomenon that began in the early 1920s, radio and record companies have played an incalculably important role in disseminating this music and in shaping its repertoire and performance style. Indeed, the electronic media has helped, more than any single factor, to introduce widespread innovations among quartet singers. Recordings must be viewed as fundamental primary documents, in the same league as sheet music or other printed means of prescriptive musical notation. While more intangible, radio broadcasts are another means by which gospel quartet performances have been brought to a wider audience.

A fourth factor is the importance of establishing the spiritual significance of this music both within the community, but also to individual singers. Time and again, these quartet singers remarked upon the fact that they "believe in feeling spiritually" (Etherlene Beans) or that "gospel quartet . . . is all about being a Christian." (Tommie Todd) This music is impossible for a white male to know from "the inside," but gaining an emic view through interviews and personal observation is not only possible, it is imperative. Understanding and then describing the spiritual nature of black gospel quartet singing remains one of the most important tasks that stand before anyone who researches black American religious music.

Finally, this study helps to fill another section of an immense puzzle that is the history and development of black American music. Although many books about blues and jazz are available, there are decidedly fewer lengthy publications about black popular music prior to the post-World War II era. The number of studies about African-American religious music is growing, but the output is discouragingly meager, and most of them remain as unpublished dissertations. I know that *"Happy in the Service of the Lord": African-American Sacred Vocal Harmony Quartets in Memphis* describes patterns, trends, and other important information that is unique to this particular musical community, but I hope that its methodology offers something to scholars who may wish to study other communities. The greater the number of carefully focused studies that we have to draw upon, the more we will know about their unique contributions to American music and culture.

In closing, I would like to thank all of the people who helped to bring this second edition to completion: Judy McCulloh of the University of Illinois Press, who originally shepherded me through the publishing gauntlet and then made sure the book found a new home. Meredith Morris-Babb of the University of Tennessee Press saw the value in keeping this study in print and patiently worked with me to reshape and broaden its scope. Lynn Abbott and Ray Allen read the revised and newly minted chapters, and offered general encouragement. My spouse, Kim Gandy, knew this book was important to me and cooperated at every turn, as did baby Cady, who slept till about 8:00 a.m. almost every morning, thus allowing me several hours of writing before I assumed my daily child-care responsibilities.

Acknowledgments

Several years of research, thought, and revising have gone into this book. Although I take ultimate responsibility for the final product, many people contributed to the project in diverse ways. I need, above all, to thank the quartet singers themselves for their untiring cooperation, patience, and interest in my work. In this regard, Elijah Ruffin, Mrs. Clara Anderson, George Rooks, and Earl Malone provided me with the most information. But there are several dozen other members of the Memphis quartet community who selflessly answered questions, loaned their invaluable photographs to be copied, and provided me with insights.

The selfless generosity of my fellow gospel quartet researchers cannot go unnoted. Lynn Abbott helped with general information, photographs, material about New Orleans quartets, and background data from various newspapers, including the *Louisiana Weekly*. Ray Funk supplied a number of photographs, numerous suggestions, newspaper clippings, and encouragement. Doug Seroff provided many critical, insightful comments at various points, helped me locate photographs, and unselfishly shared information and interviews. Their altruistic assistance helped to make this book a reality.

Three scholars at Memphis State University, David Evans, Ted Mealor, and Dick Raichelson, deserve recognition for their help in developing early drafts of this manuscript. David's thoughtful suggestions shaped the entire manuscript, while Ted encouraged my interest in the geography of music and Dick assisted me in looking at the quartet community. Riki Saltzman requires special notice for her love and moral support, as well as her help and perceptive suggestions in proofreading and revising this manuscript from its genesis.

Val Hicks pointed me toward information about barbershop quartets, and Jack Hurley generously copied many of the photographs that appear in this book. Bill Daniels provided me with invaluable, then unpublished, postwar discographical information for a number of Memphis groups. I also appreciate the efforts of the three anonymous scholars who carefully read prepublication drafts of this manuscript for the University of Illinois Press and who suggested many subtle improvements.

Special thanks also to the National Endowment for the Arts/Folk Arts and the Wenner-Gren Foundation for Anthropological Research for supporting my research and documentation of Memphis quartets while I was a doctoral candidate.

The staff of the Blue Ridge Institute of Ferrum College, especially Roddy Moore, must be cited for allowing me the extreme flexibility that I required to finish this book. Judy McCulloh recognized the promise of this project from its inception and encouraged me through several drafts, while Terry Sears patiently copyedited the final manuscript. The ongoing, selfless support of my parents, Wallace and Betty Jane Lornell, was also critical to the completion of both my education and this book. Each of these people believed in me and in what I could do.

"Happy in the Service of the Lord" is dedicated to Don Lassonde and Georgia Lundquist, both of whom died too young, and also to James Darling and the other Memphis quartet singers who did not live long enough to see their good works documented in print.

1

"One Hundred Years of Singing in Harmony"

Black American gospel quartet singing is a distinctly twentieth-century musical and cultural phenomenon, with clear roots in the traditional and popular music of the Reconstruction era. Since that time, the quartet tradition has traversed an interesting and complicated path from its predominantly southern folk roots to the heights of popular music during the 1940s and 1950s. Quartets today remain the grassroots of black sacred music, largely championed by older singers. This chapter provides an overview of the hundred-year odyssey of African-American quartets.

Despite all of the published research that has been undertaken for several decades on blues and jazz, scholars of black American music have sadly underestimated the importance within the black community of sacred music in general and quartets in particular. Thus it remains difficult to specify the precise cultural, geographical, and musical origins of religious quartet singing.

It has become evident that college jubilee groups formed during the final third of the nineteenth century provided one of the earliest sources for quartet singing. Barbershops also served as a nexus for both short-lived, informal groups and long-standing quartets.[1] More productively, however, our search begins with the all-black minstrel shows that were formed at the beginning of Reconstruction.

Minstrel shows themselves constitute a fascinating part of American vernacular culture; they are arguably the first form of American popular entertainment. Beginning in the 1830s, they presented a distorted, often exaggerated, vision of African-American plantation life to many people across the nation through music, comedy, jokes, dramatic sketches, and speeches. The lampoon was further heightened by white minstrel entertainers who appeared on stage in blackened faces. By the late 1840s minstrel shows proved to be very popular among northern audiences, who had virtually no direct contact with, or knowledge of, southern black culture. However, what began as an Anglo-American parody of black culture took on new meaning as a few blacks began to join previously all-white troupes. Shortly after the Civil War adventurous entrepreneurs formed all-black minstrel shows, which proved successful and continued to draw crowds into the early twentieth century.

By the early 1870s both black and white minstrel shows had been codified into a three-part format that has persisted for more than one hundred years and is still used by the few remaining minstrel productions, most of which are fund-raising events mounted by male-dominated civic clubs. The first part features music and humorous exchanges between several comedians (endmen) and a straightman (interlocutor). Part two, a variety section known as the olio, highlights such diverse talents as jugglers, acrobats, clowns, ventriloquists, and "stump" speakers, who pepper their act with malapropisms, mispronunciations, and other verbal missteps. The final section consists of a one-act skit, often in a plantation setting. Minstrel shows proved to be one of the most popular entertainment forms until the turn of the century. In Virginia—as in other states— Lions Clubs in Covington and Vinton put on annual minstrel shows (sometimes called variety shows, but following the same format and acts) into the late 1970s. Music of all types, but sometimes songs performed by male quartets, was integrated into these shows.[2]

The musical portion of the pre–Civil War minstrel shows included instrumental numbers performed on fiddles, jawbones, and banjos, as well as vocalists singing a wide range of traditional and popular material. Some of these pre-Reconstruction vocals were rendered by "quartettes."[3] Although few individual blacks appeared in minstrel shows prior to 1860, the importance of blacks in minstrelsy after the Civil War is much better documented and understood.[4] Reconstruction offered new opportunities for cultural, legal, and economic advancement for blacks, despite the bitter realities of the Ku Klux Klan, voter taxes, and many other barriers to equality that were erected over the next two decades.

Minstrel shows themselves reached their height of popularity in the immediate post–Civil War era. Scores of quartets appeared with these troupes, large and small, though we really know very little about them. Ike Simond, a black entertainer who worked with minstrel shows during the 1870s and 1880s listed a dozen delightfully named black American quartets associated with these traveling shows: Sans Souci, Olympic, Climax, Twilight, Garden City, Mountain Pink, Beethoven, Eclipse, Buckeye, Black Diamond, Dark Town Quartette, and Excelsior.[5] Something is known of the Excelsior Quartette, which was directed by the St. Louis singer William Coleman. In the two decades prior to 1900, they regularly worked the minstrel show and slowly evolving vaudeville circuit, traveling as far west as California from their midwestern base. Another, probably similar, group—the Excelsior Quartet—was barnstorming the upper Midwest during the spring of 1890, because a newspaper account reports them as "delight[ing] so many people in the East by their imitation of Barnum's Steam Organ are at present in Nebraska."[6] Similarly, "The Cyclone Quartette consisting of Messrs. G. L. Green, S. L. Barbour, W. A. Reid and the well-known bass singer Alf H. Lindsay, formerly of San Francisco, has just closed a two week engagement at the New State Opera, House, Spokane, Washington."[7]

As other forms of popular entertainment developed in the late nineteenth century, black vocal quartets became associated with them as well. For example, the pioneering African-American comedian Bert Williams employed the democratically named vocal quartet "Messrs. Thomas, Rex, Lightfoot, and Reed" in his hit 1909 show "Mr. Lode of Koal." One year later, Williams recorded the hit song "Play That Barbershop Chord" for Columbia, which was picked up and performed on stage by many different artists, including Gertrude "Ma" Rainey, who was then in the early stages of her career on the vaudeville circuit. Williams, along with Will Marion Cook, appreciated the wide range of black vernacular music—including vocal harmony singing—and included it on his shows on many occasions.[8]

While Reconstruction minstrel show quartets were touring the United States, predominantly black schools were creating innovative singing ensembles known as jubilee groups. In some instances, most notably Fisk University, the school and its jubilee singing group were formed within a few years of one another. Another Nashville school, the Central Tennessee College, sent out its own jubilee group—the Original Tennesseans—beginning in 1873. The majority of these institutions were located in the South and include many still-thriving institutions such as Atlanta University, Tuskegee Institute (Tuskegee, Alabama), Southern University (Baton Rouge, Louisiana), Livingstone College (Salisbury, North Carolina), and Hampton University (Hampton, Virginia).

One of the era's most demanding and difficult challenges was to educate the several million primarily illiterate blacks emancipated following the Civil War. Much of this effort was carried out on the most grassroots, informal level in schools operated either by churches or by the small communities themselves. The result was a potpourri of woefully underfunded small schools and school systems that stressed basic skills like reading, writing, and arithmetic in addition to vocational courses like sewing and shoemaking. On the postsecondary level such efforts similarly stressed basic education, often training teachers who could staff these elementary and high schools. Many of these teachers received at least a rudimentary music education in college; they, in turn, often taught their students something about sight singing and vocal techniques. Such musical training encouraged students to explore their own music with new vigor and insights, and spirituals remained one of the cornerstones of their teaching.

In 1866 the American Missionary Association of New York founded seven institutions of higher education, one of which was Fisk University in Nashville, Tennessee. Five years later Fisk sponsored the first tour of its troupe of "Jubilee Singers"—a term the university may have utilized to celebrate the freedom blacks gained after emancipation, but the name also helped to separate them from groups that appeared on the minstrel stage—to help promote and raise money for the financially strapped school. George White served as teacher, treasurer, and choir director. He traveled north with the Fisk Jubilee Singers, many of whom were former slaves. Their initial stop in Cincinnati was plagued by poor attendance, mounting expenses, and inadequate financial returns to cover their expenses. Thanks to favorable newspaper reviews, sympathetic clergy, and increased support from the African-American community, their tour gained momentum and ended as a financial and critical triumph.

This initial success proved to be just the beginning for the Fisk University Jubilee Singers, a group that continued to perform and tour, in one form or another, well into the middle of the twentieth century. Through its written and aural arrangements of spirituals (and several decades later, gospel songs) the Fisk Jubilees succeeded in moving the spiritual to a new artistic realm. They shaped the old-line spirituals into performances complete with sophisticated harmony and smooth, controlled singing. Some might protest that this process "blanched" the African-American elements, but Doug Seroff argues that this "process of reinterpretation is entirely within black choral music traditions, it is, in fact, a requisite factor in the viability of those traditions."[9]

The Fisk University Jubilee Singers broke ground for other "jubilee" groups, most of which were associated with colleges and universities; by the 1890s, however, many were professional groups that may have come up through the academic ranks but that now performed on the professional stage. The final two decades of the nineteenth century saw a wealth of black talent singing jubilee songs on the stages across the United States, Europe, Africa, and even the Orient. One of the most remarkable groups was Frederick J. Loudin's Fisk Jubilee Singers, which traded on the university's name, but was a separate entity by the 1880s. Capitalizing on its legitimate Fisk connection, Loudin's group performed across the world. The August 31, 1889, New York Age reports that "Mr. Loudin and his companions of the Fisk Jubilee Singers, so long and favorably known at Chautaugua [Chautauqua], are at present in New South Wales and have sent the sufferers of the Johnstown calamity the proceeds of a benefit concert amounting to $800. The troupe will soon go to India, and thence home via China, Japan, and the Sandwich Island[s], and spend several months on the Pacific Coast."[10] Although the Fisk University Jubilee Singers themselves took a twenty-year hiatus from touring (1879–99), the singers continued as a campus activity. In the fall of 1899 they finally toured again, this time under the direction of

Professor John W. Work, whose efforts on behalf of the group would last for decades.

The financial and critical triumphs of the Fisk singing groups did not escape the notice of other struggling, predominantly black schools. Many of these institutions looked to the Fisk University Jubilee Singers, who raised substantial sums—hundreds of thousands of dollars, in fact—as a public relations model to emulate during the late nineteenth century. Hampton University was perhaps the first of Fisk's peer organizations to take the jubilee singing movement's fund-raising possibilities seriously. In 1873 the first group of Hampton's jubilee ambassadors headed to several northern cities in order to raise seventy-five thousand dollars.The success of this sixteen-member group, organized by the chair of the music department, Thomas Fenner, is unknown. A July 26, 1941, article in the *Norfolk Journal and Guide* suggests a quartet was included as part of this initial tour, but no other evidence for this assertion exists.

Within fifteen years, however, a quartet trading on the Hampton name began touring across the United States. About 1881 four Hampton Institute students—Orpheus McAdoo, James Evans, William H. Daggs, and R. H. Hamilton—posed for a photograph, presumably as a musical quartet. McAdoo eventually launched his own jubilee troupe, which toured internationally, including trips to South Africa and Australia. Over the next several decades the Hampton Institute Quartette maintained a rigorous touring schedule; so rigorous, in fact, that the group was eventually composed of alumni. These singers became employees of Hampton Institute who, unlike students who were forced to juggle classes, school work, and singing, traveled upon demand. Known as the Hampton Institute Senior Quartette, the group toured across the United States, sometimes performing as many as 258 concerts in a single year![11]

The prosperity of the university jubilee singing groups inevitably stirred the spirit of American entrepreneurship. Within one year White, in fact, expressed his concern that the concept and the name jubilee singers were being exploited by commercial groups hoping to cash in on the widespread interest in this music. The blossoming of the Fisk and other school groups, such as those sponsored by New Orleans University, Morehouse College in Atlanta, Tuskegee Institute, and Utica Institute of Utica, Mississippi, almost certainly helped to reinforce the popularity of the minstrel quartets and jubilee groups that began to thrive during Reconstruction.

With the exception of Seroff's exhaustive work on Fisk and Abbott's New Orleans research, the true dimensions of the school jubilee singers movement are unclear, though these groups enjoyed their greatest popularity from 1870 through 1910. The *Indianapolis Freeman,* the *Chicago Defender,* the *New York Age,* and other black-oriented newspapers included many references and articles about college or university jubilee groups well into the 1930s. For example, the *Chicago Defender* noted in its August 12, 1911, issue that the "Claflin [South Carolina] University Jubilee Singers, who have been on the road for past *nine years* [emphasis added], and who have been singing in and about the city [Chicago] for the past two weeks at the big churches, will give their farewell concert next Thursday evening at 9 o'clock, August 17th." On March 5, 1927, this same paper observed that the West Virginia Collegiate Glee Club recently completed a fund-raising tour that was "attended by persons prominently connected in New York's most exclusive social, musical, and collegiate circles." Such references underscore the intent of these groups, specifically their pursuit of monetary contributions in the urban centers populated by blacks with ties to the South or white citizens interested in the music and the cause they represent. They also help us to understand that the widespread late-nineteenth-century popular interest in black American culture and music—initially the spiritual—continued well into the twentieth century.

Not surprisingly, there were some stylistic parallels between these college and minstrel black quartets, in part because both groups performed for a popular, racially mixed audience, but primarily because their music stemmed from the same wellspring of musical culture. Perhaps the best evidence of these distinctly African-American traits lies etched into the grooves of the handful of contemporary recordings made by such groups. On the most general level they all display a "call and response" (antiphonal) textual organization and the occasional use of falsetto, "growls," and other vocal devices associated with vernacular black American music. But it would be grossly misleading to suggest that black American quartet singing was limited to the minstrel stage and college-sponsored groups. There is always interaction among the various levels of culture, and the truth is that quartets played an integral part in the fabric of black folk music during the late nineteenth century. Nonetheless it is music partly shaped by formal training attained in schools, at least in those areas served by teachers with a strong musical bent. As early as the turn of the century, some "folk" quartets were conscious of some of the more technical aspects of music such as vocal "articulation" and the need to "attack" notes in a specific way.

The earliest reference to the quartet tradition in folk culture is also the first allusion to black religious singing by a "quartette." While traveling through Virginia in June 1851, Frederika Bremer reported: "I first heard the slaves, about a hundred in number, singing at their work in large rooms; they sang quartettes . . . in such perfect harmony, and with such exquisite feeling, that it was difficult to believe them self-taught."[12] Another early account of what might be heterophony among slave singers, or at the very least a foreshadowing of four-part harmony, states:

> There is no singing in parts, as we understand it, and yet no two seem to be singing the same thing; the leading singer starts the words of each verse, often improvising; and others, who "base" him as it is called, strike in with the refrain or even join in the solo when the words are familiar. And the "basers" themselves seem to follow their own whims, beginning where they please, striking an octave above or below, or hitting some other note that chords, so as to produce the effect of a marvelous complication and variety and yet with the most perfect time and rarely with any discord.[13]

By the dawn of the twentieth century, four-part vocal harmony singing was well established in black communities across the United States and appeared to be dominated by males. Seemingly, any four young black males who chanced to meet could, and often would, immediately harmonize a song. In his 1914 *Report to Dr. Frissell, Principal* the Hampton Institute director of music observed that "countless boys meet around the grounds of evenings to 'harmonize'—just for the love of it." The founder of the Piney Woods School in post-Reconstruction Mississippi, Laurance C. Jones, proclaimed that "any four coloured boys are a quartet." Famed tenor, Roland Hayes, sang in a neighborhood group, the "Silver-Toned Quartet," just after the turn of the century. In reminiscing about his

Florida childhood during the 1890s, the noted black scholar James Weldon Johnson recalled:

> Pick up four coloured boys or young men anywhere and the chances are ninety out of a hundred that you have a quartet. Let one of them sing the melody and others will naturally find the parts. Indeed, it may be said that all male Negro youth of the United States is divided into quartets. When I was fifteen and my brother was thirteen we were singing in a quartet which competed with other quartets. In the days when such thing as a white barber was unknown in the South, every barbershop had its quartet and the young men spent their leisure time "harmonizing."[14]

Gospel quartet historian Lynn Abbott goes so far as to state that "the pervasiveness of quartet singing during the 1890s and early 1900 . . . was nothing less than a national pastime."[15]

Formal, but more often informal, quartets sang in contexts as diverse as churches, "singing parties" held in people's homes, school yards, drugstores, and other points of commerce. Some of these groups no doubt formed in order to sing each week in church. Spontaneous neighborhood or street corner quartets came and went with casual indifference, while others carefully practiced and performed their sacred, sentimental, and popular songs regularly. This genre is often called "barbershop harmony singing," a name that calls attention to the importance of the barbershop in black American culture.

As Lynn Abbott has thoroughly demonstrated, the style of barbershop singing performed by white men sporting mustaches, dressed in identical outfits, and singing a sentimental repertoire is largely a historical invention. This cultural sleight of hand is largely promoted by the Society for the Preservation and Encouragement of Barbershop Quartet Singing in America (SPEBSQSA), founded in Tulsa in 1938, through its highly regimented competitions and publications such as *The Harmonizer*. In the decade before the founding of SPEBSQSA, some unfortunately uncritical and popular writers like C. T. "Deac" Martin and Sigmund Spaeth unambiguously established the myths and fictions associated with the white origins of barbershop quartets.

Barbershops, in fact, proved to be a primary crossroads for black vernacular culture beginning during Reconstruction and an important venue in promoting black quartet singing. Black Americans dominated the trade, a trend that began before the Civil War. Barbers not only cut hair, they provided a meeting ground where men could play cards, drink liquor, and discuss important business with other men. In short, turn-of-the-century barbershops were eminently respectable neighborhood hangouts and the unofficial headquarters for those who gathered to sing in harmony. The early quartet experience of W. C. Handy, the so-called Father of the Blues, centered upon a Florence, Alabama, barbershop; likewise, some twenty-five years later, the genesis of the Mills Brothers can be found in Piqua, Ohio, where John worked as a barber.

Another genre of American music, shape-note singing, also influenced black quartets. Shape-note singing consists of a system of notated music commonly using four or seven shapes in lieu of the "round notes" found in standard European notation. Each shape is assigned a solfège syllable—*fa, sol, la*—in order to facilitate learning the system. The shape-note system, which was initially popular in Virginia and Kentucky beginning in the 1830s, was generally introduced to black people in southern "singing schools" during Reconstruction. Shape-note singing among blacks has continued to be the strongest in Mississippi, Alabama, and Georgia, and its impact on black harmony quartets seems to be in its components rather than the general popularity of the tradition itself.[16] Doris Dyen's study of African-American shape-note singing in Alabama suggests two components: the tendency of these singers to "improvise separate lines of harmonic accompaniment" and their "partly improvised, orally transmitted version of written harmony."[17] It is also noteworthy that both shape-note singing and black harmony quartets stress four-part harmony, utilize a prescribed training system, and have formal performance contexts.

Although they followed in the footsteps of the larger jubilee groups and were influenced by the community quartet movement, university quartets were by no means lesser stepchildren. Most of the schools with jubilee groups ultimately also sponsored quartets, as did many of the newer institutions such as Livingstone College and Bennett College, both of which were founded in central North Carolina before 1900. Among the earliest references to quartets is the material found in the Hampton University Archive, which includes photographs of the Hampton Institute Quartette from approximately 1885, cylinder recordings of several performances dating from the turn of the century, and printed programs. The quartet apparently remained an active force in the school's fund-raising efforts until it was disbanded following the end of World War II.

Another early institutional group, the Dinwiddie Colored Quartet, was recorded by the Victor Company and became the first such vocal harmony group to make a disc. The group itself was formed in the late 1890s to sing on behalf of the John A. Dix Industrial School in Dinwiddie, Virginia, some hundred miles west of Hampton. Typically the quartet performed at school fund-raisers, though by 1902 the members had moved to the vaudeville stage.[18] Like other similar quartets, the Dinwiddie group was formed for at least two reasons: if jubilee groups could raise money for their sponsoring institutions, then quartets could do the same at a much smaller cost. Furthermore, the schools were responding to a larger trend in American vernacular music—the emergence of quartets within the black community at large. By 1900, college, minstrel, and community-based quartets had become extremely potent musical forces in the black community.

White singers also performed in both folk and popular quartets. They, too, performed in a variety of contexts before burgeoning audiences beginning in the 1880s, perhaps fueled by the popularity of the black American groups. Fraternal organizations, clubs, and even companies such as Westinghouse and 7-Up sponsored quartets. Tin Pan Alley and vaudeville were strong forces in American popular music, and these so-called barbershop quartets fit perfectly with these trends. Several of these white quartets, such as the Edison, Peerless, and American, recorded cylinders and one-sided discs. The Edison Quartette recorded just over one hundred cylinders of popular songs, religious selections, and even some selections influenced by African Americans—most notably "Cornfield Song"—during the decade beginning in 1898. As early as 1891 the Manhansett Quartette recorded their version of this "Negro melody," and in following years it was "covered" by the prolific Hayden and Imperial Quartets. Several other groups, beginning with the Harmonizers' 1922 recording "A Quartette Rehearsal," attempted to recreate the rehearsal of a black American quartet. Rather than a clear attempt to accurately replicate this phenomenon, this sketch, which was initially published by Geoffrey O'Hara and adopted by the Harmonizers, owes much to the minstrel show stage. "A Quartette Rehearsal" represents yet another attempt to present black American culture through the filter of popular trends and the vaudeville stage.[19]

While there is ample evidence to support the widespread popularity of these quartets, what else can we say about their music? Cylinder recordings by the first black American group to record, the Standard Negro Quartette of Chicago, appear in the Columbia catalog in 1895. Unfortunately, none of these recordings have survived in listenable condition. From the pioneering recordings of the Fisk Jubilee Quartet, the Dinwiddie Colored Quartet, and Polk Miller's Old South Quartette between 1902 and 1913, it is possible to make some general observations regarding performance styles. These groups stressed clear diction and precise pronunciation; and they offered little vocal embellishment or improvisation as well as only occasional instances of syncopation or rhythmic ornamentation. The vocal timbre of the singers was reminiscent of more formally trained musicians, perhaps revealing their university training or their vaudeville roots. Most of their songs were homophonic in texture; quite often the songs vacillated between major and minor tonalities.

Minstrel and institutional groups alike performed a broad, seemingly eclectic repertoire consisting of both secular and sacred songs. The secular numbers included songs composed by Stephen Foster, like "Old Black Joe" and "My Old Kentucky Home"; humorous ditties; patriotic selections; traditional material; and "coon" songs like "Old Jemima," "Little Alabama Coon," and the aforementioned "Way Down Yonder in the Cornfield." The religious songs consisted primarily of spirituals like "Roll, Jordan, Roll" and "You May Talk About Jerusalem Morning." The emerging gospel tradition, exemplified by the compositions of Philadelphia minister C. A. Tindley, is notably absent from these early discs.

The immense popular appeal of the jubilee groups, minstrel quartets, and barbershop crooners all charged the atmosphere for the widespread appreciation of small-group religious harmony singing among blacks across the entire United States. After the turn of the century, community-based black gospel groups sprang up throughout the South and urban North, and over the next thirty years greatly increased in popularity as part of a working-class cultural movement. Many blacks incorporated religious quartet singing into their everyday lives, singing not only in churches but also for special afternoon and evening programs. Kerill Rubman describes this movement:

> Factory and construction workers, porters, and other employees sang in company or union-affiliated quartets, performing at picnics, parties, dances, and other business or community events. Family members formed quartets. Negro colleges continued to sponsor such groups, and Baptist and Methodist churches often formed male quartets to sing sacred music at worship services and evening programs. In short, by the 1920s . . . harmony a cappella quartet singing was well established as a beloved and respected activity for musically adept black men [and women].[20]

These trends were directly tied to the increasingly urban character of the South's black population. During the first two decades of the twentieth century, for instance, thousands of African Americans moved into metropolitan Norfolk, Virginia, and from the surrounding rural sections of Virginia and North Carolina in search of steady, though lucrative blue-collar jobs in the rapidly growing Newport News Shipbuilding and Dry Dock Company and small factories. Others moved to Hampton Roads (this name refers to the overlapping urban areas of Norfolk, Newport News, Portsmouth, and Virginia Beach) and continued to work as fishermen or in related waterman work, such as oyster shucking and crab picking, which remained largely the domain of African Americans. The large number of military bases scattered throughout the region provided other blacks with relatively menial but steady, dependable employment that carried them through lean times. With this influx of potential talent it is not coincidental that Hampton Roads developed into one of the best-documented centers for quartet singing by the 1920s. Its significance is recalled by Thurmon Ruth of the New York City-based Selah Jubilee Singers:

> Norfolk, Virginia, that used to be a quartet town! I used to want to go to Norfolk because they told me that you could just be in bed at night and put your head out the window and guys would be on the corner blending, harmonizing. That's what the Norfolk Jubilee Singers told

me. I believe the first quartet record I heard was Melvin Smith [of the Silver Leaf Quartet of Norfolk] and he came out of Norfolk, [it was] "Sleep On, Mother." The Golden Gate originated in Norfolk and the Norfolk Jubilee Singers—they don't come any better.[21]

During the 1920s through the 1940s Hampton Roads certainly deserved its reputation as a hotbed of quartet activity. Most of these groups were formed through family ties, neighborhood connections, or church affiliations. Many adults believed that this style of religious singing was upright, positive, and worthy of a young Christian. Willie Johnson of the Golden Gate Quartet grew up in Norfolk during the early years of the Depression and recalls:

> At that time kids didn't have too much to do. And the goin' thing with most kids, or young adults you might call them, was to form some sort of singing aggregation. That way they could go, like if the church would have programs during the evening, then they could go there and sing. . . . You couldn't hardly find anybody in Norfolk at that time who could carry a tune in a bucket that wasn't affiliated somewhere with some quartet. I mean that was the general pastime.[22]

Most Hampton Roads quartets maintained their well-polished singing through weekly rehearsals and regular performances for church and community events. Some affiliated themselves with organizations outside of their neighborhoods. Vaughan Webb observed that, in addition to family groups, "harmonizers [were] tied to specific churches, such as the Second Calvary (Baptist Church) Female Quartet; lodges, such as the American Woodmen Quartet; military units, such as the 811, the Engineers Battalion Quintet; and, of course, schools. The prestige of affiliation led at least one Norfolk quartet to go so far as to name themselves the Southern Institute Jubilee Singers, even though no such school existed."[23] Others chose to celebrate their geographical heritage with names such as the Sons of Norfolk and the Suffolk Jubilee Quartet.

A small number of these groups made the bold leap into the semi-professional and professional realms. The Norfolk Jubilee/Jazz Quartet, for instance, toured on the vaudeville circuit beginning after World War I into the 1930s. Between 1921 and 1940 they also recorded scores of commercial recordings for the OKeh, Paramount, and Decca labels. In 1922 the Excelsior Quartet, who attracted singers from Norfolk and Portsmouth, displayed their wide repertoire on a brief series of recordings for Black Swan, Gennett, and OKeh that included "Sinners Crying Come Here Lord," "Down by the Old Mill Stream," and "Jelly Roll Blues." These selections, augmented by the Norfolk Jazz/Jubilee numerous recordings and the research of Vaughan Webb, clearly imply that the stage and street corner, as well as the church, all served as performance venues for Hampton Roads quartet singers. In other words, while many of these performers come from a purely sacred singing background, quite a few others represent the barbershop tradition described by Lynn Abbott.

A similar situation was developing in Birmingham, Alabama, where the rapidly burgeoning coal and iron industry helped to attract a hundred thousand blacks between 1890 and 1920. Many of these newcomers settled in the unattractive, dingy company towns of Bessemer and Fairfield located on the outskirts of Birmingham. Immigrants poured into Jefferson County in search of better lives and more lucrative employment than that afforded by their agrarian backgrounds. They traded their largely segregated rural lifestyles for residence in entirely separated quarters that left them essentially sequestered from white society. These mining camps or compounds were quite restrictive, often sitting in the shadows of blast furnaces that roared and shone eerily in the dark of night.

In a county filled with migrants from all over Alabama and adjoining states such as Georgia and Mississippi, gospel quartets helped to provide social stability. These quartets were at the heart of daily life for many of the black citizens of Bessemer and Fairfield, whose diverse backgrounds slowly came together to create a new musical culture. Doug Seroff observes: "Community life within the mining camps, company quarters, and other segregated black settlements around Bessemer [was] unusually rich in fellowship. Mass immigration brought together a variety of regional experience in the singing of traditional spirituals. Quartets were organized in the churches . . . and in the schools and places of work. Denied access to other forms of popular entertainment and diversion, quartet singing became a general pastime for Jefferson County youth."[24]

Unlike Hampton Roads, Jefferson County became a bastion for unions. These segregated unions often provided a forum for quartet singing, which helped to fulfill the need for entertainment and self-determination in a highly difficult social situation. Doug Seroff notes that during the 1930s "quartets did regularly entertain in labor temples, and their close relationship with the mine workers' and steel workers' union is epitomized by the history of the Sterling Jubilee Singers who, for many years, sang under the name CIO Singers (Congress of Industrial Organizations), providing musical entertainment at union meetings, and broadcasting a local radio show sponsored by the CIO."[25] Unions also provided a rallying point for other aspects of the black experience in Jefferson County, most notably its political life.

By the onset of the Depression, Birmingham singers had shaped their own distinctive regional style that was disseminated by way of traveling quartets and intercity migration, but most dramatically through phonograph records. The selections recorded for Columbia, Victor, and Vocalion by the Birmingham Jubilee Quartet proved to be the most influential in spreading the sound, which Lynn Abbott describes as "carefully blended harmonies and practiced enunciations embellished with tenor flourishes, rolling bass lines, generous blue-notes, syncopations, and a pressing melody-line that scored the future of gospel quartet singing."[26]

In particular, singers from nearby New Orleans came under the sway of Birmingham quartets. At first they purchased the 78-rpm records by the Birmingham Jubilee Singers, which were released between 1926 and 1930. Then some of the groups from Jefferson County began appearing in churches in Montgomery, Mobile, and, finally, New Orleans. During the Depression the Humming Four Quartet of New Orleans adopted the "Alabama style" to great local acclaim. Veteran group member Albert Veal recalls, "The people thought we were doing great, and they said 'Oh, you all sound like the Alabama Boys.' . . . They considered the Alabama Boys, that was it!"[27] But it was the Bessemer Red Rose Quartet, which arrived in New Orleans in 1932 as part of a lengthy tour, that personally brought the Jefferson County quartet style to New Orleans. The group was enthusiastically received by the local quartets, and its tenor singer, Gilbert Porterfield, decided to remain in the Crescent City. Porterfield trained many quartets during his life in New Orleans, beginning with the Duncan Brothers Quartet. Ultimately the "Alabama style" became part of the New Orleans scene, largely supplanting the university-inspired quartets that predominated up to that point.[28]

Porterfield not only trained harmony groups affiliated with churches, but also worked with quartets that were formed on the job. Many of the immigrants to southern urban areas were pulled by economic desires, and in New Orleans the sugar refineries offered employment to many blacks. Not surprisingly, these jobs provided men with the opportunity to meet others with an interest in harmony singing. Professor J. W. Williams moved from Mississippi to New Orleans in the 1920s and found work at the American Sugar Refinery. It was at work that he saw the foundation set for one of the city's best groups, the Four Great Wonders: "That's how they started, harmonizing on the job. . . . They'd start work 7:30 in the morning. And they would work till 12:00. And work was very hard then. Then they'd have half an hour for lunch; they'd run eat a little bit, then get behind a pile of sugar and start harmonizing; . . . they began to meet in different homes for rehearsal. And then started harmonizing around a couple of churches and started singing, . . . and that's how they were founded."[29]

To some degree this pattern was repeated in cities across the South and North throughout the 1920s and 1930s. While Hampton Roads, Jefferson County, and New Orleans stand out as the prime examples, other cities like Atlanta, Dallas, and Jacksonville also had strong early community quartet traditions that still await closer scrutiny. Following the "great migration" of southern blacks to urban centers in the North during the teens and twenties, Detroit, Chicago, and New York—among others—gradually emerged as strongholds for quartet singing. Ray Funk has documented that singers from the Birmingham-to-New Orleans connection migrated northward, perpetuating this fascinating musical tradition in Cleveland during the 1940s and 1950s.[30]

Significantly, schools at all levels played a strong role in encouraging black religious harmony singing—considered dignified and worthwhile by black American schoolteachers, most of whom were educated at southern black colleges. Numerous quartet singers received their initial harmony singing instructions in school as early as their primary and secondary years. Many outstanding, nationally respected quartets began as informal groups that met on the playground of their school yards; the Golden Gate Quartet began singing together as students at the Booker T. Washington High School in Norfolk, Virginia, in the middle 1930s. A few years later the Five Blind Boys of Mississippi first began to harmonize while they attended the Piney Woods School.

The experience of R. C. Foster of Bessemer, who began training quartets in Jefferson County, Alabama, during World War I, clearly illustrates the importance of schools in training singers, many of whom later performed in community-based quartets:

> I was in school under a young man graduated from Tuskegee who learned to sing there, and he taught me quartet music. Professor Vernon W. Barnett . . . was a black man and he come out to teach a little small school; that was Charity High Industrial School in Lowndes County, Alabama. A certain portion of the day we had practice. We called it voice culture. You could hear the four voices but they was so even that if you were sitting out there you couldn't hardly tell who was singing what. And it come down just like one solid voice and it sounded just like a brass band.[31]

Perceived as respectable because it was so closely associated with positive aspects of American culture—education, family, place of employment, and the church—young blacks were often encouraged to pursue harmony singing. The involvement of blacks with vocal quartets also made the transition from their rural birthplaces to the nation's urban centers easier. Blues singing was yet another musical form that helped to ease the social dysfunction felt by African Americans moving to the city, especially one as segregated as Birmingham, Alabama. This seemed to be especially true for younger males, many of whom turned to the "devil's music" for comfort and self-expression, and because it was popular. Other singers vacillated between the two worlds, and it is important to remember that the recorded repertoire of some groups, most notably the Norfolk Jazz/Jubilee Quartet and the Birmingham Jubilee, included both the sacred and the salacious. But quartets performing Christian music provided black Americans with an important, acceptable social and musical outlet.[32]

Along with the collegiate and minstrel show quartets, these grassroots quartets provided singers with yet another a musical outlet. Community-based quartets incorporated stylistic elements from these and other allied traditions to form a new genre. The gospel quartet style that emerged early in this century—indeed, gospel music itself—was a hybrid based on many facets of black America's musical culture. Unlike their academic predecessors, gospel quartets stressed rhythmic inventiveness, especially through their increasing sense of syncopation that was permeating all of black music at this time. They also incorporated many of the vocal techniques, such as guttural growls and the use of their falsetto range, found in their folk roots. These groups also began to include many newly composed gospel songs along with the traditional songs, mostly spirituals, that made up the repertoires of earlier quartets. It must have been quite striking to hear a spiritual such as "Rollin' Through an Unfriendly Land" sung for the first time in the newly evolving gospel style.

The widespread and rapidly growing popularity of these quartets was not lost on the United States' mass media, particularly the record industry. Despite the fact that Columbia recorded the Standard Quartette as early as 1895 and Victor followed with the Dinwiddie Colored Quartet in 1902, these cylinders and discs faced twin problems in dissemination: limited production runs and very poor distribution. Only a few thousand of each of these early recordings were manufactured and ultimately sold through a slowly developing system for distribution, which remained largely confined to the furniture stores that also sold machines and through mail order. Furthermore, these fledgling record companies did not know how to market recordings to its rapidly growing market of African-American purchasers. It was not until the early 1920s that record companies began to gradually exploit the wealth of black religious (and secular) quartet singing.

As the companies themselves expanded their horizons, these quartet recordings were part of a larger trend that included the documentation of many forms of traditional American and ethnic music. All of the pre-1922 gospel and quartet recordings were issued as part of a general release series that included dance band, popular vocalists, comedians, and piano soloists. In 1922, following a minor depression in the industry, companies such as OKeh, Columbia, and Paramount slowly began recording more black folk musicians. Within four years each of these companies was selling records on specially segregated "race" series. The Columbia 14000, OKeh 8000, and Paramount 12/13000 releases featured blues, gospel, and jazz musicians as diverse as Louis Armstrong, Barbecue Bob, Arizona Dranes, Reverend J. M. Gates, the Harlem Footwarmers, Lonnie Johnson, the Memphis Jug Band, King Oliver, Victoria Spivey, and Wood's Famous Blind Jubilee Singers.[33]

Among the earliest and most prolific of the community quartets to record commercially was the Norfolk Jazz and Jubilee Quartet. The quartet's initial selections were made for OKeh in 1921, for which they recorded twenty selections as wide ranging as "Preacher Man Blues," "Who Built the Ark?" "When I Walked Up I Was as Sharp as a Tack," and "Strut Miss Lizzie." By 1923 the group had switched to the Paramount label, and one of its earliest records, "Father Prepare Me" / "My Lord's Gonna Move This Wicked Race" (Paramount 12035), proved to be so popular that it remained in the catalog for nine years, until the company went out of business in 1932. The success of these early quartet records inspired the companies to explore this genre, and dozens of community and semi-professional quartets eventually recorded at the permanent studios or the southern field sessions that became common practice among record companies by the late 1920s. These twice yearly sweeps (usually in the spring and fall to avoid extreme weather) brought the major companies into southern cities such as Atlanta, Dallas, Memphis, and New Orleans, where many types of local talent, including quartets, were documented.

Radio gradually emerged as the second most important outlet for the promotion and dissemination of black gospel quartet singing. Regularly scheduled commercial radio broadcasts began in 1920 when Pittsburgh's KDKA signed on the air. Quartets began performing on "live" broadcasts about the same time as they recorded in larger numbers for the commercial record companies. Virtually all of the programs on these early radio stations were live and included programs that featured talent such as hillbilly musicians, drama, dance bands, comedy acts, and popular quartets. In Roanoke, Virginia, for example, the N&W [Norfolk & Western Railroad] Imperial Quartet was broadcasting over WDBJ as early as 1928, a feat mirrored in Hampton Roads, where local groups like the Silver Leaf Quartette of Norfolk and the Golden Crown Quartet began their radio work about the same time.

Local businesses quite often underwrote these daily or weekly fifteen- to thirty-minute radio shows, which brought the singing groups wider exposure among both a white audience and members of the black community, as well as among urban and rural listeners. As the number and geographical distribution of harmony quartets performing on local and regional (usually 50,000-watt "clear channel" that covered several states) stations prior to World War II grew, the broadcasts' impact also increased. During the 1930s several quartets began appearing on nationally syndicated radio programs. The Utica Jubilee Quartet was featured on one of the first such programs, broadcasting over the National Broadcasting Network in 1927. Their groundbreaking exposure was soon followed by many other groups, including the Southernaires, whose show, "The Little Weather Beaten Church of the Air," ran from 1933 until 1944.

Grassroots gospel quartets had grabbed the musical imagination of black Americans by the time the pall of the Great Depression had settled over the United States. Although the record industry was decimated by the Depression (Paramount went bankrupt in 1932), Columbia and OKeh continued to distribute recordings by a few select, largely unknown, groups like the Campbell College Quartet and the Central Mississippi Quartet. Meanwhile, the radio broadcasts of other quartets continued to reach hundreds of thousands of listeners, no doubt including a significant number of white Americans. Thus black gospel quartet singing began its rapid transformation from a religious, regional genre to a form of popular entertainment that was slowly crossing the invisible borders that demarcate the United States along racial and geographical lines.

The gospel quartet tradition soon established itself as a vibrant, exciting, and rapidly changing style of religious music. Its far-flung appeal partially began when the older spirituals and hymns were synthesized and infused with extended, innovative, and unconventional (by the standards of common-practice Western art music) harmonies that are embellished far beyond the basic triads, which included much crossing of the inner voices. Vocal improvisations, rendered by a prominent bass singer or a strong falsetto from the baritone or high tenor, set apart this new style from older, more formal gospel vocal practices. Many of the these harmony groups also sang slightly "behind the beat," which increased the rhythmic tension and interest. A few groups even added a second lead singer, which allowed for lead switching, though this caught on even more after World War II. Even though the four parts for singers were carefully worked out, they still allowed for the freedom of semi-improvisation that helped to create a slightly new performance each time. Quartets were also quick to include many of the popular religious songs newly composed by Thomas A. Dorsey and Kenneth Morris as well as Memphians Herbert W. Brewster and Lucie Campbell, whose influence is discussed more fully later in this book.

This distinctive combination won many fans for black gospel quartet singing. The confluence of the quartets' widespread popularity with mass media's attention soon promoted this music beyond its initial audience of southern black Americans. By the mid- to late 1930s, some black gospel quartets began heading toward full-time professional status. While groups from Texas, such as the Soul Stirrers, and Birmingham's Famous Blue Jay Singers and Kings of Harmony were the key quartets during this time of change, the Golden Gate Quartet from Norfolk emerged as the single most influential group to take this major step.

Most scholars and quartet singers credit the Golden Gate Quartet with reinfusing the jubilee style with new life by adding an infectious, highly rhythmic aspect to gospel singing. Contemporary singers often still refer to them as "fathers" who not only defined but perfected the style. This extremely syncopated rhythmic drive caught on with fans and singers alike, creating a sensation that brought the Gates (as they were called) to the forefront of African-American gospel music. Willie Johnson, founder of the Golden Gate Quartet, described it as vocal percussion that Johnson likened to a tempered percussion instrument—"It was just like a drum, but it had notes to it, it had lyrics to it . . . like a bunch of guys beating a tom-tom somewhere . . . it all had to be done sharply and together." Johnson further articulated his own definition, albeit brief, of jubilee gospel singing: "Any music that had a beat and had a joyful sound to it. It was a joyous sort of thing. I mean it was a thing you patted your foot by. It wasn't a thing that made you want to cry like 'my mama's dead and gone.' . . . It was all light really, entertaining. And it had some merit, like in the narrative tunes, a lot of people had never heard about all the Biblical heroes. They could hear the story start and they'd see when it reached the middle and they'd see it reach the apex and then quit."[34]

This jubilee style of gospel quartet singing, which emerged nationwide in 1936 and 1937, contained both lyrical and musical innovations. The words of jubilee quartet performance often told a coherent story based on a parable from the Bible; for instance, two of the Golden Gates' best-known songs describe the temptations of Jezebel, the trials of Job, and Noah's wrangle with the epic flood. "Job," for example, begins with a spiritual, "I'm on My Way to the Kingdom Land," before Johnson launches into his own half-spoken *cante fable*—like opening, almost a "come-ye-all" that introduces the gradually unfolding story. The fact that jubilee songs featured a narrative story line appealed to listeners, who were tickled to hear familiar Bible stories told in this fashion and because storytelling was so integral to black American culture. Except for the African-American ballad tradition that brought us epics about "John Henry" and "Stackolee," most black American music—blues and rap come to mind—is nonlinear and coheres through emotional logic. Jubilee songs are closer to Protestant sermons that are presented in a more thematic or narrative form.

Expanding from its home base in Norfolk, Virginia, the Golden Gate Quartet began touring across the Middle Atlantic states and the Southeast. By 1936 the group was on the road much of the time, veering close to professional status; late in the year they landed a regular spot on Columbia, South Carolina's powerful WIS. Within a year the Gates had gained not only a nationally syndicated radio broadcast that originated in Charlotte, North Carolina, but a contract with Bluebird Records, for whom it recorded for three years. Just before World War II the group switched over to Columbia Records and, in the early 1940s, continued to broadcast regularly over the NBC radio network. The Golden Gate Quartet gradually expanded its repertoire in order to move into the lucrative pop music field and, by the middle 1940s, had toured with several white and black swing bands, sung at the White House, performed at New York City's famous Cafe Society, and appeared in the films "Star Spangled Rhythm" and "Stage Door Canteen." In short, by the close of World War II, the Golden Gate Quartet had become "the most artistically innovative, widely imitated, and the most commercially successful of all twentieth-century religious quartets."[35]

The role of gospel quartets such as the Famous Blue Jay Singers and the Soul Stirrers during the late 1930s transition period to full-time, professional status proved to be critical to groups that followed in their footsteps. During the middle 1930s the Famous Blue Jay Singers and the Kings of Harmony moved their base of operations from Jefferson County, Alabama, to Dallas, Texas, where they soon met Houston's Five Soul Stirrers. These three groups were among the first to give up the security of full-time employment in exchange for the potentially lucrative but untried life of professional gospel quartet singing. After touring for several years and slowly expanding their audience base, the Kings of Harmony remained with their southern audience; however the Famous Blue Jay Singers and the Soul Stirrers decided to explore a different path. Just as World War II began to ravage western Europe these two groups relocated to Chicago—home of a major gospel publishing house and composers like Thomas A. Dorsey—which gave them ready access to a large and receptive audience of transplanted southerners who had moved to the urban Midwest.

Though not as well recognized as the Golden Gate Quartet, the Famous Blue Jay Singers and the Soul Stirrers helped to alter the sound of popular quartet singing by exploring their own innovations. They expanded the concept and use of "switch leading," which called for more than one lead singer during the performance of a song. Role switching in midperformance often ignited the lead singers, helping to create a very competitive atmosphere and leading inevitably to an even more emotional exhibition of spiritual fervor. Silas Steele of the Famous Blue Jay Singers emerged as the first master of this fervent lead singing. Black Christians flocked to the programs featuring Steele, at least in part to hear his magnificent lead singing soaring over the background harmony, which gave his hard-edged vocals power similar to a shouting, Pentecostal preacher. Such lead singing provided audiences with a taste of the "hard gospel" singing that would become common a decade later. Dual lead singing also expanded many quartets from four to five members, offering new opportunities to talented young singers who wished to explore these new avenues. The growing popularity of these innovative groups also led to the practice of advertising shows as "song battles," in which some of these younger groups would attempt to raise the crowd to its feet with increasingly excited and passionate performances. The quartet that garnered the largest applause "won" the contest. These new performance techniques, creative marketing tactics (such as multiple "star" billings on a single program), and successful records and radio programs by the Golden Gate Quartet, the Heavenly Gospel Singers, Mitchell's Christian Singers, Selah Jubilee Singers, and others laid a very firm foundation for the mass popularity for quartets.

The onset of World War II slowed the rapidly growing interest in quartets. Gasoline rationing, a shortage of rubber for tires, and the diminished production of automobiles greatly inhibited travel. Quartets stuck closer to home, many traveled by rail, and quartets mostly performed in churches and other venues close to their home. The record industry also slowed considerably due to a shortage of shellac, and during all of 1943 and much of 1944 a bitter dispute between the musicians' union and the record companies all but shut down the entire industry. The only public aspect of quartet singing not affected by the war was radio broadcasting; in fact, groups sought out even more radio exposure due to the travel and recording restrictions. Many local quartets continued with their radio broadcasts, and a few even thrived due to increased radio exposure. One group that particularly benefited from the continued boom in broadcasting was Nashville's Fairfield Four: "They began broadcasting over 50,000 watt WLAC in 1942, after winning a local contest sponsored by Sunway Vitamins. Their WLAC program was transcribed and broadcast over powerful sister stations from Philadelphia to Salt Lake City, Utah, effectively blanketing the nation. Their broadcasts were so popular that the group was in constant demand for personal appearances and soon became the South's greatest box office attraction."[36]

These radio broadcasts themselves were not very lucrative. The pay, in fact, was minimal; however, the live engagements that resulted from such exposure provided them with the core of their income. And the Fairfield Four was not an isolated example of radio's power to expand a group's popularity among black Christians. The Four Harmony Kings, formed in West Virginia in 1938, built their reputation through radio work and personal appearances. Within several months of their formation the group had moved rapidly from a low-profile, weekly Sunday morning broadcast to a fifteen-minute daily radio program on WNOX in Knoxville, which covered much of the southeastern United States. After the Swan Bread Company began sponsoring the radio show, the group changed its name to the Swan Silvertone Singers and firmly established its reputation.[37] Simultaneously the Selah Jubilee Singers built their career by way of daily radio work over WPTF, a clear-channel 50,000-watt station in Raleigh, North Carolina. This pattern was well established by the late 1930s, though the overwhelming number of quartets remained tied to local stations and performed on a circuit that permitted them to retain their regular, daily employment.

Beginning in mid-1944 the record industry began to reopen. Unlike the days before World War II, which were dominated by a handful of major companies, scores of independent record labels sprang up following the close of the war. The shellac shortages and the musicians' union ban had shaken the industry to its core. The gradual availability of reel-to-reel magnetic tape recorders also freed these entrepreneurs from the extremely high cost of purchasing disc-cutting machines that were the industry standard until the 1947. During 1943 small companies, such as Savoy and Regis, began with limited operations around the greater New York City area. The fever gradually spread as the war ended and a handful of companies like Peacock (Houston), King (Cincinnati), and Capitol (Los Angeles) emerged as major labels. Most of the postwar labels, however, remained tiny operations that released a handful of records before going out of business or being folded into another company.

Despite such factors as a lack of promotion, questionable or nonexistent accounting practices, and inferior pressings, most quartets sought out the opportunity to record their singing, while a few assiduously avoided the recording studios, apparently fearful that they would be defrauded or that some other group might steal an arrangement from one of their records. In most ways, though, the radio and record industries served the interests of quartets by getting their names and music before a wider audience. Both of these media helped to expand the groups' audience, but live performances at churches, schools, and neighborhood centers actually provided nearly all of the quartets with their true source of income. It was the rare group, indeed, that actually made money directly from radio programs or the sales of their records.

What did all of this media attention mean to the general interest in African-American gospel quartet singing? Prior to World

War II only a select few of the thousands of black gospel quartets performed professionally; however, beginning about 1945 the popularity of quartets skyrocketed—the cultural, musical, and economical climate had grown ripe for full-time performing. Interest in this type of music became so intense that within a few years there were "hundreds of quartets making lengthy tours, travelling around the country singing in churches, school auditoriums, and concert halls."[38] The organizational, social, and cultural fiber of black quartet singing underwent a critical transformation as a result of this newfound mass appeal. The large, complex network of community quartets continued to function, but many singers joined or formed groups with the intention of testing their vocal talents and general popularity by quitting their day jobs and going on the road as professionals. The weekend (Thursday through Monday) schedule of late July 1947 for the Chosen Five, which was published in a local black newspaper, the *Louisiana Weekly,* typifies the work available to the group that

> have been acclaimed as "New Orleans' Most Famous Singing Group": Hear the Chosen Five in person, July 25 and 26 at the Masonic Hall in Ocean Springs. La. On July 27, 2:30 pm, the Chosen Five and Mighty Pilgrim Travelers of Los Angeles, Calif. will meet in a song battle at Booker Washington Auditorium, and at 8:30 pm on the same date the Chosen Five and the Pilgrim Travelers will meet in a battle at Big Zion Methodist Church, Roseland, La. July 28 they will be at the Hartzell Methodist Church, 2024 Caffin Ave.[39]

Quartets during this era had to provide an interesting repertoire that included not only a few older spirituals and many jubilee songs, but also a few of the even more fashionable "shouting" numbers that could bring a holiness fever to their performance. By the late 1940s and early 1950s there were so many fine jubilee-style harmony groups around that only the very best caught the audience's attention for very long.[40] Jubilee singing continued to predominate among gospel quartets during the years immediately following the end of the war. In fact, jubilee quartets spawned many imitators across the United States, but especially on the East Coast. The Golden Gate Quartet, in particular, became the model for innumerable local and semiprofessional quartets in the Carolinas, Virginia, and Maryland, in addition to groups in the urban corridor between

Washington, D.C., and New York City. Many of these groups attempted to copy Willie Johnson's biblical narratives and syncopated bass arrangements.

By the late 1940s a new style, "hard gospel," began to catch on with black American gospel singers in general, but especially with quartets. This style refers to the emotional, powerful lead singing epitomized by Ira Tucker of the Dixie Hummingbirds and the Sensational Nightingales' Julius Cheeks. The Dixie Hummingbirds were, in fact, one of the most successful quartets that furthered this innovative style. Organized in Greenville, South Carolina, in 1928, the group worked locally and semiprofessionally throughout the 1930s and came under the sway of the Heavenly Gospel Singers, who often sang in churches between Charlotte, North Carolina, and Columbia, South Carolina. Near the close of World War II they relocated to Philadelphia, and it was the postwar version of the Dixie Hummingbirds that achieved national prominence. Lead singer Ira Tucker, along with master "basser," William Bobo, proved themselves to be at the heart of the group. Tucker's impassioned lead singing often provided the highlights to their live performances and is documented on their Apollo recordings from the late 1940s. Highlighting lead vocals in quartet singing represented an innovation in quartet singing and acknowledged the influence of solo gospel singers like Mahalia Jackson, Sister Rosetta Tharpe, and Alex Bradford.[41]

Hard gospel quartets often mixed their repertoire in order to reflect their own interests and to appeal to a wide range of fans. They usually combined older spirituals such as "Wouldn't Mind Dying If Dying Was All," "I've Been in the Storm Too Long," or "Motherless Children Have a Hard Time" with some of the gospel songs composed during the 1920s, 1930s, and 1940s. Despite the varied background of these songs, they were generally cast in emotionally evocative arrangements that "worked" the crowd in an attempt to raise them to higher states of religious fervor. In addition to the singing itself, the lead singers often moved among the folks who attended the program, strutting and talking to their adoring fans. This movement off the stage was facilitated by the gradual widespread use of amplified sound systems that also allowed groups to perform in larger venues and still be heard. Silas Steele of the Famous Blue

Jay Singers was the master of exploiting the spiritual zeal of his listeners, especially as he moved around the stage. Lynn Abbott observed that most New Orleans quartet singers generally credit Steele "with inventing the 'preacher-style' lead as he broke from the old 'flatfooted' formation to pace the stage, 'worrying' his listeners with two-fisted antics and gravelly vocal intonations that usurped the traditional emphasis on harmony with direct appeal to emotion."[42] Many of the popular, progressive quartets also added musical instruments (first guitars and pianos, then bass and drums), which important groups as diverse as the Swan Silvertone Singers and the Five Blind Boys of Alabama had incorporated by 1950.

By the early 1950s jubilee and hard gospel elements both proved so important that many groups included two separate lead singers—one for jubilee, the other for hard gospel. Sometimes groups with contrasting styles, for instance, the Trumpeteers and the Pilgrim Travelers, might appear on the same bill, as part of a "song battle" in order to stimulate community interest in the program. This combination brought out even more black Christians who wished to listen to and wildly cheer these popular groups. Such traveling, packaged shows underscored the already intense competition found among the many fine grassroots, semiprofessional, and professional quartets singing after World War II. The very existence of so many black religious vocal harmony groups that were able to fully or partially support themselves through singing also reinforces the fact that they had reached a special plateau of public acceptance; in retrospect, the years around 1950 represent the apex of popular interest in quartets.

Other extramusical factors reflect this trend. The propensity to dress in sharply tailored clothes, present a highly polish stage act using well-rehearsed choreography, and the addition of amplified instruments illustrates the quartets' desire to uphold a "professional" appearance. Audiences judged them every time they appeared at a church or auditorium, thus placing their financial well-being and professional integrity on the line at least several times a week. Their failure to please the black American Christians who came to hear them would put them at risk. Such pressures led to a gradual, perhaps inevitable, institutionalization or standardization in dress, stage presence, and performance style paralleling those other professional entertainers. The importance of these trends was not lost on Thurmon Ruth of the Selah Jubilee Singers when he reminisced about this era.

> I remember the time when groups dressed in black suits and white shirts and bow ties. Then we got to the place with red suits, green suits, loud as we could get. Once upon a time I said I wouldn't wear certain colors and we ended up with some kelly green pants and some beige coats we had made in Chicago. Everybody said it was so sharp, you know . . . it impressed the ladies.
>
> We were entertainers, let's put it that way. We didn't try to get the folks to shout all that much; we entertained the folks—had a lot of novelty stuff. . . . They would call us "spirit killers," [because] we would do "Gospel Train," we'd shovel the coal; "There's Fire Down Below," we'd push him in the oven, throw him in the fire. It was hard for a group to beat us . . . [when] we could come along with our novelty stuff and cool 'em down.[43]

The Pilgrim Travelers, Soul Stirrers, and Spirit of Memphis Quartet were in many respects the African-American religious equivalent of Duke Ellington's famous Cotton Club "Jungle Band," Whoopie John Whilfarht's Polka Band, or Bob Wills and the Texas Playboys. All of these moderate-sized music organizations enjoyed professional status, commercial recording contracts with important labels, and radio work that kept their creative work in the consciousness of a faithful and proud racial, ethnic, or regional audience. During the time of the Korean War, black gospel quartets enjoyed such a strong base of popular support across the United States that it must have seemed as if the musical genre would last forever.

The decade ending in 1955 marked the pinnacle of commercial success for this music. Touring and personal appearances provided the primary financial support for major quartets such as the Dixie Hummingbirds, the Fairfield Four, the Harmonizing Four of Richmond (Virginia), and the Sensational Nightingales. These and other similar groups worked urban centers across the country as well as the small towns and churches throughout the South. Other figures in black gospel music—the Ward Singers, Roberta Martin, Brother Joe May, and Alex Bradford—enjoyed enough strong financial and popular support that they were able to dedicate their lives to performing, promoting, and writing gospel music. A spirit of commercialism and showmanship pervaded all of black American gospel

Table 1. *The Emergence of Professional Quartets, 1935–60*

1935–40

Golden Gate Quartet	Norfolk, Virginia
Soul Stirrers	Houston, Texas
Kings of Harmony	Birmingham, Alabama
Famous Blue Jay Singers	Birmingham, Alabama

1940–50

Dixie Hummingbirds	Spartanburg, South Carolina
Spirit of Memphis	Memphis, Tennessee
Swan Silvertone	Charleston, West Virginia
Five Blind Boys of Mississippi	Jackson, Mississippi
Harmonizing Four	Richmond, Virginia
Fairfield Four	Nashville, Tennessee

1950–60

Flying Clouds of Joy	Detroit, Michigan
Bells of Joy	Houston, Texas
Sensational Nightingales	Greenville, South Carolina
Highway QCs	Houston, Texas

music as everyone tried to catch their share of the money and the glory generated by this intense, widespread interest.

By the early 1950s, semi- and fully professional quartets could be found throughout the South as well as in the urban areas that served as home to a significant black population. Table 1 lists the names and geographical origins of fourteen of the most important touring professional quartets. The lure of full-time quartet singing attracted many talented singers, even though touring meant leaving the secure confines of home for new places, different ideas, and temptations never before encountered. For young singers who had lived their entire lives in small, distant, rural communities like Dimebox, Texas; Bobo, Mississippi; or Difficulty, Tennessee, such opportunities seemed heaven-sent. It gave them the chance to see places of which they had never even heard and sing the praises of God to other like-minded Christians. Life on the road proved to be unpredictable and forever changing, and financial security was never far from the singers' thoughts, for many of them had families to support. Doug Seroff observes: "When a group goes out on the road as a full-time occupation, money and its proper division among members can become a serious point of contention. Money was the cause of many bitter breakups during the 'Golden Age.'"[44]

Finances became an even greater factor as the business end of quartet singing grew more lucrative and the stakes increased. Programs headlined by major groups usually included three or four other local or regionally recognized acts and brought in thousands of dollars in a single night. Multistar events, sometimes known as caravans, included as many as three or four big names and were not limited only to quartets. These big-money programs took place in major venues of big cities like New York City's Apollo Theater or Birmingham's Civic Center. Caravans were well advertised and heavily promoted in newspaper advertisements, over local radio stations that featured gospel music, and on posters and placards placed throughout the African-American community. Members of the local participating groups not only personally sold tickets to their friends, but they also made certain that they were readily available (at a discount for advance purchase) through neighborhood grocery stores, barbershops, and record stores. During the program itself they also encouraged fans to buy some of the merchandise, usually records and autographed photographs, of the each of the groups. No doubt about it, this was a lucrative enough business that each member of the quartet carefully scrutinized all of the financial transactions.

Most programs followed a prescribed format. They often lasted five or six hours, sometimes longer if some of the quartets were particularly successful in working the crowd into a spiritual frenzy. The well-known, out-of-town quartets always closed the program; they were often kept on stage for extended periods because the crowds rarely got to hear them in person. Audience members showed great respect for all of the groups, from local quartets whom they heard regularly to the greatest crowd-pleasers whose records were well known to them. Throughout these programs the audience clapped their hands, stomped their feet, and danced near their seats and in the aisles in ethereal ecstasy when the singing reached its height of religious passion. And "spirit raisers" such as Clarence Fountain of the Blind Boys or Claude Jeter of the Swan Silvertones were always proud of their ability to induce this type of ritual behavior among quartet fans. Although the program was an unambiguously, totally religious event, it was also an occasion to celebrate popular music and culture.

The crowds' outward reactions were hardly alien to those of fans of the era's best-known black pop singers—Louis Jordan, Hank Ballard, Dinah Washington, or Nellie Lutcher. And it created tension among members of the extended community of gospel singers, fans, and promoters, almost all of whom were devout Christians who attended Protestant churches. This level of popularity brought out a type of adulation that sometimes bordered on the sexual. Tony Heilbut also took note of this aspect of quartet performing when he wrote about the Soul Stirrers during the early to mid-1950s when Sam Cooke sang lead for them: "Its performers sing with their bodies and move with a thrilling grace and physical abandonment. This sexuality is taken for granted, and is, I think, largely innocent. . . . But Cooke's sex appeal had nothing to do with friendly local sponsors. It was the allure of the professional showman. Even in gospel, he was a bobby-sox idol, the first singer to bring in the younger crowd as well as the older shouting saints."[45] Surely this was not the type of program or response that the Soul Stirrers themselves or the Famous Blue Jay Singers expected when they began touring fifteen years ago.

It was not enough to tour and sing professionally; quartets also felt strong, continuous pressure to bring their music into the homes of fans. Some were able to keep up their network radio broadcasts, while many others turned to the recording industry to help them remain in the fans' consciousness. Recording for a local label was fine, but the professional quartets needed well-distributed records in order to truly spread their name across the entire United States. The lack of a major record contract proved to be the downfall of many semiprofessional or professional groups who wished to remain on the touring circuit that provided them with a stable income. The fate of the New Orleans Chosen Five provide a case in point:

> As "hit" records for independent labels like Specialty and Peacock were taking the Soul Stirrers, the Pilgrim Travelers, and the Five Blind Boys to gospel stardom in the early '50s, the New Orleans Chosen Five found itself fenced in. Their firm reputation in Chicago kept them in demand there, but Northern tours which used to run open-ended now barely lasted a week. "We went there five or six times,"

says Neal Kimble, "but the rest of the time we was going to Mississippi; Jackson, Meridian, McComb, like this, and then back to New Orleans." This was the old Route 51 territory that they had started out canvassing a decade ago. To make ends meet, group members started taking day jobs.[46]

Even with gospel quartets enjoying stunning popularity, many of these harmony singers might have admired the professional groups but were not interested in following the glitter associated with full-time singing. They preferred the security of their own communities, jobs they already knew, and a familiar social milieu. However proficient and well trained they might be, the vast majority of jubilee and hard quartets were content with local or regional fame, a ready-made and established audience, and, if they could arrange for it, a weekly radio broadcast. Many of these quartets no doubt had the talent, but lacked the inclination to pursue full-time careers in harmony singing. Grassroots quartets continued to prosper in their own communities, and the general success of quartet singing helped to reinforce their own popularity.

By the middle 1950s commercial interest in black American gospel quartets began to slide, in part due to changes in musical tastes but also because of the inevitable saturation of the marketplace. The lead singers of the best-known quartets had not only stepped out to the front of their own groups, but to a more prominent position in the fans' eyes. Many of these singers became as well known as their groups, and flyers for caravans were often billed as "Claude Jeter *and* the Swan Silvertone" or "Julius Cheeks *with* the Sensational Nightingales." The change in emphasis from quartets to a harmony ensemble with a featured lead singer signaled the renewed, popular interest in solo performers, including such formidable talents as Sister Edna Gallmon Cooke, Mahalia Jackson, or Marian Williams, who had been around for years. A trend toward even larger ensembles, particularly mass choirs and choruses of a score of voices or more, began. This movement evolved slowly—it had actually begun in the late 1940s—but by the early 1960s it blossomed outward into the public's consciousness. Choirs were led by Clinton Utterbach and James Cleveland in the East and Midwest, while Edwin Hawkins's Singers came to the fore in California. By the late 1960s recordings by these choirs and groups like the B. C. and M. Choir and the Southern California

Community Choir topped the charts followed by those interested in black popular religious music.

Equally significant, many of the most visible lead singers left the gospel field completely to try their hands at popular music. Over an eight-year period the Soul Stirrers' Sam Cooke, for instance, gradually moved from simply being a group member, to headliner, to pop crooner before his shocking death in 1964. Many other black pop singers began their careers performing with quartets, including Lou Rawls (Pilgrim Travelers), Brook Benton (Bill Langford Quartet), Joe Hinton (Spirit of Memphis), "Little" Johnny Taylor (Highway QCs), and O. V. Wright (Spirit of Memphis). This trend was particularly notable in cities already well known for popular music:

> Johnny Adams of the Consolators, Ernie Kador of the Golden Chain Jubileers, and Chris Kenner of Noah's Ark were among the more successful New Orleans gospel singers to swing into the secular arena. . . . Walter Budgett [another long-standing quartet singer] resisted, "You know, people were following me from New York to Florida trying to change me over, like at the same time Sam Cooke and all these guys were changing over, but . . . I never went for it. I tell my wife now, 'Look at Lou Rawls and these guys,' say, 'You see where I could have been!' But I just loved gospel singing too much.'"[47]

Entire quartets also left gospel music for the greater financial rewards of popular music. In the early 1940s one of the Hampton Institute quartets dropped out of religious music and became the Deep River Boys. Another long-standing quartet, the Selah Jubilee Singers, switched to rhythm and blues about 1953, recording as the Larks for Apollo, Timely, and other New York–area record companies. Similarly, the New Orleans Humming Four, one of the Crescent City's outstanding quartets, became the Hawks and recorded for Imperial Records during the middle 1950s.[48] This profound switch from gospel quartet to pop vocal group often came at the insistence of record company executives, who made convincing pitches, wooing the singers with righteous tales of lucrative contracts that would bring them not only more cash, but women, cars, and an even larger audience. Most of the groups turned them down, although Don Robey (Peacock/Duke Records) and Lew Chudd (Imperial Records) were legendary in their ability to convince gospel quartets to convert to secular music. Conversions were not new, of course; in the 1880s college jubilee groups associated with Fisk University split from their collegiate ties in order to reach a larger audience both in this country and abroad. And as early as the late 1920s, some of the church-based groups, such as the Silver Leaf Quartet of Norfolk, were pressured to record blues. But the large financial stakes and recording opportunities of the 1950s only provided a greater incentive to switch from the sacred to the secular realm. Although the seductive lure of popular music by no means destroyed the black gospel quartet field, it became increasingly difficult to differentiate between black secular and sacred harmony groups. Both religious and popular quartets were utilizing instruments to accompany their singing; because of the size of the venues and increasing technology, coupled with lower prices, amplified guitars and keyboards became more commonplace. Their performance styles had evolved into carefully choreographed, quick-paced rituals, complete with emcees, and designed to squeeze as much emotional response from as large a crowd as possible. This fascination and flirtation with popular trends may have increased the revenues of some groups, but it also helped to bring about the decline of black gospel quartets. The opportunities for live performances dropped off dramatically after 1955, and a significant number of quartets stopped touring. Many full-time groups dropped from these ranks to those of semiprofessionals, while others returned to community quartet status, finding employment outside the music field. The decade that began with the close of World War II had been rewarding for some quartet singers, and perhaps too healthy in the eyes of some black churchgoers.[49]

The long-burning bright light that had focused on quartet singers inevitably opened them up to criticism from some of the more conservative African-American church members. These spiritual folks slowly became dissatisfied with the increasing secularization of gospel music by quartets. They saw quartet singers being treated like stars of popular music—riding in large, expensive automobiles, wearing finely tailored clothes, and making generous salaries. Behind the scenes many fans also heard the rumors about "outside" women and too much liquor, which further clouded the image of quartet singers. Many church members felt that some of the big-time quartets had moved too far from the spirit of God and the ideals of the Lord's teachings, causing them to look with disfavor upon the more commercial, ostentatious groups.

Although very few quartets, most notably the Dixie Humming-birds, the Blind Boys, the Might Clouds of Joy, and the Soul Stirrers, remained on the road after 1960, four-part harmony groups remain a significant, albeit old-fashioned, force in African-American religious music in the United States. Many older, once full-time professional groups, such as the Harmonizing Four of Richmond (Virginia) and the Spirit of Memphis, retreated to semiprofessional status and remained popular regional groups into the 1980s. Several other grassroots quartets have been active for at least fifty years. Although none of them ever reached the semiprofessional ranks, the Royal Harmony Four (Memphis, Tennessee), the Sterling Jubilees (Besse-mer, Alabama), and the Alabama and Georgia Quartet (Chicago, Illinois) have been singing since the early 1930s. With few exceptions, the careers of these and most other quartets are largely undocumented because few of them were ever known outside of their communities.[50]

Because quartet singing is all but defunct in the free-wheeling commercial marketplace, its future support must inevitably lie within the black Christian community itself. With the exception of the veteran Fairfield Four and Five Blind Boys of Alabama, both of which have recorded for major labels and toured nationwide in the early 1990s, few signs exist that this music will ever again enjoy a strong base of commercial support. Although a few younger a cappella groups, most notably the Birmingham Sunlights, have gained attention on the festival and concert circuit, the community support for the older, more traditional quartet singing discussed in this chapter is more sentimental than fact. Today's popular black "quartets" that continue to tour into the 1990s, such as the Mighty Clouds of Joy, have all but dropped their bass singers, often feature three-part harmony, and sound more like a small choir with organ, piano, and percussion accompaniment. The rest of this book underscores the irony that, at least in Memphis, black gospel quartet singing has moved full circle from the folk tradition to popular culture and then back to its folk roots again. It is doubtful that the cycle will ever repeat itself.

NOTES

1. The most substantial work on this particular subject is found in Lynn Abbott, "'Play That Barber Shop Chord': A Case for the African-American Origin of Barbershop Harmony," *American Music,* 10 (Fall 1992), pp. 289–326. This article, as well as personal conversations with Abbott, inform not only the section on barbershops but this entire chapter. Likewise, Doug Seroff's unpublished paper "The Continuity of the Black Gospel Quartet Tradition—In Harmony with the Black Community," read at the Baptist Sunday School Convention, Nashville, Tennessee, October 1982, helped to shape my thinking on this subject.

2. Robert Toll, *Blacking Up: The Minstrel Show in Nineteenth-Century America* (New York: Oxford University Press, 1974), remains the best minstrel show history.

3. This reference infers the presence of four-voice vocal groups in minstrel shows as early as the 1850s. See Carl Wittke, *Tambo and Bones* (Durham, N.C.: Duke University Press, 1930), p. 177.

4. See, for instance, Toll, *Blacking Up,* chap. 5.

5. Ike Simond, *Old Slack's Reminiscences and Pocket History of the Colored Profession from 1865–1891* (Chicago: by the author, 1891), p. 26.

6. My profound thanks for Lynn Abbott, Ray Funk, and Doug Seroff's reading of the *Indianapolis Freeman* and other turn-of-the-century black newspapers for information about blues, quartets, and other forms of black popular entertainment. The background information and details for this section are deeply indebted to their research. This quote is drawn from their published research "100 Years From Today: A Survey of Afro-American Music in 1890 as Recorded in the Black Community Press," *78 Quarterly,* vol. 1, no. 6 (1992), p. 54.

7. Ibid., p. 61–62.

8. Abbott, "Play That Barber Shop Chord," p. 311.

9. Doug Seroff, "How Shall We Sing The Lord's Song in a Foreign Land?" (Nashville: Gospel Arts Day Catalogue, 1989), p. 3. This essay is drawn from a book-length manuscript in progress that Seroff has nearly completed on the first thirty years of the Fisk University Jubilee Singers.

10. Lynn Abbott, Ray Funk, and Doug Seroff, "100 Years from Today: Selected Items of Musical Matters Drawn from the Black Community," *78 Quarterly,* vol. 1, no. 5 (1991), p. 59.

11. Vaughn Webb, an unpublished essay to accompany BRI 011 "Hampton Roads Quartets," p. 10.

12. Frederika Bremer, *The Homes of the New World: Impressions of America* (New York: Harper and Brothers, 1853), as quoted in Dena Epstein, *Sinful Tunes and Spirituals* (Urbana: University of Illinois Press, 1977), p. 164.

13. William Allen, Charles Ware, and Lucy Garrison, *Slave Songs of the United States* (1867; rpt., New York: Oak Publications, 1965), p. v.

14. James Weldon Johnson, "The Origins of the 'Barber Chord,'" *The Mentor* (February 1929), p. 53.

15. Abbott, "Play That Barber Shop Chord," p. 290.

16. The most comprehensive work on black American shape-note singing is Doris Dyen, "The Role of Shape-Note Singing in the Musical Culture of Black Communities in Southeastern Alabama" (Ph.D. dissertation, University of Illinois, 1977). See also John Work, "Plantation Meistersinger," *Musical Quarterly,* 39 (1941), pp. 40–49; Walter Byrd, "The Shape Note Singing Convention as a Musical Institution in Alabama" (M.A. thesis, University of Alabama, 1962); and Joe Dan Boyd, "Judge Jackson: Black Giant of the White Spirituals," *Mississippi Folklore Register,* 4 (1970), pp. 7–11.

17. Dyen, "Role of Shape-Note Singing," p. 5.

18. *Louisiana Weekly,* March 2, 1929, 15.

19. A tip of the hat to Lynn Abbott for his lengthy discussion of this phenomenon in "Play That Barber Shop Chord," pp. 301–8.

20. Kerill Rubman "From 'Jubilee' to 'Gospel' in Black Male Quartet Singing" (M.A. Thesis, University of North Carolina, 1980), p. 35.

21. Thurmon Ruth, interviewed by Kip Lornell, Birmingham, Alabama, October 16, 1980.

22. Willie Johnson, interviewed by Doug Seroff, Los Angeles, California, January 23 and 25, 1980.

23. Vaughn Webb, p. 18–19.

24. Doug Seroff, "On the Battlefield," in *Repercussion,* ed. Geoffrey Haydon and Dennis Marks (London: Century Publishing, 1985), pp. 35–36. For more information about Birmingham Quartets see Brenda McCallum, ed., "Birmingham Quartet Anthology" (Birmingham: Alabama Arts Council, 1982).

25. Doug Seroff, "Two Worlds—One Heart," *Home of the Heroes* (Montgomery, Alabama: Ladysmith Black Mambazo and Traditional Gospel Quartets Catalogue, 1990), p. 13.

26. Lynn Abbott, "The Soproco Spiritual Singers: A New Orleans Quartet Family Tree" (New Orleans: National Park Service, 1983), p. 11.

27. Ibid., p. 19.

28. Ibid., pp. 14–28, for more information about this phenomenon.

29. Ibid., p. 32.

30. Further information about these migratory trends can be found in George Davis and Fred Donaldson, *Blacks in the United States: A Geographic Perspective* (Boston: Houghton Mifflin, 1975). Some of this research is being disseminated by way of extensive liner notes for audio products, such as Ray Funk's essay for "Cleveland Gospel," Gospel Heritage Records HT 316, which discusses the connections among Birmingham, New Orleans, and Cleveland.

31. Seroff, "On the Battlefield," p. 37.

32. This concept is more fully explored by Kip Lornell, "Banjos and Blues" in *Arts in Earnest: North Carolina Folklife,* ed. Daniel Patterson and Charles Zug (Durham: Duke University Press, 1990), pp. 216–32.

33. For a general survey of this aspect of the American recording industry, see John Godrich and Robert Dixon, *Recording the Blues* (London: Studio Vista, 1970); and Ronald Foreman, "Jazz and Race Records 1920–1932" (Ph.D. dissertation, University of Illinois, 1968).

34. Willie Johnson, interviewed by Doug Seroff.

35. Doug Seroff, "The Continuity of the Black Gospel Quartet Tradition—In Harmony with the Black Community," p. 14.

36. Ibid., p. 17.

37. Rubman, "From 'Jubilee' to 'Gospel,'" p. 88.

38. Seroff, "Continuity of the Black Gospel Quartet Tradition," p. 17.

39. This announcement appears in Abbott, "Soproco Singers," p. 101.

40. To hear some of these recordings and learn more about the history from this "Golden Age," please seek out Lynn Abbott "New Orleans Gospel Quartets," Heritage 306 (Sussex, England, 1985); Ray Funk, "Detroit Gospel," Heritage 311 (Sussex, England, 1986); "Atlanta Gospel," Heritage 312 (Sussex, England, 1987); or "Cleveland Gospel," Heritage 316 (Sussex, England, 1987); and Vaughan Webb, "The Hampton Roads Quartet Tradition," BRI 011 (Ferrum, Virginia, in press).

41. For more about Ira Tucker, see Tony Heilbut, *The Gospel Sound* (New York: Simon and Schuster, 1985), chapter 3.

42. Abbott, "Soproco Singers," pp. 44–45.

43. Kip Lornell, "Thurmon Ruth Interview," *Journal of Black Sacred Music,* 3 (Fall 1988), p. 31.

44. Seroff, "Continuity of the Black Gospel Quartet Tradition," p. 18.

45. Tony Heilbut, *The Gospel Sound,* p. 76. He also discusses similar topics in chapters 3 and 7.

46. Abbott, "Soproco Singers," p. 121.

47. Ibid., p. 135.

48. For more information about this transition see Lynn Abbott, "The New Orleans Humming Four," *Whiskey, Women, and . . . ,* 13 (1983), pp. 4–8.

49. Viv Broughton, *Black Gospel: An Illustrated History of the Gospel Sound* (Dorset, England: Blandford Press, 1985), pp. 61–91, succinctly recounts the overall picture of black gospel music and the internal conflicts between 1945 and 1960.

50. A few exceptions exist; see Lynn Abbott's work on the Soproco Singers and Joyce Jackson's dissertation.

2

"We Are the Spirit of Memphis"

By the 1930s Afro-American gospel quartets were popular across the South and in northern urban centers. Radio stations were broadcasting live quartet performances and all of the major commercial record companies listed quartets among their roster of artists. Recent research has shown that the most influential early groups came from two of the strongholds for community-based quartets: Jefferson County, Alabama, and the Virginia Tidewater. But what of quartets in other parts of the South and in northern cities? Among southern cities Memphis, Tennessee, has proven to be one of the most tenacious and influential hearths for blues, rhythm and blues, and soul music. Gospel quartets also have been an integral, albeit largely overlooked, segment of Afro-American music in Memphis.

Predepression quartet singers in Memphis performed without instrumental accompaniment. The I.C. Glee Club, for instance, featured only a cappella numbers, and there are no accounts of any groups using instruments until the late 1930s. Although the I.C. group was the only local quartet to record during this era, it was one among many active music groups during the 1920s. Older singers also recall the Harmony Four, the Old Red Rose Quartet, the L. and N. (Louisville and Nashville Railroad) Quartet, the Hollywood Specials, and the Mount Olive Wonders. (The heritage of one other quartet, the Spirit of Memphis, also extends back to the 1920s and will be covered later in this chapter.) While there must have been many other quartets active prior to the Great Depression, their histories have been lost to the vicissitudes of time.

The black musical culture of the 1920s is not a complete enigma, however, for we do know something more substantial about the I.C. Glee Club, which the Illinois Central Railroad sponsored. At the time of their recordings for OKeh, the quartet was composed of C. H. Evans, a porter, as first tenor; R. S. Saunders, a laborer, as second tenor; E. L. Rhodes, a springman, as baritone; and L. S. Brown, a pipefitter's helper, as bass. Organized in 1927, the club existed until some time in the late 1930s. According to a spokesman for the railroad, the quartet sang for "churches, lodges and . . . for ICRR employee events at the Memphis shop."[1] That its members named their ensemble for a local company is not unique. Testimony that such a practice benefited both parties is evident in two other Memphis groups—the Orval Brothers (Construction Company) Quartet and the S. and W. (Construction Company) Quartet. Elsewhere one finds the TCI (Tennessee, Coal, Iron Company) Quartet of Birmingham, Chicago's Stevedores Quartet, and the N. and W. (Norfolk and Western Railroad) Imperial Quartet in Roanoke, Virginia.

Although other companies had musical associations, it is especially interesting to note that the Illinois Central Railroad in Memphis sponsored at least three other groups, including the I.C. Hummingbirds, the I.C. Harmony Boys, and the I.C. Quartet (Number Two). The most specific information on this complex of ensembles comes from Haywood Gaines, a retired Illinois Central employee who sang with the I.C. Quartet (Number Two) between 1928 and 1939. He suggests that the railroad felt quartets helped improve its corporate image by association with such upstanding Christian music organizations. Gaines further notes that while the Illinois Central's support for the groups was usually literally in name only, the company's rewards were far more substantial:

> The purpose of the company to have quartets was bringing back business to the I.C. passenger [trains]. Business had left, and that was bringing them back. Folks thought little of the railroad at that time —the passenger service. . . . To get them to come and ride with us, we had booster clubs and singers. The booster club was . . . an organization that gave different parties or entertainment. They would entertain and invite the general public. When we got them there,

we would impress upon them the necessity to use the railroad as transportation. We gave dances . . . had 500 or 600 people! That brought business back to the railroad.[2]

Another responsibility of the I.C. quartets was singing on the trains themselves. Gaines recalls that "the singing groups was active riding up and down the road. Folks would come in to hear them, and some would ride the train with them. They'd go from Chicago to New Orleans. Wherever they'd go, they'd have to have extra cars."[3] Not all of the quartets actually traveled "up and down the road" on such prestigious missions, however. The railroad company called upon only the I.C. Hummingbirds for this task, while other groups entertained people at booster club meetings in and around Memphis. Although the Missouri-Pacific Railroad, which also served Memphis, echoed this pattern of corporate boosterism, we know virtually no details of its workings.[4]

Not all of the early Memphis quartets affiliated with businesses. Most were allied with community churches or specific neighborhoods and stayed out of the more commercial network that was beginning to develop. The only direct impact from outside the city was personal contact with nearby rural quartets that occasionally traveled to Memphis for weekend performances. Such travel became more prevalent during the 1940s and 1950s when quartet singing reached its popular peak. That local black quartets frequently affiliated with specific churches was not surprising given the central role of the church in Afro-American social, economic, and religious life. For example, the Mount Olive Wonders, the first quartet with which Theo Wade sang in the late 1920s, consisted of church members who provided a cappella harmony singing for their congregation, for programs at other churches, and at "box-lunch" social events held at church members' homes.[5]

For those predepression quartets not directly connected with a church, there was nearly always some neighborhood or community affiliation. The Harmony Four are recalled as one of the most respected singing groups in south Memphis at the time. Led by Gus Miller, the quartet performed for neighborhood community groups and in churches throughout the city. The Old Red Rose Quartet from north Memphis also frequently sang in local homes during the evening. Another quartet from north Memphis, the Royal Harmony Four, was founded by Jack Miller and James Spriggens in about 1930 and remains active under Miller's leadership with primary support from a network of local inner-city churches.

The members of these and other similar groups worked in full-time extramusical jobs. Harmony quartet singing was one example of religious feelings that could be expressed during weekly rehearsals and at Sunday programs. The era of part-time singing and quartet activity that centered upon the church, neighborhoods, or businesses lasted well into the 1940s. For quartets like the Royal Harmony Four, Memphis's Afro-American gospel community has been their lifeblood for over fifty years.

The Spirit of Memphis in many ways encapsulates the history of gospel quartet activity in Memphis. The group, which included "Quartette" in its name for many years before dropping it in the late 1940s, is unquestionably the best known and most commercially successful home-grown black gospel group. Although the Spirit of Memphis celebrated its fiftieth anniversary in 1980, the passage of so many years has obscured the precise date of its origination. In the memory of the sole surviving founding member, James Darling, the quartet was established in the gloom of the early depression and consisted of Darling, Burt Perkins, Arthur White, and Arthur Wright.[6] The roots of the Spirit of Memphis are in the T. M. and S. Quartet, a name derived from the initials of the *T*ree of Life, *M*ount Olive, and *S*t. Matthew's Baptist churches, which the various group members attended (Darling himself belonged to the Tree of Life Baptist Church). If this quartet was indeed the first incarnation of the Spirit of Memphis, then the group can more accurately be dated to 1927 or 1928.

Such genealogical problems result from the ever-changing personnel of quartets, the lack of written records, and hazy memories. The founding date of a group is an important event for Afro-American gospel quartets, however, because lavish celebrations are held to honor and commemorate the anniversaries. Prestige is also attached to the number of years a group has remained together, which further heightens the group's importance.

Irrespective of the precise details, it appears that the Spirit of Memphis altered its name around 1930 in memory of Charles Lindbergh's 1927 flight across the Atlantic in the *Spirit of St. Louis.* James Darling relates the story:

When the group was named . . . it was named after the initials of the churches; and when we decided to organize into a quartet, we had to bring in some names. The night we had to bring in some names, I hadn't thought up a name until we got almost to [the house at] Looney and Second Street. That's where we were meeting, at Burt Perkins's house. I had a pocket handkerchief, had the Spirit of St. Louis in the corner. That's where the name really originated. I put down the Spirit of Memphis from this Spirit of St. Louis pocket hand-kerchief, you know, the design in the corner.[7]

This transformation in name, which symbolized a very conscious move from a church-allied group to a quartet representing the city in which the members lived, foreshadowed some of the changes that were to take place in Memphis quartet singing. It was a presentiment that quietly signaled the gradual rise of professionalism, which was the single most important alteration in the tradition. By publicly aligning itself with a well-known "worldly" event, this former church ensemble set the foundation for the slow evolution from grassroots to popular entertainment. It took nearly twenty years for Memphis groups to complete this process.

At the time the Spirit of Memphis adopted its present moniker, quartet singing was becoming more popular in the city. Although no Memphis groups are known to have recorded during the 1930s, the sheer number of groups indicate that quartet singing was widespread. Quartets active between 1930 and 1940 included the Orange Mound Harmonizers, the North Memphis Harmonizers, the Lake Grove Specials, the Gospel Writers, the Four Stars of Harmony, the Middle Baptist Quartet, the Busyline Soft Singers, the True Friends Gospel Singers, the Veteran Jubilees, and the Independent Quartet. (A complete list of quartets is found in Appendix I.)

One of the more formidable groups from this era was the Middle Baptist Quartet, organized in 1935 and held in awe by most quartet veterans around Memphis. It was certainly one of the most revered of the unrecorded local quartets. In the late 1930s the quartet included James Darling, Mose Hill, Elijah Jones, and James Harvey, each reputedly a first-rate singer; in fact many people still recall with wonder Harvey's lead singing. The group, which also at various times included Gus Miller (the dean of the local trainers), James Strong, Sam Miller, and Horace Fisher, served as a training ground for singers who left to join other respected harmony ensembles. It also was the foundation for yet another legendary quartet, the Gospel Writers.

The Gospel Writers played a critical role in Memphis gospel quartet history. The respect accorded them by their fellow singers testifies to their importance. But it was the leadership of their founder, Elijah Jones, who trained many harmony singers during his fifty-year career, that made the Gospel Writers a group of renown just prior to World War II. As a quartet trainer Jones helped to shape a distinctive local tradition through his suggestions regarding repertoire, vocal techniques, harmony, and arrangements.

The archetypal "sound" of Memphis quartets from the pre-World War II period is difficult to establish since the only recordings available from this period are the I. C. Glee Club's fourteen sides. It is possible to augment these vintage performances with songs recorded by four contemporary groups—the Harps of Melody, the Harmonizers, the Royal Harmony Four, and the Gospel Writers—who still consciously keep the older, a cappella style alive. (All but the Royal Harmony Four can be heard on discs released by High Water Records.)

The repertoires of these early unaccompanied quartets tend to rely heavily upon traditional material. For example, if the recordings by the I. C. Glee Club truly reflect their performing repertoire, then they mixed older spirituals with original songs based on traditional themes. The former category includes well-known pieces such as "I Shall Not Be Moved," "So Glad Trouble Don't Last Always," and "Lord Have Mercy When I Die"; into the latter category fall "If I Could Hear My Mother Pray Again" and "When They Ring Dem Golden Bells." Several other songs—"I'm Going Home on the Chickasaw Train," "Riding on the Seminole," and "Panama to Chi"—underscore the group's affiliation with the Illinois Central Railroad. It is also interesting to note that the motifs utilized in these songs, trains and travel, are two of the most popular images in black religious and secular folk music.[8]

Similar comments apply to the repertoires of the Harps of Melody, the Harmonizers, and the Gospel Writers of the 1980s. The principal difference in their singing is the inclusion of many more composed gospel songs like "I Need Thee," "I'm Leaning on the Everlasting Arms," or "Peace in the Valley." Nonetheless, most of their repertoires still consists of the traditional songs or spirituals.

The Harmonizers, for example, regularly perform "Steal Away" and use "Rollin' through an Unfriendly Land" as their theme song and introductory number. Elijah Ruffin, the Harmonizers' founder and trainer, knew that these songs were old, but he was surprised to learn that they were first "collected" during Reconstruction.[9]

The Gospel Writers still sing many of the arrangements that Elijah Jones taught them when he worked with the group during the late 1970s. According to George Rooks, who heard the "old" Gospel Writers forty years ago, the current arrangements of "Gospel Writer Boys Are We" (the group's theme song) and "Blind Bartamus" are virtually unchanged. Much the same can be said of the songs performed by the Royal Harmony Four and the Harps of Melody, for they, too, include many familiar spirituals like "Roll, Jordan, Roll" and "Old Time Religion." In short, these four groups maintain repertoires that fairly accurately reflect the style of singing widely performed in Memphis prior to the addition of musical instruments to quartets after World War II.

The best way to hear and appreciate this music is to experience it "live" and in the context of a rehearsal or church program. Since this is not possible for all but the most ardent fans and scholars, I will describe some of the music's most important traits using recorded examples as a guide.[10] These examples are listed in the Discography at the end of the book, and many are readily available on commercial records issued on the High Water label.[11]

All but one of the 1928–30 I. C. Glee Club recordings and the recent selections by the Gospel Writers, the Harps of Melody, and the Harmonizers are sung without instrumental accompaniment. The meter is almost always duple, either in 2/4 or 4/4, which is true of most prewar-style quartet recordings in Memphis. The only exception occurs when the ensemble momentarily drops out and the lead singer is left to improvise more spontaneously. In these unusual instances, such as the Harmonizers' "Trampin'" or the Gospel Writers' "Up above My Head I Hear Music in the Air," the meter is somewhat freer. The tonality is overwhelmingly major, the only exception among these groups being the Gospel Writers' "Wade in the Water," which is clearly derived from a 1950s recording by the Harmonizing Four of Richmond, Virginia (the earlier version is also performed in a minor key).

Four-part harmony consisting of alto, tenor, baritone, and bass is heavily stressed in this music. On rare occasions the group leaves the leader on his own or the singers alter their parts to form a three-part harmony, which is accomplished by "doubling" on one voice. One of the finest examples of four-part harmony is heard on the Harmonizers' showcase piece, "Roll, Jordan, Roll." Crossing of the inner voices also is fairly common, as in the final chord of the Harmonizers' "I'm Leaning on the Everlasting Arms." During this sustained chord the alto (lead) and tenor voices cross one another to end on the same note. This type of crossing results in parallel octaves, but it can often produce parallel fifths.

Quartets sometimes include more than four singers, in which case one is featured as a lead or two voices double on a single part. The Gospel Writers use a lead singer on "New Born Soul" and "I'll Fly Away"; their "Meet Me in Gloryland," which essentially has two tenor singers, offers another instance of doubling. Most quartets include a well-developed bass part, often interpolating a line distinct from the other voices; in fact, a pronounced bass is one of the most distinctive features of prewar Memphis quartets. One has but to listen to the chorus of "Riding on the Seminole" by the I. C. Glee Club, "Sing and Make Melody unto the Lord" by the Harps of Melody, or the final chorus of the Harmonizers' "My Lord Is Writing" to recognize the importance of this voice.

The lead singer and chorus are generally kept separate in quartet music, and it is quite clear which singer has the preeminent role. But on several songs, such as "I Am a Pilgrim and a Stranger," by the Harmonizers, overlapping does occur. The texture is usually homophonic, although simple polyphony is sometimes heard, and there is generally little melodic independence in the four parts sung by these groups. Extreme examples of this are "Steal Away," by the Harmonizers, and the I. C. Glee Club's "Come On, Don't You Want to Go?" Simple polyphony is evident on the I. C. Glee Club's rendition of "When They Ring Dem Golden Bells."

The mid- to late 1930s witnessed the beginning of a transition in Memphis's gospel quartet music from a primarily folk expression to a popular one. An element critical to this intermediary stage was the increasing number of out-of-town quartets appearing in Memphis. Many nonprofessional quartets had visited the city for church programs as early as the mid-1930s. Elijah Jones recalls that the True Loving Five from Little Rock, Arkansas, and the Lonesome Moaners of Hot Springs, Arkansas, appeared at the Columbus (Street) Baptist Church about 1933.[12] Such groups usually made two appearances—one on Saturday evening and the other on Sunday afternoon—with an admission charge of ten or fifteen cents per person to help defray the group's travel and other expenses. By the late 1930s, however, professional talent was coming to Memphis on a regular basis.

Local singers themselves helped to promote many out-of-town quartets, primarily because these Memphians were acquainted with the other singers. James Darling claims: "Well, I booked the first out-of-town groups into the city. The first group that came in was the Birmingham [Famous] Blue Jay Singers. That was before the Soul Stirrers came into Memphis. They were out on the road . . . [and] I booked them at the auditorium on Main Street."[13] Although the exact date of this program is not clear, it was no earlier than 1937 or 1938, which is when both the Soul Stirrers and the Famous Blue Jay Singers began touring full-time. Because it was the first such booking, Darling recalls it well:

> That was the first program we had for a dollar. All the programs before that had been twenty-five cents or fifty cents. This was the first major one. . . . Crump [the mayor of Memphis] had for some reason gave orders for colored and white not to mix at the show on Main Street. For that particular reason we couldn't have white people to attend this show. There was a whole lot of them wanted to come to the program, but he gave them orders not to come.[14]

Despite "Boss" Crump's intrusion, the first Memphis program by a professional black gospel quartet brought a large number of people into the auditorium. This success opened the gate for other groups interested in Memphis engagements. Within a year groups such as the Pilgrim Travelers and the Golden Gate Quartet were appearing in Memphis every few months. These professional programs had a profound influence on Memphis quartets, with perhaps the most significant being the realization that such musical religious events could be held outside the church for the singers' own profit. This was a critical change in perspective from the earlier attitudes about singing religious music for private gain. Although such a practice was unknown in Memphis as late as the middle 1930s, the first signs of private enterprise in quartet singing were quite evident by the late 1930s among local groups who brought in professional ensembles.

The performance style and general stage-image that professional groups presented signaled another important shift for Memphis quartets. Local harmony groups normally rendered programs in a very dignified and restrained manner. After all, their singing was part of a conservative Church of Christ, National and Progressive Baptist, or Methodist worship service and a reserved demeanor was appropriate in this context. Public appearances by them paralleled the groups' singing style, meaning suits or dresses appropriate for church or some other prominent social event.

Groups like the Famous Blue Jay Singers helped to change these customs, however, with their simple but expensive matched suits, known as "uniforms," and their dramatic stage presence. Where Memphis quartets once stood "flat-footed" and simply sang, these other groups began to move while performing, using hand gestures and vivid facial expressions to intensify the emotions expressed in their songs. Memphis groups soon incorporated these changes in performance style and dress so they would appear modern, progressive, and professional, and by the onset of World War II such innovations were widely embraced.

There were other signs, too, of professionalism among Memphis quartets. One was the expanding opportunities for groups to sing on local radio stations. By the 1950s all of the most important and influential local stations featured quartet singing, a phenomenon that was critical to the growth of the Memphis quartet tradition (see chapter 5). Black-owned and white-owned businesses observed the popularity of this music and began exploiting its commercial appeal by the late 1930s. One example of this was the cosponsorship by the Littlejohn Taxi Company and Pate's Men's Shop of the Spirit of Memphis's radio broadcasts. The business community's interest in quartet singing also took other forms, as Theo Wade explains: "We used to sing for Wallace Johnson, the man who owned Holiday Inns. We used to sing for him up on the wagon beds; go to where he had houses. He used to call and tell us to send the group. He would send a truckbed and we would get up on the truckbed and sing for two hours. Of course, he would pay us, you know, for advertising his homes [for sale]. Some days we'd sell four or five houses for him!"[15] This tactic apparently proved successful, for Johnson later brought the Gospel Writers to Mississippi to help sell homes and churches there.

Not only were local groups more visible around Memphis, but they also began to perform throughout the Mid-South. The Spirit of Memphis, for instance, traveled to Birmingham, Alabama, as early as 1935 to appear on programs promoted by a Jefferson County entrepreneur named Puckett, who was to help the group with their initial recording. Other groups, like the Gospel Writers and the Four Stars of Harmony, also began expanding their audiences by traveling more often to Mississippi and western Tennessee on weekends. Clara Anderson, who helped organize and sang with the Golden Stars between 1938 and 1943, tells of her experiences:

> When we were with the Golden Stars, we were very young and we stayed out of town a whole lot. We would book programs . . . knew every cow path in between here and Birmingham! We'd go into the town . . . to the school and sing a couple songs. Then they'd give us dinner, [and we'd] get dressed up for the night's performance. We would stay there that particular night and get up the next morning . . . go on our way and go on to the next town. This wouldn't be more than fifty miles apart. Then it would be the same thing.[16]

At the time singers like Jethroe Bledsoe, Earl Malone, and Robert Reed of the Spirit of Memphis, Jack Franklin and James Harvey of the Southern Wonders, and Doris Jean Gary and Elizabeth Darling of the Songbirds of the South were all in their late teens or early twenties. Although these singers and their quartets were to become among the most influential Memphis groups, they began at an age when the new out-of-town quartets, with their fresh ideas, would have a lasting influence on them. "Jet" Bledsoe vividly recalls his earliest impression of a professional quartet: ". . . they were at the Manassas High School and we went to hear them. We had never seen a professional group with uniforms on, because we didn't sing with no uniforms! We just got out there and sang with what we had on. . . . so that's what kind of motivated us—the Blue Jays."[17]

Changes in singing style and physical appearance paved the way for the professional quartets, yet no Memphis group explored the possibility of singing for a living until the end of the 1940s. The

The Gold Stars in 1945: Mary Ruth Youngblood, Clara Anderson, Mary Louise Wilson, Hazel Cole, Sylvia Anne Garrett. *Courtesy of Clara Anderson.*

A Memphis neighborhood group, the Friendly Brothers Quartet, which was fronted by John and Robert Maddrie (second and third on the left) in the early 1940s. *Courtesy of Sylvia Smith.*

The Gospel Writers were one of Memphis's top groups in the late 1930s: (*top*) James Strong, Roy White, Elijah Jones; (*bottom*) James Joy, James Harvey. *Courtesy of Doug Seroff.*

In the mid-1940s the Southern Junior Girls sang in local churches. *Courtesy of Cleo Satterfield.*

The M. N. Gospel Singers began performing on WMPS radio about 1946: (*standing*) R. D. Rogers, Ozell Webster, Silas Hughes, Will Rodgers, Andrew Kelly, Nathaniel Breakenridge; (*seated*) Roosevelt Webster, Roosevelt Muse. *Author's collection.*

The True Friend Gospel Singers in 1946: Mose Walker, Louis Satterfield, Willie Gillon, R. C. Dixon. *Courtesy of Louis Satterfield.*

M and N Junior Girls about 1949: Virgy Kelly, Jesse Ruth, Willie Mae Gray, Cleo Satterfield, Elizabeth Kelly, Mildred Gage. *Courtesy of Cleo Satterfield.*

One of the best groups in north Memphis in the late 1930s was the Four Stars of Harmony: Edward O'Brian, Elijah Ruffin, Willie Partee, Demsy Harris. *Courtesy of Elijah Ruffin.*

The city's most famous group, the Spirit of Memphis, as they appeared about 1936: Freddie Johnson, Ramond Sanders, Hermon Paul, Lewis White, Robert Reed, Earl Malone, Jethroe Bledsoe. *Author's collection.*

The Spirit of Memphis, in 1948, about one year before the members became fulltime professionals: (*top*) Earl Malone, "Jet" Bledsoe; (*middle*) Theo Wade, James Darling; (*bottom*) Reverend Crenshaw, Robert Reed. *Courtesy of Cleo Satterfield.*

Quartet trainer and founder of the
Gospel Writers, Elijah Jones, about
1945. *Courtesy of Doug Seroff.*

The Songbirds of the South, on the verge of turning professional in 1949: (*top*)
Dorothy Murff, Elizabeth Darling; (*middle*) Julia Pruett; (*bottom*) Cassietta
George. *Courtesy of Doug Seroff.*

The Famous Golden Stars

of Memphis, Tenn.

Presents Musical Recitals.

For information write

Clara Mae Anderson, Pres and Mgr.
930 Woodlawn Street or
Phone 8-8381

Mary Louise Wilson, Secretary

Season's   Greatest   Attraction
Mr. J. A. Gray and His
FAMOUS LIVE WIRE SINGERS
Presents
THE FAMOUS GOLDEN STARS
Of Memphis Tenn
Sunday Aug. 25th, 1946   at 8:30 P M
at the Carver House   3035 Bell Ave.
Advance $ 1;00   At Door $ 1-25

THE GOLDEN STARS AND MT. PISGUAH
GOSPEL SINGERS
..Presents The..
FAMOUS BARONS of HARMONY
GOSPEL SINGERS
Of Chicago Ill.
W. S. B. C. Radio Artists
Will Appear At The
PLEASANT GREEN M. B. C.
Cor. Life and Nicholas St
Thursday Nite Aug. 2nd. 1945.   At 8:00 P. M.
Rev. J. M. Madison, Pastor
Admission, Adult--50c.

ATTENTION! THE FAMOUS
Golden Star Quartette
of Memphis, Tennessee, is presenting a
MUSICAL RECITAL
at the DUSABLE HIGH SCHOOL
SUNDAY, JULY 15th, 1945
Program Begins at 3:00 P. M.
Ticket $1.20

ATTENTION !
The Famous GOLDEN STAR QUARTET
Showcased, Radio Artists of Memphis, Tenn., in a
Great Musical Program
WEDNESDAY EVENING, JULY 11th, 1945
at the Y. M. C. A., 1918 Maxwell Street
Program starts at 8:30 P. M.
There will also be other Great Gospel Singers appearing
on the same Program, so if you want to hear
good singing don't miss this gala event.
For information Call MRS. CHRISTIAN—Canal 4279
Donation 75c

Tickets for performances by the Famous Golden Stars. *Author's collection.*

fact that it *could* be accomplished, however, was amply demonstrated ten years beforehand. Although commercialism in gospel quartet singing was becoming more and more evident, most Memphis ensembles continued singing only in their home churches and neighborhoods. A few groups began moving slowly toward the professional route, but most were not so inclined. According to Clara Anderson, who prior to forming the Golden Stars in 1938 sang with a community quartet, the Busyline Soft Singers:

> As a kid, we had a little neighborhood quartet. They just wanted to be busy in religious work and they called themselves the Busylines. We were a group dedicated to singing gospel songs and it didn't matter if we actually got anything out of it. We did a lot of singing during the week. We've played a lot of night programs, too. A lot of people told us we really should have gone professional, but we just liked singing and didn't want to go out for it.[18]

Many Memphis quartets apparently shared these feelings. Highly regarded groups, like the Royal Harmony Four, the M and N Singers, and the Jolly Sunshine Boosters Club Quartet, occasionally sang outside of Memphis and the Mid-South, but their primary audience was within the city. They supported the churches and congregations that had listened to and appreciated them over the years.

Despite such "unbusiness-like" motives, by 1941 Afro-American gospel music in Memphis and the rest of the country was inexorably moving toward professionalization. All of the key elements were present: a general, widespread interest in quartet singing, mass media support, a sense of commercial popularity, and the groups' willingness to travel for public appearances. This trend was stymied and virtually stopped by World War II, however. Gasoline rationing greatly curtailed traveling for performance, and the war's virtual monopoly on materials and production shut down the record industry between mid-1942 and late 1943. Once the war ended, this music skyrocketed in popularity and Memphis was caught up in the fervor.

The Spirit of Memphis played an important role in popularizing and professionalizing quartet singing during the years following the close of the Second World War. Up through this stage of its career, the group was one of the most highly respected quartets in and around Memphis. During the war its members continued to travel to the surrounding states for weekend programs. When travel restrictions eased about 1945, they were eager to increase their out-of-town engagements, and James Darling rejoined the Spirit of Memphis to facilitate this:

> Well, I am the man that started them traveling. I [could] book them all over the country and that's one of the reasons that the Spirit of Memphis wanted me to take them over . . . the connections that I had across the country from booking my wife's group [the Songbirds of the South]. I finally agreed after Elizabeth talked me into it. I booked 'em with the Fairfield Four . . . [and] quite often with Mr. Harris in Detroit, the Shields Brothers in Cleveland, all those different groups.[19]

Darling added another significant facet to the group when alternating lead singers Silas Steele and Little Ax (Wilbur Broadnax) were brought into the fold. Darling recalls that Steele and Little Ax were fully blended into the group by early 1948:

> Silas Steele had talked with me long distance and told me that his fellows was getting old and not well. They couldn't go on the road anymore and he didn't know nothing but singing, had never did nothing else. He asked me if I thought I could get him with the Spirit of Memphis. . . . So I talked with the boys and they said yes. It was 'bout six months after that I got Little Ax, when we were in Pittsburgh. Bledsoe had done all the leading and I wanted to get him some help anyway . . . 'cause we were pretty hot at that time [with] "Days Past and Gone" and "Happy in the Service of the Lord." Those [songs] were really burning![20]

Steele had for many years been with the Famous Blue Jay Singers of Birmingham and was intimately acquainted with the hazards and benefits of full-time performing. The members of the Spirit of Memphis were quite willing to listen to him and to Darling and to learn from their vast experiences.

The Spirit of Memphis was now on the threshold of a major commercial and artistic breakthrough, but it could not quite break free of the confines of the Mid-South performance circuit it had worked for many years. Jethroe Bledsoe vividly recalls that the group journeyed throughout "Mississippi, Arkansas, Alabama, Knoxville . . . places like that. We didn't take it on as a job, professionally. We didn't go out professionally until Silas Steele got with us. At that time we were scared to go out there. We were liable to starve to death! Couldn't lose our jobs!"[21] The final, critical factor that pushed the group into the professional ranks was the release of their first commercial record, "I'm Happy in the Service of the Lord" / "My Life Is in His Hands" in the fall of 1949. Issued on the local Hallelujah label but almost immediately leased to De Luxe, this record had an immediate regional impact and provided the group members with all the impetus they needed to finally quit their extramusical jobs and go on the road.

The triumphs of the Spirit of Memphis were not lost on other local quartets. Perhaps the second most popular group was the Southern Wonders, who began singing in Memphis about 1942 as the Renowned Southern Wonders—a name that distinguished the group from a contemporary Blytheville, Arkansas, quartet named the Southern Wonders. The initial members of the group were Jack Franklin, James Harvey, Bill Jones, Andrew Black, and James Darling. True to the tradition, they began by singing in neighborhood churches and remained a popular, strictly local group for about ten years, during which they went through the standard maze of personnel changes. By 1950 the core of the group, which was soon to turn professional, was in place. According to Jack Franklin, the Southern Wonders' cofounder, ". . . it was after World War II that the later Southern Wonders were organized. It consisted of R. L. Weaver, Ernest McKinney, who is a pastor in town now, Artus Yancey, and Ernest Moore. L. T. Blair was our musicianer, our guitar player."[22]

As with the Spirit of Memphis, the key to the Southern Wonders' transition to a professional quartet was the addition of a single member, James Darling. Darling had been a founding member of the Southern Wonders but was enticed to rejoin the Spirit of Memphis in 1945. Due to a severe ulcer that limited his ability to travel, he decided to rejoin the Southern Wonders in 1952. Franklin credits Darling, with his vast number of professional contacts and his road savvy, as the primary force in guiding the Southern Wonders through its transition to a full-time touring quartet. By 1953 a fully recovered James Darling was providing invaluable assistance in booking programs, setting up the group's itinerary, organizing finances, and utilizing his network of professional contacts.

Some interesting parallels between the careers of these two

groups illustrate the changes in Memphis quartet singing. Both began as community or church-affiliated quartets whose traveling for performance increased just after the end of the war. The critical factor in each group's decision to turn professional was the addition of a member with extensive experience, who joined at a time when the general musical climate was favorable toward black harmony singing.

The interest local radio stations displayed in quartet singing also increased during the postwar era. Because the number of local quartets performing regularly on Memphis radio was quite substantial, they served to strengthen the music's popularity throughout the Mid-South. "Jet" Bledsoe recalls: "It surprised me . . . how the group kicked off because I didn't think we'd ever get twenty miles out of town to be booked. 'Course the radio stations helped a lot. When WDIA went 50,000 watts [in July 1954] that's what blew the top! We were getting letters from all over, far as the station would reach."[23]

All of these factors encouraged a third group, the Sunset Travelers, to join the Southern Wonders and the Spirit of Memphis on the professional circuit. Formed in 1950 by Grover Blake, the Sunset Travelers performed throughout the Mid-South for about three years before carefully moving up to professional status. Blake himself was highly motivated to make this change and had a very clear idea of what he wanted from his music:

> We [Blake and a friend] tried to get with other groups when we came here [from Mississippi in 1945], groups such as the Spiritual Four. They wanted us to go like other groups. I never wanted to sing like no other group. . . . they wanted us to mock the Pilgrim Travelers . . . but I didn't want to do that.
> . . . during that time, the music the people liked was the CBS Trumpeteers. They was real hot at that type of singing. Our singing was somewhat based like that. . . . There's just one group that I admired down through the years, and we may sound somewhat like that group, and that's the Dixie Hummingbirds.[24]

These statements reflect Blake's attitudes toward quartet singing as well as his own involvement with music, which was rooted in an extremely religious upbringing. He proved very capable at forming a strong quartet with popular appeal, a unique musical personality, and then taking it on the road full-time. Furthermore, Blake was a shrewd businessman, always willing to exploit the personal contacts he made with the out-of-town groups performing in Memphis: "We started dealing with the Sensational Nightingales and different groups like that. Then we began to move! Like the Traveling Echoes, they carried us all over the country and we took up with them. They carried us places we didn't know about!"[25] By the middle 1950s his numerous contacts and his business acumen earned the Sunset Travelers a recording contract with Don Robey's Duke label and a spot among the other professional quartets. The group's success places it alongside Detroit's Violinaires or Chicago's Kelly Brothers as second-echelon groups whose members made a comfortable living as singers but were never as popular as the Fairfield Four from Nashville or the Harmonizing Four of Richmond, Virginia.

The Spirit of Memphis, the Southern Wonders, and the Sunset Travelers toured at a time when many quartets were working the same basic circuit of cities and towns. Because of its strategic location and size, Memphis had its share of programs by traveling gospel quartets. Local quartets, particularly the Spirit of Memphis, "sponsored" (booked and promoted) many of these programs. These events most often featured at least one headline group, such as the Highway QCs, the Pilgrim Travelers, or the Caravans, who were supported by three or four other local or regional ensembles. The programs were most frequently held in the Mason's Temple, a 7,000-seat facility located just off Crump Boulevard in southwestern Memphis. Countless gospel music extravaganzas were held there throughout the 1950s, as fans packed into the building to listen to and applaud their favorite groups. According to announcements that appeared in the *Memphis World* and the *Tri-State Defender,* there was a major concert in this facility about every two months.

The Spirit of Memphis's manager through the 1950s, Jethroe Bledsoe, recounts a few of the "packages" he assisted in arranging: "When they started booking four professional groups together, I'm the one that put them together. [I] got a bus. That's what made the song battle, that's what started it. . . . We went all down in California, everywhere—the Soul Stirrers, Pilgrim Travelers, and the Swan Silvertones."[26] These kinds of tours quickly became very popular and were a standard feature of gospel programs by the early 1950s. People loved hearing all of the exciting groups in the demanding, high-tension atmosphere created by "song battles." Such battles pitted popular quartets in head-to-head competition, which was intensified by having the crowd's applause determine the winner.

During this period of frequent tours and competitions, the singers enjoyed a high status within the black community. Quartet programs were very popular, generating thousands of dollars in revenues. Quartet singers in the highest paid professional ranks, like the Spirit of Memphis, commanded weekly salaries of as much as $200, which meant it was possible to perform religious music *and* have a substantial income. The lure of glamour and financial well-being proved strong, and many local Memphis singers were encouraged to pursue careers with professional gospel quartets.

Another reason for the rapidly burgeoning popularity of quartet singing in Memphis during the 1950s was the music's increased documentation on commercial recordings. Although they do not provide a complete picture, these aural documents illustrate the important transformation that occurred in Memphis gospel quartet singing between the middle 1930s and the middle 1950s. One dramatic aspect of quartet singing that changed was that of repertoire. Most of the material sung by the early quartets consisted of either traditional songs or original songs cast in traditional formats. This canon remained an important component of postwar quartets but was augmented by an ever-growing number of composed gospel songs. For example, of the ninety-four songs recorded commercially by the Spirit of Memphis, the Southern Wonders, the Sunset Travelers, and the Brewsteraires during the 1950s, approximately one-half are newly composed. The rest of their recorded repertoires consists of more traditional or traditional-sounding songs, such as "Wish I Was in Heaven Sitting Down," "On the Battlefield," and "Take Your Burden to the Lord."

The addition of composed gospel songs is not surprising given their increased popularity among blacks and whites in the 1940s. Thomas A. Dorsey's "Precious Lord" and "Peace in the Valley" proved enormously popular. Two other prominent Afro-American gospel composers, Rev. W. Herbert Brewster and Lucie E. Campbell, were Memphians,[27] and both were active as songwriters during the second two decades of gospel music—1940 through 1960. At least two of Reverend Brewster's songs, "Move On Up a Little Higher" (1946) and "Surely God Is Able" (1950), have become gospel standards, while another, "Old Landmark" (1948) remains popular in Memphis. Campbell was not as prolific as Brewster, although "Just to Behold His Face" (1951) is still widely performed. With two such important composers in their own city, it was hardly surprising that Memphis quartets fortunate enough to record during the postwar boom readily incorporated into their repertoires these and other composed gospel songs. (In fact, the title of the first edition of this book was derived from "I Am Happy in the Service of the Lord," written in 1945 by Faye Ernestine Brown and made popular by the Spirit of Memphis through their 1949 recording debut.)

Although it is evident that newly authored gospel songs were an integral part of the repertoires of postwar Memphis quartets, ascribing their authorship is problematic. Some of them, such as Roberta Martin's "Swing Down, Chariot" (1956), are unquestionably based on traditional themes. At least one song title, "I'm Going to Move On Up a Little Higher" is credited to more than one author—Reverend Brewster and Kenneth Morris—though Memphis groups generally sing the Brewster composition. Finally, there is no comprehensive resource book to check such credits. (The songs for which authorship is known are cited here with the publication date and sometimes the author's name.[28])

Memphis's black gospel quartets were quite different in 1950 from the I. C. Glee Club that traveled to New York to record its songs. "Cold War" doldrums may have settled across the country, but quartets soon helped to ignite the atmosphere with their flashy suits, exciting choreography, and extravagant programs. The singing itself changed as the groups kept up with current trends. For example, most groups now use some instrumental accompaniment, although each group performs at least a few a cappella numbers, such as the Southern Wonders' "Come Over Here," or "Just to Behold His Face" by the Spirit of Memphis. Quartets commonly are accompanied on guitar, and they also make use of drums and piano.

The role of the bass singer has lost some of its importance in black gospel quartet singing. Most groups deemphasized strong bass singers and prominent parts for bass singers during the 1950s, augmenting or replacing them with guitars. The bass singer is still important, though, for a cappella numbers and up-tempo "jubilee" songs such as the Spirit of Memphis's "Working til the Day Is Done," or "Wish I Was in Heaven Sitting Down" by the Sunset Travelers. These songs highlight "pumping" bass singing that is often syncopated, very percussive, and quite striking.

Tonality now is primarily major, although minor keys are occasionally heard. Two exceptions are "Storm of Life" and "Blessed Are the Dead" by the Spirit of Memphis. There are also a few instances in which a song modulates between major and minor keys: for example, "Let My People Go" by the Sons of Jehovah. The prewar duple meter continues to predominate, but two new time signatures, 12/8 and 6/8, are now often used. This so-called gospel meter began to be heard in all types of black American gospel music throughout the 1940s. An example among the "modern" Memphis quartets is the Pattersonaire's "Surely, God Is Able," one of the earliest popular gospel songs regularly performed in 12/8 time.

Background (or chorus) singing most often consists of four-part harmony, though sometimes there are only three distinctive parts, as in the Sunset Travelers' "I Am Building a Home" and the Brewsteraire's "Jasper Walls" (Rev. W. Herbert Brewster, 1953). The predominant four-part harmony consists of bass, alto, and two tenor voices, and the background singers often utilize percussive techniques during the chorus. One of the most noticeable elements of Memphis quartet singing from the 1950s is the use of these percussive effects, which heighten the rhythmic interest and tension. Willie Johnson of the Golden Gate Quartet pioneered this singing technique, which was adopted by Memphis singers. Earl Malone and Robert Reed (from the Spirit of Memphis) use some of the following techniques on their recordings: syncopated phrasing; repetitive, clipped, single syllable words; and emphasized, explosive vowels. Their versions of the "Swing Down, Chariot" and "Working til the Day Is Done" illustrate these techniques, as does the Sunset Travelers' "Traveling Shoes."

Among gospel quartets there is an increased emphasis on lead singing, possibly due to the importance of solo singers like Sister Rosetta Tharpe and Mahalia Jackson during the 1940s. By the 1950s Memphis quartets featured more singing by a designated lead singer, and most groups had more than one lead singer who alternated the lead or was featured on a specific number. For example, the Southern Wonders' ten Peacock sides spotlight three different lead singers: James Darling, R. L. Weaver, and Sammie Dortch. Both lead and background singers also more frequently use improvisatory techniques, one of the cornerstones of local quartet singing during this period being its highly ornamented style. Lead singers such as Silas Steele, Jethroe Bledsoe (the Spirit of Memphis) and O. V. Wright (the Sunset Travelers) utilize melismatic, falsetto, and sforzando vocal techniques to heighten the emotional impact of a song. Bledsoe's vocal on "Lord Jesus" provides a striking example of this, as does Wright's singing on "Lazarus."

Most instances of overlap occur between the leader and the chorus, a stylistic trait that has become common among black quartets. Perhaps the most important reason for this was the increased emphasis placed on improvisatory lead singing. This type of vocal arrangement usually means that the lead singer's improvisation carries over into the chorus, as in the Southern Wonders' "As an Eagle Stirrith Her Nest." The song structure of these groups also tends to be more repetitive, which facilitates lead singing. Memphis quartets of this period most often used an ABABAB format. The A section is the chorus, which is generally quite stable, while the B section is usually an improvised lead. Singers sometimes refer to the B section as the part where the lead singer can "stretch out" and display his or her arsenal of vocal approaches and tricks. The Spirit of Memphis typifies this structure in "If Jesus Had to Pray (What about Me)."

While only three Memphis quartets operated as full-time groups, there were perhaps a half-dozen others striving to attain this status. Although none of them reached their goal, they were able to capitalize on the widespread popularity of this music. Almost any group with a good sense of organization, a willingness to promote itself, and at least a modicum of talent could make money arranging local programs. These semiprofessional quartets were willing to trek as far as Chicago or Dallas for a weekend and then return to Memphis in time for work on Monday morning.

One man who belonged in this category is Julius Readers, who came to Memphis from nearby Clarksdale, Mississippi, in 1949 and quickly immersed himself in the burgeoning quartet scene. He became a singer and manager for the Spiritual Travelers between

1953 and 1958. Like a cadre of Memphis quartets that included the Sons of Jehovah, the Dixie Nightingales, the Gableaires, the Jubilee Hummingbirds, and the Jones Brothers, the Spiritual Travelers had professional aspirations; they just were never able to make it to the top. Readers recalls:

> The Gabelaires and the Jubilee Hummingbirds was my favorite groups to work with. At that particular time, the Jubilee Hummingbirds . . . were working under the name of the Harmony Echo. We traveled every weekend. We did a lot of stuff in Little Rock, St. Louis, and Chicago. We didn't do no daily shows, just weekends. We have been as far away as Dallas, Texas, [or] New Orleans and back for a weekend. We traveled some long trips and we mostly lose every Monday [from work].
>
> I had to go out and set up the engagements. Go from town to town, get sponsors to work with you on programs. Actually you were some like "meat and bread"; if you don't make no money to pay them, then automatically they didn't make no money.[29]

Instead of working with major groups in these large cities, Readers and others worked with the local semiprofessional quartets, setting up programs in large churches or small auditoriums. These bookings constituted a circuit that paralleled quartets. Those programs featuring semiprofessional quartets were held only on weekends because the singers had to maintain their regular jobs in order to support their families. Thus, Readers and his peers directed much of their energy toward securing engagements in churches near or in the larger towns scattered throughout the Mid-South.

> Back in the '50s . . . quartets were very popular. We could draw about as many people as any pastor could draw at his church on Sunday morning because people used to go out and hear quartet singers. We did stuff around Blytheville, Arkansas; Portageville, Missouri; Jackson, Tennessee. That was the backbone of gospel singing. [Programs were held] on Saturday afternoon, [again] at 7:30 P.M. and then again Sunday afternoon. Then we do a Sunday night. A lot of times we do four—Friday, Saturday, and Sunday, double on Sunday. We only sung at home maybe once or twice every ninety days.[30]

What separated these groups from the professional quartets probably had as much to do with good fortune, contacts, and karma as anything else. The Spiritual Pilgrims, the Jordan Wonders, and others had almost everything going for them: a strong desire for professional status, contacts with professional quartets and promoters, the ambition to work toward that goal, and a knowledge of how the booking system worked. They possibly lacked some of the inherent singing ability and polish possessed by their professional counterparts, but without aural evidence this remains a supposition. Readers assesses the situation this way: "The only reason we didn't go professional . . . we couldn't get on a professional [record] label. That's what held us back. We had the professional contacts. We had the guys with intention of being professional. They sung professional and they were respected as professional singers . . . but they never could get on the right track to be on a national label."[31]

Readers's viewpoint certainly has merit. Despite the number of recordings made by Memphis groups during the late 1940s and 1950s, not every worthy group had the opportunity to get into the studios. Whether or not this inhibited the careers of certain groups is very difficult to verify, yet it is almost certainly true that the lack of recording exposure denied them did not help. However, the ambiguous status experienced by so many of these semiprofessional ensembles in no way diminishes their substantial niche in history. They represented the dreams of many singers who aspired to be part of "name" groups at a time when black gospel music was both commercially prosperous and a respected expression of Afro-American religious culture. If nothing else singers like Readers, Frank Perkins of the Sons of Jehovah, and Doris Jean Gary of the Songbirds of the South were able to perform music they loved, see places they may never have seen otherwise, as well as sing on the same bill as the Dixie Hummingbirds or some other out-of-town professional group.

The increased popularity and commercialization of quartets signaled other changes in performance style and the stage presence of local groups. Along with the increased emphasis on theatrics came another dramatic element, the "sermonette." This is an emotional narration that accompanies a gospel song, either as a prologue or during the course of the performance itself. Sermonettes, a direct outgrowth of the biblical stories that were so important to the jubilee quartets, were often performed as *cante-fables* and had a stirring impact on the audience. Out-of-town groups introduced these sermonettes to Memphis quartets during the late 1940s. Silas Steele, who helped pioneer their use, popularized them within the city, as Earl Malone of the Spirit of Memphis attests:

> What can I say about Silas Steele . . . he was beyond compare! He was inspirational to a lot of lead singers. He brought out a style that nobody had and they capitalized on what he did singing. [Steele was known for] narrating through a song and the different lead singers picked up on that style. They started doing it, but Silas Steele was the first to sing a song and just narrate through with that inspirational feeling.[32]

This style quickly proved popular on records, too. One of the Spirit of Memphis's best-selling discs is "Lord Jesus," a sermonette recorded live at the Mason's Temple in 1952 which literally pulsates with a fervor that would have been impossible to replicate in a studio.

Despite the numerous steps taken by many Memphis quartets toward a popular base and away from their folk roots, these trends were not all-pervasive. Throughout the postwar years there was a vital and active grassroots movement that supported the more traditional quartets. For each of the professional and semiprofessional ensembles mentioned in this chapter, there were many more community-based quartets active in the city. Without exception, all of the professional singers in Memphis began performing in community or church quartets and moved on only when they could grasp an opportunity to shift and attain a different realm of musical worship. But most of the quartets in Memphis remained firmly rooted within the communities or churches that spawned them. The principal interests of groups like the Harps of Melody, the Evening Doves, and the Majestic Soft Singers were their musical ministry and the people they could reach in Memphis. These groups also have tended to endure over many years, providing musical and spiritual sustenance for their peers.

By 1960 quartet singing in Memphis had lost much of its popular support base, a shift in interest that was not unique to Memphis (see chap. 1). Popular music and culture are by definition ephemeral, and it was only a matter of time before interest in gospel harmony singing had to wane. For more than a decade, though, quartet singing proved to be one of the most favored forms of music in Memphis's black community. Why, then, did it suffer such an immense diminution in popularity? Perhaps the simplest and most direct answer is overexposure. There were literally dozens of quartets performing in Memphis following World War II. Appearances by touring groups at the City Auditorium or the Mason's Temple every six or eight weeks augmented the weekly singing of local quartets. If one considers the number of opportunities offered Memphians to hear this music "live" and adds to that the regularly scheduled radio broadcasts and availability of commercial phonograph records by quartets, it quickly becomes clear how quartet music saturated the market. Because quartet singing was immensely popular for so many years, artists like Jethroe Bledsoe have only come to understand in retrospect that "after a while they went to running it into the ground. That's what it was, too much!"[33]

While it is indisputable that the popularity of this music was inherently ephemeral and that quartets eventually suffered from overexposure, the increasing secularization that pervaded every phase of black gospel music is another strong reason for its decline.[34] Quartet singing began as a community event, but by the 1950s it had often moved away from its original context. Professionally promoted programs were frequently held in secular settings that drew thousands of enthusiasts who paid an admission fee. Such trends proved very distressing to some Memphians, who felt that gospel quartets had left their ideals behind. Such sentiments became stronger among the conservative members of the Afro-American religious community as this music grew in popularity. Harry Winfield, a former gospel pianist who played on many religious programs during the 1950s, articulates the concerns of the more conservative churchgoers:

> The gospel during those early 1950s . . . [was] traveling more and more towards rock and roll music. They were changing their style and they were dancing on stage. They were now, more or less, giving performances. They were now walking on benches and getting sort of ridiculous. Quartet singers were now processing their hair and riding in Cadillacs, doing very much of the things that the gospel people attributed to the world, you know, drinking. We see you now on stage, can't hardly stand. The support they were formerly

getting from many people . . . was church people. They felt they were being deceived. . . . lot of things happened that started people totally against what was happening in the gospel field, as far as quartet was concerned.[35]

Winfield's points are incisive and well taken. By 1960 gospel quartet music had drifted far from its sacred roots and into a decidedly secular world. Programs highlighted by touring professional quartets entertained and diverted as much as they delivered a religious message. This treatment of religious music eventually turned many stalwart churchgoers from quartets toward different forms of gospel music. One type featured soloists, who were beginning to regain some of the prominence they had lost following World War II. Singers like "Professor" Alex Bradford, Bessie Griffen, Mahalia Jackson, and Memphis's own Queen C. Anderson are just four solo performers whose careers prospered during the middle 1950s and into the 1960s. Another popular genre was the ensemble, such as the Caravans and the Clara Ward Singers, which featured six or eight singers accompanied by a keyboard player or a rhythm section. In Memphis, the Brewster Singers, who were named for Rev. W. Herbert Brewster, reigned supreme.

By the late 1950s many of the harmony quartets from across the nation found that they could no longer support themselves by touring. The situation in Memphis once more mirrored trends outside the Mid-South. The Southern Wonders, wracked by personal problems and conflicts, were on the road for five years before giving up in 1957. In 1960 "Jet" Bledsoe pulled the Spirit of Memphis off the road, while the Sunset Travelers managed to scrape by until 1962. But despite the dramatic decline in its general popularity, Afro-American gospel quartet singing in Memphis is by no means moribund. At least a half-dozen older-style quartets still sing in churches throughout the city, some of them, such as the Willing Four Soft Singers and the Harps of Melody, having served their community for more than thirty years. Both the Spirit of Memphis and the Royal Harmony Four have moved beyond the fifty-year mark.

Several other groups popular in the 1950s, most notably the Jubilee Hummingbirds, the Dixie Wonders, and the Southern Jubilees, no longer emphasize harmony singing and perform more contemporary gospel tunes to the accompaniment of a full rhythm section. These groups enjoy a greater following than do the older harmony quartets because they have made a conscious effort to keep up with current trends in gospel music. Both the Jubilee Hummingbirds and the Dixie Wonders still perform "live" every Sunday over WDIA, and until 1980 the Jubilee Hummingbirds also had a weekly half-hour television show over WREG in Memphis. Although none of the current Memphis groups have recorded on a label of national prominence, many of them have issued recordings on local labels like Designer and Philwood.

Although the quartet harmony style may be out of vogue, there are several noteworthy examples of older singers who have deliberately formed new quartets to perpetuate prewar styles: the Harmonizers, founded by Elijah Ruffin in 1976; the revamped Gospel Writers, revived by their founder, Elijah Jones, in 1977; and two female groups, the Vance Ensemble and the Holy Ghost Spirituals, established in 1978 and 1979, respectively. In 1987 George Rooks organized the New Gospel Writers, choosing the name to honor his mentor. Community churches in Memphis still strongly support such groups, each of which performs regularly. The fact that these contemporary quartets sing almost exclusively in churches throughout the city helps to underscore the fact that this music has gone full circle—from its folk roots to the popular realm and back again. Above all, the cultural and musical history of Memphis gospel quartets directly relates to this grassroots support and its unique community of singers—a concept to be explored in chapter 4.

NOTES

1. Personal correspondence, Robert O'Brien to Kip Lornell, July 27, 1982.

2. Haywood Gaines, interviewed by Kip Lornell, June 24, 1982. Unless indicated otherwise, all interviews were conducted by the author in Memphis, Tennessee. Transcript copies and tapes are on deposit at the Mississippi Valley Collection, Brister Library, Memphis State University.

3. Ibid.

4. Frank Miller, interviewed via telephone from St. Louis, Missouri, August 8, 1982.

5. Theo Wade, interview, October 1979.

6. James Darling, interviewed via telephone from Los Angeles, California, July 21, 1982.

7. Ibid.

8. Norman Cohen, *Long Steel Rail* (Urbana: University of Illinois Press, 1983), cites examples of these images, as do the contemporaneous recorded sermons by Afro-American preachers such as Rev. J. M. Gates and Rev. J. C. Burnett.

9. These older spirituals appear in the following collections: William Allen et al., *Slave Songs of the United States* (1867; rpt., New York: Oak Publishers, 1965) and J. B. T. Marsh, *The Story of the Jubilee Singers* (Cleveland: Cleveland Printing and Publishing, n.d.).

10. Some scholars would argue for the use of Western notation to transcribe these selections. However, Mantle Hood, in *The Ethnomusicologist* (Kent, Ohio: Kent State University Press, 1984), pp. 50–123, carefully points out the general limitations of this system.

11. The specific problems inherent in using this approach in transcribing Afro-American gospel music are noted by William Tallmadge, brochure notes, *Jubilee to Gospel—A Selection of Commercially Recorded Black Religious Music, 1921–1953,* JEMF-108 (Los Angeles, 1980), pp. 7–8. The descriptive system used here is similar to that employed by George Herzog, "The Yuman Musical Style," *Journal of American Folklore,* 41 (1928), pp. 183–231; and George Ricks, *Some Aspects of the Religious Music of the United States Negro* (New York: Arno Press, 1978).

12. Elijah Jones, interview, October 1979.

13. Darling interview.

14. Ibid.

15. Wade interview.

16. Clara Anderson, interview, April 18, 1982.

17. Jethroe Bledsoe, interview, January 21, 1981.

18. Anderson interview.

19. James Darling, interview, August 2, 1983.

20. Ibid.

21. Bledsoe interview.

22. Jack Franklin, interview, June 21, 1980.

23. Bledsoe interview.

24. Grover Blake, interview, July 10, 1982.

25. Ibid.

26. Bledsoe interview.

27. The Best Source for information on both Brewster and Campbell is found in a book of essays edited by Bernice Johnson Reagon, *We'll Understand It Better By and By: Pioneering African American Gospel Composers* (Washington, D.C.: Smithsonian Institution Press, 1992)

28. The most important source for this information is Irene V. Jackson,

comp., *Afro-American Religious Music: A Bibliography and a Catalogue of Gospel Music* (Westport, Conn.: Greenwood Press, 1979).

29. Julius Readers, interview, May 28, 1982. For additional information on this strata of Memphis quartets see Hank Davis, "Sun's Jones Brothers," *Whiskey, Women, and . . . ,* no. 16 (Spring 1987), pp. 16, 17.

30. Ibid.

31. Ibid.

32. Earl Malone, interview, October 11, 1980.

33. Bledsoe interview.

34. Tony Heilbut, *The Gospel Sound—Good News and Bad Times* (New York: Simon and Schuster, 1984), pp. 281–307.

35. Harry Winfield, interview, July 14, 1982.

CHAPTER

3

"I've Got on My Traveling Shoes"

Black gospel quartet singers in Memphis have always been highly mobile, spreading their music throughout the Mid-South and beyond. This mobility has created unique patterns of movement that are of special interest to cultural geographers.[1] Most important, the singers have left their imprint on the spatial landscape by developing special travel patterns that were largely correlated to their degree of amateur or professional status. Secondarily, the names of gospel quartets, their song titles, and their lyrics reflect themes of environmental perception and sense of place.

The movement of people and the process itself is multifaceted because migration involves more than a simple shift from one geographical location to another. Nearly 85 percent of the approximately fifty Memphis gospel quartet singers I interviewed were born in the Mid-South; of the rest, nearly all moved from other parts of the South to Memphis as children. Virtually all of them relocated to Memphis directly from small towns or rural areas located within approximately one hundred miles of the city (Figure 1). The fact that Memphis was the final destination for these singers underscores its position as the most important urban center in the Mid-South. Somewhat surprisingly, none of the singers moved specifically to join a quartet, nor did any groups migrate en masse.

Avery Savage, founder in 1937 of the Zion Hill Spirituals, followed the typical pattern. Savage spent most of his childhood on his parents' farm in eastern Arkansas. In 1936 he moved to Osceola, Arkansas, but was not able to land a steady job and within a matter of months journeyed to Memphis in search of secure employment, which was quite elusive during the late days of the depression: "When I first got to Memphis, I worked for Q. S. Transfer Company. From there to Happy Feed Company. . . . after they ran low and laid off, I left . . . and went to Fisher Body Company. Fisher laid off and I went to Kelsy Wheel Company, shipping wheels. When they laid off, I went to Buckeye, which is a subsidiary of Procter and Gamble. That's when I hit it! I worked for them forty-one years and then retired."[2] Savage's experiences were echoed some ten years later by Robert Royston, of the Wells Spiritual Singers, who moved to Memphis from Holly Springs, Mississippi: "I had just gotten out of the service and felt I wanted to move from down there. There were better jobs [in Memphis]. . . . I wouldn't say they were so much better, but I *did* find work at the H. C. Taylor Company down there on Front Street. Finally I got a job down at the Defense Depot; been there ever since."[3]

Of the black gospel quartet singers who relocated to Memphis, most were primarily motivated by the harsh realities of a bleak rural economy. Attracted by a job market that at least offered blue-collar work, they generally arrived in Memphis with poor or nonexistent educational backgrounds and eagerly accepted whatever work they could find. This was especially true throughout the 1930s, until World War II pulled the country out of the depression. Memphis also offered social and cultural amenities like restaurants, movie theaters, libraries, and night clubs. The pace of city life was generally quicker and more varied than in the settings from which these singers had come. As Elijah Ruffin, who moved to Memphis from Sardis, Mississippi, in 1929, states: "I always did like the city. . . . I just got tired of it down there [in Mississippi]!"[4] This simple observation articulates what many rural blacks probably felt and also indicates some of the "push" and "pull" factor for rural black migration into Memphis.[5] George Davis and Fred Donaldson, two geographers with an interest in migration patterns involving the rural South and northern cities, have paid special attention to black migration. They have observed that black Americans who moved from Arkansas, Mississippi, and Tennessee during the 1950s favored Chicago as a northern destination but that Mem-

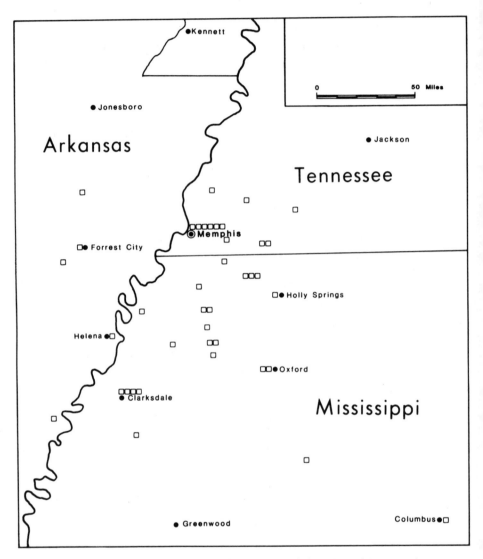

Figure 1 locates the birthplaces of thirty-nine of the Memphis gospel quartet singers interviewed. Most of these singers were born in small towns or rural hamlets located within 100 miles of Memphis. The spatial distribution underscores the importance of rural to urban migration, which later influenced performance travel patterns.

phis was the "important local destination" for this same group.[6] (The significance of this link between the rural and urban South and cities in the North for Memphis quartet singers will soon become apparent.)

While the migration of blacks and black quartet singers to Memphis almost always represented a permanent move, the routes they traveled for out-of-town performances have been predictably multidirectional and fall into two basic categories directly related to the group's professional, semiprofessional, or nonprofessional status. These categories also reflect the amount of travel and the time each group could devote to out-of-town engagements. All but about ten of the eighty documented groups that have performed in Memphis since the 1920s have been nonprofessional, and as such their travel patterns have generally been limited to the Mid-South. While the place names and precise locations of the small towns and rural communities differ, most Memphis gospel quartets have trod remarkably similar terrain over the past forty to fifty years. They seem to have sent representatives to almost every black church located within one hundred miles of the city.

Typical of such quartets active in Memphis during the 1940s and 1950s are the Southern Jubilees, the Zion Hill Spirituals, and the Orange Mound Specials. According to Floyd Wiley, the Southern Jubilees have given innumerable programs throughout the Mid-South, particularly in Mississippi, since 1938. Most of the performances have taken place on the weekends in small churches located in the Yazoo Basin (e.g., Rosedale, Beulah, and Shelby). At one time the group even performed in the "boot-heel" area of Missouri, singing in towns like Hayti and Saxon. However, these out-of-state trips became less frequent in the mid-1950s when the Southern Jubilees' popularity in Mississippi began to grow.

Similarly, the Zion Hill Spirituals, who represented the Zion Hill Baptist Church from 1939 until 1972, traveled a modest distance outside Memphis to sing. Unlike the Southern Jubilees, though, the Zion Hill Spirituals' performance territory included eastern Arkansas as far west as Little Rock. Most of the programs were held in the east quarter of that state, particularly around Osceola and Blytheville. The group occasionally performed in small towns in northwestern Mississippi and sometimes sang as far south as Greenwood, nearly one hundred miles south of Memphis.

The Orange Mound Specials existed from about 1936 until the outbreak of World War II. A former member, Elijah Ruffin, recalls that the group traveled in all directions from Memphis. In Arkansas they often performed in West Memphis, Forrest City, Brinkley, Blytheville and Osceola, while their Mississippi trips took them to Como, Mount Pleasant, and Holly Springs. Western Tennessee was also within their domain; they sometimes journeyed as far away as Jackson and Covington.

Figure 2 gives the general location of performances by the Golden Stars, the Harps of Melody, the Orange Mound Specials, the Zion Hill Spirituals, the Southern Jubilees, and the Spiritual Pilgrims between 1940 and 1955. A comparison of this figure and Figure 1 reveals a strong correlation between the birthplaces of quartet singers I interviewed and the locations of later performances of six of the most popular groups. The two maps clearly indicate that northwestern Mississippi was the favorite location for performances by nonprofessional quartet singers, which implies that directional biases are closely related to long-standing kinship-friendship ties with childhood communities.

Where a group traveled to perform often resulted from ongoing contacts in the singers' former homes. Indeed, the quartet performance network largely depended on friends and relatives who contacted various Memphis groups to request an appearance. These rural dwellers provided an extremely important emotional and musical link between country and city, creating a vital bond with the singers' childhoods and another aspect of "down-home" life that was probably experienced by every black Memphian who moved in from the country. Most of the Memphis singers eagerly anticipated the trips back to Mississippi because of the chance to see old friends and relatives and to feast on home cooking. In many ways these intangible networks were closely related to the migration patterns observed by Davis and Donaldson.[7]

Floyd Wiley, the first president of the Memphis chapter of the National Quartet Convention, describes how the quartet network functioned: "Sometimes we would have relatives or maybe another group down there. You might contact them or maybe they contact you and say they wanted to get you down there. Some days you might be up in Missouri and somebody from down in Mississippi might be visiting there and they hear you and contact

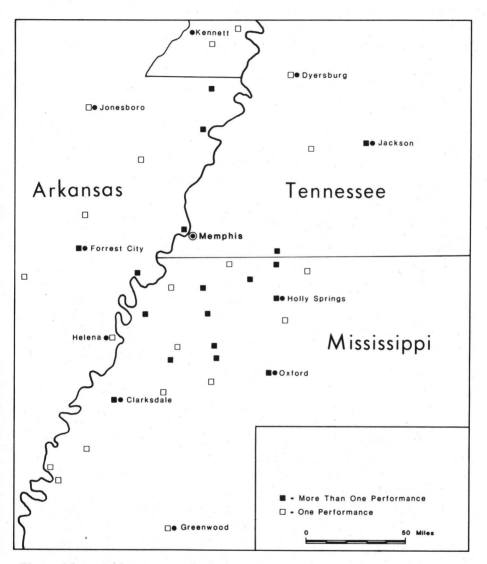

Figure 2 locates the sites at which the Golden Stars, the Harps of Melody, the Orange Mound Specials, the Southern Jubilees, the Zion Hill Spirituals, and the Spiritual Pilgrims performed between 1940 and 1950. Many gospel quartet singers performed in or near their places of birth, the result of kinship contacts and other networks that facilitated bookings for performances.

you."[8] Churches, schools, and small auditoriums provided the settings for most of these programs, which, as a general rule among most nonprofessional Memphis quartets, occurred once or twice a month. Longer trips outside the Mid-South usually took place only once or twice a year.

Since the late 1920s radio broadcasts have also affected this network. Beginning with the I. C. Glee Club in 1928 and continuing regularly through the early 1960s, quartets performed over the airwaves. People residing in rural areas wrote either to the quartets themselves or to the radio station, requesting that the singers appear at their local church or auditorium. Mary Davis of the Majestic Soft Singers recalls how this worked:

> From Memphis, Tennessee . . . down to Mississippi, far as you could go: Marks, Como, Hernando, Clarksdale. . . . All over Arkansas, I can't name all those little places—I done forgot. We went so many places! Every Sunday or so, we were gone. . . . At one time we was broadcasting [and] a lot of times they would say, "We heard you on the air." They would call me or write me a letter . . . ask us was we booked up for a certain time.[9]

The Songbirds of the South and the Dixie Nightingales, in particular, developed a significant following as a result of their radio broadcasts and subsequent personal appearances.

The social and musical kinship network also played an important part in the long-distance performance travel of quartets. Although groups like the Harmonizers and the Jolly Sunshine Boosters Club Quartet never sang outside the Mid-South, forty or fifty other Memphis quartets did travel longer distances. To a great extent these groups utilized the same networks that brought them to rural Arkansas, Mississippi, Tennessee, and Missouri. The primary difference in the networks is that these new routes followed the long-established migration routes from the South to cities in the North.

The Pattersonaires, for example, have been making regular pilgrimages to churches in the North since the middle 1950s. Their main contact was initially through the Reverend Charles J. Patterson, after whom the group is named. Reverend Patterson, now deceased, was a Baptist minister in Memphis before he moved to Lansing, Michigan, in 1955. For many years he booked the Pattersonaires in the Detroit area. Now the group makes an annual one-week to ten-day tour there each summer.

Another nonprofessional Memphis group, the Golden Stars, made regular trips north between 1940 and 1945. As Clara Anderson explains: "We went to Chicago on our own. One of the girls had some sisters in Chicago. . . . They were up in Chicago and they had a group . . . [and] booked us at DuSable High School and around in different churches. We even got our picture in the *Chicago Defender!*"[10] The Golden Stars also made trips to St. Louis, appearing on programs booked by friends who had moved there, thus extending the Memphis-area network.

Many other groups, including the Pilgrim Spirituals and the Campbellaires, made annual or semiannual journeys north during the 1940s and 1950s. Like the Golden Stars, these nonprofessional quartets usually sang on programs that former neighbors, friends, relatives, or other quartet singers who had permanently settled in cities like South Bend, Chicago, or Detroit had arranged. The groups made these trips over long weekends or during vacations in order not to lose time from work.

A different, though related, network developed for local semiprofessional and professional quartets—a status to which the overwhelming majority of quartets in Memphis neither aspired to nor achieved. Only the Spirit of Memphis, the Southern Wonders, and the Sunset Travelers worked as full-time quartets, while the semiprofessional ranks consisted of the Sons of Jehovah, the Dixie Nightingales, the Dixie Wonders, and the Spiritual Travelers. The three professional quartets spent much of the 1950s touring the country full-time—a level of commitment about which semiprofessional groups only dreamt.

Instead of a cadre of friends, relatives, and local groups, Memphis semiprofessional and professional groups relied upon a small number of booking agencies and some of the other touring quartets for most of their dates. This created radically different travel patterns from the majority of the other quartets in Memphis. Based on interviews with Grover Blake of the Sunset Travelers and Jack Franklin of the Southern Wonders, it is possible to reconstruct something of their performance itineraries. Grover Blake explains how he arranged extended tours: "Sometimes we'd book two or three months or some dates further than that. Just scattered dates, you know; then we'd try and fill in. After I learned about booking

. . . it's like if we leave here going to California, I'll book my way all the way from here into California. Then I'll book myself all the way out of California. If I go to New York, I'll book myself there and I'll book myself back."[11]

As for the routes themselves, Blake recounts a lengthy, meandering trip his group made about 1956:

> We came out of Key West and sang in Jacksonville, Pensacola, Mobile, Hattiesburg, New Orleans, Baton Rouge, Shreveport. Then we got into Dallas, next we go into Oklahoma. We leave Oklahoma, I think we sang in Kansas City. We come out of Kansas City and into Odessa and Amarillo, Texas. Then we sing in Albuquerque, New Mexico. Then into Phoenix, then into Los Angeles and into Bakersfield. We sang in White Springs, California; then we moved into Oakland. Then we sing in Reno, Nevada—into El Paso [and] in Houston.[12]

Such travel was wearing, tedious, and demanding. Quartet singers had to be dedicated to their careers and to singing, for as Blake explains, life on the road had many hardships along with the financial and spiritual rewards: ". . . you got to pay your dues on the road! There are times when the crowds are thin, but you still got to go on. Then you go places and sometimes your shows are cancelled when you get there. Then you move on and the next program is good. . . . You've got to have some guys who are willing to stick-up and follow what they believe."[13]

While the Sunset Travelers appeared on programs throughout the southern half of the United States, particularly in the Deep South and Southwest out to the West Coast, the Southern Wonders booked their engagements elsewhere. Most of their programs took place in the south-central states, and according to Jack Franklin, the Southern Wonders also were favorites in "Arkansas—Little Rock, Hot Springs, Pine Bluff, Hughes, Helena, Forrest City, and Mariana—and in Mississippi—Vicksburg, Natchez, Jackson, Grenada, Aberdeen, Ponotoc, Tupelo, Columbus, Indianola, Greensville, and Clarksdale. Great big cities!" he observed with a laugh.[14]

The Southern Wonders' dates were arranged through the Buffalo Booking Agency in Houston, Texas, home of their record label, Peacock Records. This agency, which also booked such important national artists as the Bells of Joy and the original Five Blind Boys, set up programs for the Southern Wonders in midwestern cities. Franklin recalls that they were booked into such places as

Racine, Wisconsin, Waterloo, Iowa, and Mayfield, Kentucky—not locations one would usually think of as critical performance points for black quartets. But professional quartets traveling in buses or automobiles often sang in many smaller cities because these dates helped to fill the gaps between the more lucrative programs in big cities.

The travel patterns of the local semiprofessional groups are even more difficult to establish. While these singers tended to perform in the Mid-South, they were often booked in more distant cities like Dallas and New Orleans. Julius Readers of the Spiritual Pilgrims recalls trekking to Chicago or Detroit every other month during the mid-1950s. Most of these trips were limited to weekends because the group members all held full-time jobs and sang partly to augment their incomes. Perhaps the wildest trip was made by the Jordan Wonders in about 1952 when they drove to Rochester, New York, for a single Saturday night engagement and were back in Memphis for work on Monday morning! The only quartet whose performance routes are possible to track precisely is the Spirit of Memphis. Jethroe Bledsoe, the group's business manager from the 1950s, kept a travel diary listing each place the quartet sang in during the spring and summer of 1952 (see Appendix II), at the apex of its commercial success. During the most favorable travel months—April through September—the quartet performed as far west as Oakland, California, and as far east as Newark, New Jersey (see Figure 3).

A large automobile or touring limousine was the usual mode of transportation for these groups. During the 1950s the Sunset Travelers owned four limousines and drove them all into the ground. The Spirit of Memphis toured so much between 1950 and 1955 that no group member can recall the number or model of cars they used. If the spring and summer 1952 itinerary is exemplary of their nationwide bookings for the early 1950s, then the Spirit of Memphis drove in excess of 50,000 miles each year, or at least half a million miles in one decade.

At first glance the travel patterns of Memphis quartet singers appear to be random, but they were clearly influenced by many underlying economic, cultural, and social factors, including group members' places of birth or who wrote for a quartet booking as the result of a radio broadcast. The patterns are also the result of choices, such as the groups' nonprofessional or professional status.

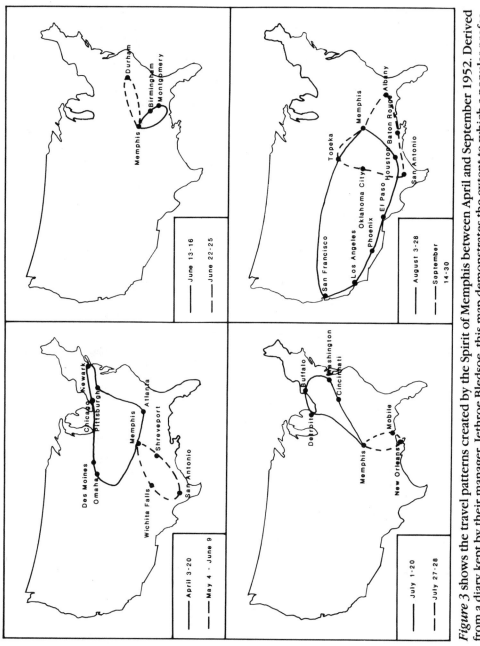

Figure 3 shows the travel patterns created by the Spirit of Memphis between April and September 1952. Derived from a diary kept by their manager, Jethroe Bledsoe, this map demonstrates the extent to which a popular professional group traveled during the height of interest in black gospel quartets.

Hence, the basic ingredients shaping these spatial patterns are of interest not only to geographers but to anyone seeking to understand the human factors related to music. It is also worth observing that geographical themes are significant to the spatial study of this type of music. Among Memphis groups two different components—names of quartets, and song titles and lyrics—underscore a subtle polarity. Simply stated, quartet names often reflect a real geographic location, while song titles and lyrics frequently maintain a more ethereal orientation. To fully explore this dichotomy it is necessary to look at the names that Memphis quartets have used over the past sixty years. These names function on at least three levels of geographic orientation, and all reveal important clues to the singers' sense of place.

Many groups in Memphis chose generic religious names such as the Four Kings of Harmony, the Pilgrim Spirituals, the Willing Four Soft Singers, the Christian Harmonizers, or the Sons of Jehovah. Significantly, other quartets selected monikers with definite geographic implications. On the most general level are names reflecting a regional orientation toward the South: the Songbirds of the South, the Southern Bells, the Southern Wonders, the Dixie Nightingales, the Dixie Wonders, the Southern Jubilees, and the Southern Harmony Boys. Other Memphis quartets' names clearly establish their sense of identity with that city, the most obvious example being the Spirit of Memphis. But at least two other groups, the Memphis Spiritual Four and the Delta Friendly Four of Memphis, also bear the city's name. On an even more specific level, other gospel quartets picked names referring to locations within Memphis. Some, such as the Orange Mound Specials, the North Memphis Harmonizers, the Magnolia Specials, and the Orange Mound Harmonizers, chose their names from readily identifiable neighborhoods or sections of the city. The most explicit example is the Wells Spirituals, whose members rehearsed on Wells Street.

Interestingly, many secular black groups in Memphis have used a similar naming system. Several important blues groups from the 1920s—the Beale Street Jug Band, the Beale Street Sheiks, and the Beale Street Rounders—openly identified with the city's best-known, most notorious street. Two other noted blues singers, Minnie McCoy and Peter Chatman, performed and recorded as Memphis Minnie and Memphis Slim, respectively. Finally, there was the loose, easy-going conglomeration of musicians called the Memphis

Jug Band, well known throughout the Mid-South during the 1920s and 1930s from their live performances and numerous recordings for the Victor and OKeh labels.

Of course, not all Memphis gospel musicians were so geographically inclined. Some groups adopted their employer's names, such as the various groups associated with the Illinois Central Railroad: the I. C. Glee Club, the I. C. Harmony Boys, and the I. C. Hummingbirds. This practice occurred because the workplace often served as a common meeting ground as well as a practice site. The Orval Brothers (Construction Company) Quartet was active during the late 1920s, and the Keystone Masters of Harmony took their name from the sponsor of their late-1940s radio broadcasts—the Keystone Beauty Products Company. Still other groups chose a more pedestrian path by selecting the name of their "home" church to represent their group. This resulted in quartets like the Middle Baptist Quartet, the Lake Grove (Baptist) Specials, the Mount Moriah (Baptist) Wonders, the T. M. and S. (Baptist) Quartet, and the M. and N. (Baptist) Singers. At least two other Memphis quartets chose the name of their spiritual leader: Rev. Charles J. Patterson inspired the Pattersonaires, while Rev. W. Herbert Brewster, a noted songwriter and pastor of the East Trigg Baptist Church, was similarly honored by the Brewsteraires and the Brewster Singers.

It is clear from these examples that a significant percentage of black gospel quartet names in Memphis reflect geographic alignments. In fact, of the eighty quartets listed in Appendix I, approximately 35 percent selected names that identified them directly with Memphis, and nearly 10 percent chose names that aligned them with the South (the remaining 55 percent displayed no apparent geographic sense of place). All of this underscores how often people identify with names that reflect a feeling of belonging and a spirit of pride in a specific place—a phenomenon not limited to black gospel quartets in Memphis, of course. For instance, state university nicknames like the University of Florida "Gators," the University of Nebraska "Cornhuskers," or the University of Maine "Bears" can evoke a strong response from fervent, loyal alumni, whose pride is reflected in such visible, public ways as bumper stickers, beer mugs, and sweatshirts.

Although the names of many Memphis gospel quartets suggest a definite worldly orientation, their songs often express a yearning to reach an ethereal realm—an abstract heaven rather than their present home. This opposition underscores the ambivalence many people feel toward mortality. Memphis quartet singers acknowledge these human limitations through group names and songs by simultaneously balancing the concept of heaven with earth's reality. Furthermore, it is just one more way in which these singers cope with the daily dilemma of how to reconcile their spiritual and worldly lives. This celestial inclination is most readily apparent in titles like "Wish I Was In Heaven Sitting Down" (the Sunset Travelers), "Home in the Sky" and "Automobile to Glory" (the Spirit of Memphis), "Highway to Heaven" (the Harmonizers), "Meet Me in Gloryland" (the Gospel Writers), "Heaven Is My Goal" (the Holy Ghost Spirituals), and "I Am Bound for the Promised Land" (the Harps of Melody). Such titles follow the strong Christian willingness to trade this life for a locale far removed from south Memphis, Orange Mound, Wells Street, or any other place on Earth.

Memphis quartet song lyrics often express similar sentiments. The Brewsteraires, for example, wish to "just move on up the King's highway" because "it's a highway that leads up to heaven"; the "King" refers, of course, to Jesus. Similarly, the I. C. Glee Club associates Memphis and heaven when it sings of the "ride home on the Chickasaw train." One of the most powerful and direct heaven-bound metaphors found in this corpus is "Milky White Way" by the Spirit of Memphis:

> Yes, I'm going to walk the milky white way,
> One of these old days.
> Gonna walk up and take my stand,
> Gonna join that Christian band,
> Woah, woah, one of these old days.

Metaphors, allusions, and related images of travel and movement are an important part of the language that quartet singers in Memphis use. These devices are also commonly found in other forms of Afro-American folk music, most notably in the blues.[15] Such similarities are not surprising in light of the important oral tradition and backgrounds shared by many blues and gospel singers.

Literary scholars have long applied the methods of textual analysis to poetry, short stories, and novels in order to gain a greater awareness of implicit cultural and personal values. Other scholars have used semiotics to understand the symbolism that underlies many everyday objects like the American flag. An analogue is the expensive, matched suits and ornate uniforms worn by the quartets which signify a deeper cultural, musical, and religious unity and dignity. From the geographer's perspective, a close examination of the names selected by these quartets and the songs they perform helps us to better understand the singers' often subconscious perceptions of their own environment.

NOTES

1. For a comprehensive, annotated bibliography of this scholarship see Kip Lornell, "Diffusion, Migration, and Sense of Place: The Geography of American Folk and Popular Music," *Current Musicology,* 37/8 (1984), pp. 127–35.

2. Avery Savage, interviewed by Kip Lornell, March 22, 1982. Unless indicated otherwise, all interviews were conducted in Memphis, Tennessee, by the author. Copies of the interview tapes and transcripts are deposited in the Mississippi Valley Collection, Brister Library, Memphis State University.

3. Robert Royston, interview, April 21, 1982.

4. Elijah Ruffin, interview, March 2, 1981.

5. Paul T. Bechtol discusses this phenomenon in "Migration and Economic Opportunities in Tennessee Counties" (Ph.D. dissertation, Vanderbilt University, 1962), pp. 81–102.

6. George O. Davis and Fred O. Donaldson, *Blacks in the United States: A Geographic Perspective* (Boston: Houghton Mifflin, 1975), p. 44.

7. Ibid., pp. 30–34.

8. Floyd Wiley, interview, March 15, 1982.

9. Mary Davis, interview, May 10, 1982.

10. Clara Anderson, interview, April 18, 1982.

11. Grover Blake, interview, July 10, 1982.

12. Ibid.

13. Ibid.

14. Jack Franklin, interview, May 31, 1982.

15. These scholars examine the language and lyrics of blues singers: Samuel Charters, *Poetry of the Blues* (New York: Oak Publications, 1963); Norm Cohen, *Long Steel Rail: The Railroad in American Folksong* (Urbana: University of Illinois Press, 1983); David Evans, *Big Road Blues: Creativity in the Folk Blues* (Berkeley: University of California Press, 1982); and Jeff Todd Titon, *Down Home Blues Lyrics* (Boston: G. K. Hall, 1982).

The Gospel Writer Junior Boys had achieved semiprofessional status by 1953: (*top*) Willie "Pop" Jones, Roy Neal, Willie Neal, Clyde Howard; (*bottom*) Ollie Hoskins, Willie Pettis, Thomas Caldwell. *Courtesy of Marie Walton.*

One of America's most popular quartets of the early 1950s, the Five Blind Boys of Mississippi. *Author's collection.*

Beginning in the late 1940s the Famous Pilgrim Travelers toured the country from their Los Angeles base. *Author's collection.*

By 1946 the Soul Stirrers had been an innovative and influential quartet for nearly a decade. *Courtesy of Cleo Satterfield.*

The Golden Gate Quartette, circa 1948, perhaps the single most respected quartet for two decades, beginning in 1937. *Author's collection.*

In 1952 the Sunset Travelers were about to enter the studios for Duke
Records: (*top*) Lonnie Walton, Bill (?), Adam (?), Sam Miller; (*bot-
tom*) McKinney Jones, Walter Pittman, Grover Blake. *Courtesy of Marie
Walton.*

Beginning in 1949, thousands of Memphis residents tuned in to "Cousin" Eugene Walton's daily gospel programs, circa 1954. *Author's collection.*

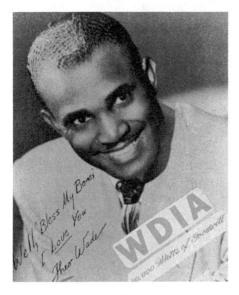

A singer and booking agent for the Spirit of Memphis, Theo Wade was best known as a WDIA disc jockey, circa 1952. *Author's collection.*

WDIA gospel disc jockey Ford Nelson, circa 1952, began his broadcasting career in the late 1940s. *Author's collection.*

In 1951 WDIA was featuring regular broadcasts by the Spirit of Memphis: "Little Ax" Broadnax, "Jet" Bledsoe, Robert Reed, James Darling, Earl Malone, Silas Steele. *Author's collection.*

The Spirit of Memphis reached the height of their popularity about 1953: (*top*) Fred Howard, "Jet" Bledsoe, Earl Malone; (*bottom*) Robert Reed, Silas Steele, "Little Ax" Broadnax, Theo Wade. *Author's collection.*

The Southern Wonders, circa 1953, did many remote broadcasts on WDIA sponsored by Pet Milk: (*standing*) L. T. Blair, Ernest McKinney, James Darling, Jack Franklin, R. L. Weaver, Artis Yancey; (*seated*) Ford Nelson. *Courtesy of Essie Mae Wade.*

The Southern Wonders, seated on stage, performed at a benefit to purchase a new wheelchair for the young woman on the left. *Author's collection.*

A WDIA remote broadcast featuring Ford Nelson and the Southern Wonders, from the Foote Homes in Memphis, circa 1952. *Author's collection.*

By 1953 the Southern Wonders recorded for Peacock Records: (*top*) Jack Franklin, Artis Yancey, R. L. Weaver; (*bottom*) Ernest McKinney, L. T. Blair, James Darling. *Author's collection.*

An unknown quartet performing on a WDIA remote broadcast, circa 1952. *Author's collection.*

The Spirit of Memphis posing with heavyweight boxing champion "Jersey Joe" Walcott, about 1953: Theo Wade, Fred Howard, Walcott, Robert Reed, Earl Malone, "Little Ax" Broadnax, "Jet" Bledsoe, Silas Steele. *Courtesy of Essie Mae Wade.*

The Dixie Nightingales, circa 1960, evolved from the Gospel Writer Junior Boys: (*top*) Ollie Hoskins, Willie Neal, Bill Davis; (*bottom*) Melvin Malone, Nelson Lesure, Rochester Neal. *Author's collection.*

The Sunset Travelers, about 1962, recorded for Peacock Records: (*top*) Clyde Beyers, Grover Blake, Robert Lewis; (*bottom*) Daniel Scott, Rev. Jeff Brown. *Courtesy of Doug Seroff.*

By 1956 the Spiritual Travelers had become a semiprofessional quartet: Levi Williams, Henry Bishop, L. D. Tennel, J. W. Williams, Sam Jones, Julius Readers. *Author's collection.*

SOUVENIR PROGRAM
1956
WDIA
Goodwill Revue
All-Star Charity Show

8:00 P.M. December 7th   Ellis Auditorium

Souvenir program, 1956 WDIA Goodwill Revue. *Author's collection.*

The WDIA Goodwill Fund

In 1949, Radio Station WDIA presented the first Goodwill Revue to provide aid to needy Negro children. This was the birth of the Goodwill Station policy to "help people to help themselves."

For the first four years, all profits were turned over to established Memphis charity funds. As the shows grew larger, the Revue moved into North Hall of Ellis Auditorium, and a larger charity project was sought. In 1954, the Fund was incorporated and plans made to enable WDIA to purchase, and operate special buses in order that Negro crippled children could get proper education. Now the Keel Avenue school is being operated by the Memphis Board of Education at the suggestion of WDIA.

In addition to this service for Negro Crippled Children, the year 1955 saw Goodwill at work in the field of juvenile sports. The Fund purchased 198 baseball uniforms and equipment for 14 teams—the WDIA Little League, first of its kind in the United States. This year, almost 400 youngsters played in the League.

This past summer, on July 3rd, the first annual "Starlight Revue" was presented at Martin Stadium before more than 11,000 people . . . who came and contributed to the Goodwill Fund.

These charity shows are produced and presented by the WDIA staff with the help of America's top recording stars who come to Memphis at their own expense. Absolutely NO ONE RECEIVES A CENT FOR HIS SERVICES. All money goes to the WDIA Goodwill Fund.

These projects are Goodwill at work . . . helping people in communities all over the Mid-South to help themselves to better education — better standards of living — better understanding—and better opportunity. Your ticket money is your contribution to all of these. This is Goodwill At Work.

Program

Part One: "A Pilgrimage To The Holy Land"

Ford Nelson	Theo Wade
Cornell Wells	Ernest Brazzle
Aunt Carrie	

The Brewsteraires	Dixie Nightengales
Unison Voices	Reed Singers
Sons Of Jehovah	Friendly Echoes

THE SPIRIT OF MEMPHIS
REV. CLEOPHUS ROBINSON
MADAME ROBINSON
THE HAPPYLAND BLIND BOYS

****

Part Two: Early American Rock'n Roll
Blues and Pop Stars

WDIA Goodwill Revue All-Star Band

RAY CHARLES..Atlantic Records
THE MAGNIFICENTS...Vee-Jay Records
B. B. KING..WDIA-RPM
THE MOONGLOWS...Chess Records

THE CAST

Great Googa Mooga (Medicine Man)........Nat Williams
Sweet Mama...Willa Monroe
Big Chief Moohah..Moohah
Chief Rockin' Horse.....................................Rufus Thomas
Princess Premium Stuff.................................Martha Jean
Crazy Man Crazy...Honeyboy
Bad Stuff...Cathryn Johnson
Braves and Squaws............................Teen Town Singers

Costumes: Mattie Lee Russell, Martha Armstrong, Betty Mattis, Yvonne Brown.

THE STORY: Big Chief Moohah is an old-fashioned Indian who does not approve of rock'n roll. This new musical influence has been brought into Choctaw tribe by Chief Rockin' Horse who has run off and married Princess Premium Stuff, daughter of Big Chief. For that, Rockin' Horse and all braves have been banished from tribe.

WDIA Goodwill family portrait. *Author's collection.*

The WDIA Goodwill Story

From 1070 on your radio dial, you hear the friendly voice of RADIO STATION WDIA in Memphis, broadcasting with 50,000 watts of power-- the most powerful radio station possible -- on the air from 4:00 A. M. to 12 midnight.

You hear the wonderful programs and sparkling stars that have made WDIA the favorite station of more than half a million Negroes in and around Memphis for more than six years!

WDIA, The Goodwill Station, is the FIRST -- and the ONLY 50,000-watt station programmed exclusively for Negroes, -- truly one of America's GREAT radio stations!

But WDIA has many other "firsts" to its credit, too. It pioneered in Negro programming and was the first station to devote all of its time to serving Negroes. WDIA had the first all-Negro staff of broadcast stars, "Brown America Speaks" (the first all-Negro forum for the free and open discussion of Negro problems), and the first Negro woman broadcaster in America. WDIA is first in public service promotion for Negroes, and has received outstanding recognition and awards.

WDIA has the largest Negro audience in America; a listening audience wanting the best entertainment and programs in the nation. Known as "The Starmaker Station" for development of Negro talent, WDIA has discovered such recording stars as B. B. King, Johnny ACE, Rosco Gordon, Earl Forest and Bobby Bland. WDIA was directly responsible for the development of gospel groups such as Teen Town Singers, The Spirit of Memphis Quartet, The Southern Wonders, The Songbirds of The South, -- all presently heard on WDIA. Every week, you hear the Southern Jubilee Singers, The Brewsteraires, Brother Cleophas Robinson, The Friendly Echoes, The Jones Boys, The Gospel Writer Jr. Boys, and many other outstanding singers.

WDIA has been called "the sensation of the nation" by many, but WDIA calls itself YOUR GOODWILL STATION, and by that name it is known by the 3,800,000 people in its tremendous listening area.

First in Negro programming with 50,000 watts, -- first in the hearts of its listeners, WDIA is YOUR station. DAYTIME and NIGHTTIME, TOO -- 1070 on your radio.

1070

55   60   70   90▼   110   130   150

Set Your Radio Dial

The Spirit of Memphis's popularity continued well into the late 1950s: (*top*) Robert Reed, Fred Howard, "Jet" Bledsoe, Earl Malone; (*bottom*) O. V. Wright, Berry Brown. *Author's collection.*

TNT Braggs, Don Robey, and Bobby "Blue" Bland (*left to right*), circa 1955. *Courtesy of Michael Ochs Archives/Venice, California.*

CHAPTER

4

"A Family of Singers"

Over the years the black gospel quartet singers in Memphis have
evolved into a highly complex, extended family by virtue of birth,
marriage, geographic proximity, religious affiliation, and shared
social values and status. These singers, the organizers of gospel
"quartet unions," and the quartet trainers are among the core
members of the unique musical community to be explored in this
chapter.

To date, few American studies utilizing the concept of a musical
community have been published.[1] Such a community can be described as a loose-knit, often eclectic group of people coalescing
around a shared, specific musical interest. We have, for example,
Alan Merriam and Raymond Mack's analysis of "the set of people
who share an interest in jazz, and who share it at a level of intensity such that they participate to some extent in the occupation
role and ideology of the professional jazz musician. They learn and
accept at least some of the norms which are particular to the jazz
musician: norms regarding proper and improper language, good
and bad music, stylish and unstylish clothing, acceptable and unac-
ceptable audience behavior and so forth."[2] Bill Ferris has studied,
among other groups, the musical community of blues singers that
existed in Leland, Mississippi, during the 1960s. He remarks that
"the blues community grew up like a family with a kinship of love
for music and good times together."[3] These comments reflect some
of my own thoughts regarding the Memphis gospel quartet com-

munity, which encompasses not only the singers themselves but disc jockeys, preachers, record company officials, and fans, as well as relatives of the singers. Indeed, anyone with more than a casual connection with Memphis gospel quartets is part of this unique musical community.

Quartet and other gospel singers often speak to one another using the ritualistic church greetings "brother" and "sister." Doug Seroff, who has also written about black gospel quartets in Memphis, observed that "it would not be misleading to describe Memphis' gospel singing community as a 'family.' The local gospel scene was rather insular and surprisingly homogeneous."[4] His suggestion that gospel singers form a "family" is quite often literally true: many of the local quartet singers have married others who have also been in singing groups; in fact, of the fifty singers interviewed for this book, 60 percent had married within the Memphis quartet community. Cleo and Louis Satterfield are a typical quartet couple. They first met in 1941 at a gospel quartet program—Louis was a member of the True Friends Gospel Singers and Cleo sang with the Union Soft Singers. Within two years they had wed. Elijah Jones and his first wife, Jimmie Martin, became acquainted in the late 1930s when he led the Gospel Writers and she performed with the Gospel Writer Junior Girls. Some of the most important and influential singers in Memphis—Jethroe and Shirley Bledsoe, James and Elizabeth Darling, Floyd and Florence Wiley—also were involved with gospel quartets both before and after their marriages.

Kinship patterns within the quartet community are not limited only to married couples, however, for many siblings have been involved with singing. Willie and Rochester Neal began their careers in the late 1940s as members of the Gospel Writer Junior Boys under the direction of their stepfather, Elijah Jones. They continued with this group throughout the 1950s and 1960s, weathering many personnel changes and a switch in name to the Dixie Nightingales. When the group turned to popular music in the middle 1960s, both Neal brothers left to join the Pattersonaires. Clara and Essie Anderson were sisters who began singing together with the Busyline Soft Singers during the mid-1930s and sang with a neighborhood quartet until Essie's death in 1938. Clara remained in singing and went on to form the Golden Stars and then the

Harps of Melody. Doris Jean Gary was a vital member of the Songbirds of the South between 1949 and 1956, while her brother
Willie sang first with the Rust College Quartet and then helped to
found the Pattersonaires in 1953.

Although familial involvement in black gospel music is not limited to quartets or to Memphis—for example, the Staple Singers
from Mississippi and Alabama's Ravizee Singers, two long-respected
black American gospel groups, have been composed entirely or almost entirely of members from the same family—it is nonetheless
striking how pervasive kinship systems are within the Memphis
musical community. Despite the size of the city, its position as a
transportation hub, and its importance as a destination for migrants in the Mid-South, the quartet community in Memphis has
remained largely free of outside influence.

The Memphis quartet community has long extended well beyond kinship systems into more practical concerns of cooperation,
one of the most visible and interesting being the formation of
"unions" to cultivate quartet singing within the city. While organizations like the National Convention of Gospel Choirs and
Choruses, Inc., which Thomas A. Dorsey founded in Chicago in
1932, existed to promote large ensembles, smaller groups also
formed to encourage unity among quartets. For example, in Chicago, just before the Great Depression, Norman McQueen began a
quartet union that was probably America's first such organization.

The first quartet organization in Memphis was the City Quartette Union, founded by "Doctor" Frost in 1939. Although not a
singer himself, Frost took a lively interest in harmony singing. He
helped to organize and promote weekly programs within the city
and often served as master of ceremonies. The City Quartette Union
lost his valuable services in 1943 when Frost migrated to Detroit
for a more lucrative daytime job. Another charter member of the
organization, James Darling, assumed Frost's responsibilities for
about four years. Then Huddie Moore replaced Darling, holding
the presidency of the City Quartette Union until its dissolution in
about 1953. Moore explains the ideology and organization of the
union: The idea was "to get a lot of singers together and cooperate,
and have more people participate on your programs. When you
had the City Quartette Union and the quartets, you had your pro-

gram. All you had to get [was] the church and render your program. We'd have the City Quartette Union [chorus] open the program and let the quartets come on later."[5]

Although it was the first organization of its kind in Memphis, the City Quartette Union was not the only group to serve as the community's rallying point and clearinghouse for quartet singing. Most of the older singers I interviewed mentioned two similar groups— the South Memphis Singing Union and the North Memphis Singing Union—which existed briefly during the mid-1940s but proved to be so ephemeral that nothing more can be learned about them. Just after the end of World War II, however, another more substantial, influential cooperative, the United Singing Union, was formed. Several singers suggested that this organization sprang up in the wake of the South Memphis Singing Union. Regardless of its origins, the United Singing Union was a very significant force in organizing the Memphis community-based quartets throughout the late 1940s and 1950s.

The guiding strength behind the United Singing Union, from its inception until the early 1980s, was Lillian Wafford. Although greatly burdened by her husband's severe stroke in 1978, Mrs. Wafford worked tirelessly to keep the union together and functioning smoothly. During her tenure she served as the union's president and its spiritual leader. Mrs. Wafford nursed her husband until his death in March 1982, and within ten days she herself was dead. With its principal leadership gone, Memphis's last gospel quartet cooperative disbanded.

The principal purposes of these unions were to encourage solidarity among members, promote quartet singing, and assist members in booking their programs. While their goals were concrete, the organizations themselves were not always so stable. According to Mary Davis, cofounder in 1944 of the Majestic Soft Singers, the ranks of the United Singing Union were always in flux: "The original group was the Majestic Soft Singers plus the Spiritual Pilgrims. Then came the Wells Spirituals . . . then the Morris Special Singers . . . [and] four or five years later, the Brewsteraires. Then we had the Walker Specials to join in. In other words, we had several groups to going in, but several of them didn't stay too long."[6] These continual changes created a fluid organization whose precise ranks are impossible to establish. Mrs. Wafford left no formal, written records, though it appears that only the Wells Spirituals, the Majestic Soft Singers, and the Spiritual Pilgrims remained union members for an extended period.

It is apparent that once the United Singing Union established its reputation as a clearinghouse for booking quartets in the late 1940s, it served an important and useful purpose in Memphis. Mrs. Wafford, who oversaw the union's finances, had a formula for splitting fees between the host group and the quartet. Basically, progams held in Memphis paid 50 percent of the money to the quartet and 50 percent to the host church, while programs held outside of Memphis paid 60 percent to the quartet, with the host church receiving 40 percent; the difference reflected the travel expenses involved. Out of the revenues from programs booked by the United Singing Union, each quartet contributed some money to the union for organizational expenses. Mrs. Wafford herself accepted no salary; she considered her work as a contribution to the union as well as a means of assisting others in spreading this musical ministry.

The spirit of cooperation and mutual assistance that characterized the City Quartette Union and the United Singing Union was emblematic of a more general sense of a synergetic partnership that permeated the black American gospel quartet community in Memphis. Although singing was the focal point for their energies, group members were also deeply involved in service to the community at large. Both major quartet unions fit into a larger mosaic of the city's black religious community that served as the center of social and community work long before President Johnson's cry for the Great Society brought us a codified welfare system and Aid to Dependent Children. In this respect the unions deserve to be viewed in the same light as African Method Episcopal (A.M.E.) women's auxiliary groups or local civic and fraternal organizations, which also served as self-help groups in the black community. The church and its many allied support services have been the backbone of black social and religious life for many decades, extending their community work in Memphis far beyond a strictly sacred context.

The comments of Cleo Satterfield illustrate the important role of gospel quartet unions in the social and cultural fabric of black life:

Frost [of the City Quartette Union] was the type of person who
could keep a program so alive that everybody wanted to hear him
talk after the singing. He was nice about helping someone if he knew
they were sick or somebody in the group or in the church was sick.
It somebody tell him about it, he would raise an offering for them.
If they knew that something was wrong with someone they knew,
they would always reach out and give a helping hand. We never had
that much, but what we had, we'd give it freely. If you were in the
city, if you got to a program, you always help somebody.[7]

Huddie Moore recalls that the City Quartette Union "would do a
program for somebody who had gotten burned out or something
like that. We would put on programs to raise money to help that
family or different things like that. Somebody was always in necessity."[8] He also observed that a share of the money from each
program the union sponsored went into a special fund, and at
Christmas union members would deliver baskets of food to needy
families.

The aid provided by these gospel groups included spiritual sustenance as well, particularly in the form of free programs held at
rest homes and senior citizens' centers. Some quartets even performed in local prisons and jails, the idea being simply to spread
the ministry of God in song. Etherlene Beans explains how she and
her group, the Willing Four Softline Singers, worked:

They contacted us because they find that we were just a group that
liked to sing. We didn't sing for finances . . . [but because] we like to
sing and we always want to share what we had with other people.
We was really a spiritual group. We like to sing and get happy and
let other people get happy. We just would go where we thought that
the spirit was needed. We would go to the workhouse and sing . . .
also sing for sick people, cripple children's hospitals, and to help
churches.

I like to sing quartet singing because I'm a Christian person and I
believe in feeling spiritually. I sing until I feel good . . . and feel like
I've helped somebody. I want to try and save a soul, see, through my
singing.[9]

By the late 1940s a nationwide group, the National Quartet
Convention, was founded by the Famous Blue Jay Singers and the
Soul Stirrers for the purpose of "professionalizing" gospel quartets.
Headquartered in Chicago, chapters were quickly established

throughout the country. In 1949 a Memphis chapter was formed; its first president was Floyd Wiley. The impact of this nationwide group on Memphis quartets was significant, though it had a different premise from that of the local singing organizations. While the City Quartette Union and the United Singing Union were primarily interested in supporting local groups and providing social assistance, the National Quartet Convention stressed a professional stance toward quartet singing. The convention's annual meeting featured workshops and sessions devoted to helping groups develop or improve their organizational and business skills. A member of the National Quartet Convention since the early 1950s, Flozell Leland, explains: "We have workshops that train you how to do a whole lot of things; how to meet people, how to address an audience, how to perform, how to dress, and, really, how to sing; how to do a lot of [related] things: carry meetings, make motions and what not. A lot of people don't even know how to be a secretary or write a 'minute.' That's very important." [10]

The efforts of the National Quartet Convention to promote professionalism among quartet singers were not lost on Memphis, though it was a lesson that many local groups had already learned. Like the whole community of singers, the quartets themselves generally follow formal rules of protocol and procedure similar to those found in social and civic clubs. Quartets contain anywhere from four to eight members who delegate among themselves the duties and responsibilities necessary to operate. Memphis quartets tend to divide the responsibilities among four parties: manager, secretary, treasurer, and president. The manager is in charge of choosing uniforms, sound equipment, and any other similar items required by the group. The manager also helps with the details of transportation to and from the program, decides if infractions, such as chewing gum in church or missing a rehearsal, deserve fines, and serves as one of the liaisons between the group and anyone wishing to book programs.

The primary role of the quartet president is to oversee meetings and rehearsals. This includes reading minutes from the previous meeting, calling for new business, reading the roll call, and clarifying any questions or problems that arise. The president is also the quartet's public spokesperson. If the president is ill, then the manager fills in. The secretary records each meeting's minutes, including the time and location, which members are absent, and what fines are levied. Another duty is to keep track of the bylaws, to which new rules can be added or old rules deleted, according to a vote of the membership. The quartet treasurer accounts for all funds and keeps track of all travel expenses, the cost of uniforms, fines, dues, income from programs, and so forth. He or she is also charged with collecting money and dispersing funds.

To complement this formal hierarchy, local quartets have a set of rules (either written or tacitly understood) by which they govern themselves. Some rules pertain strictly to the procedural matters needed to run meetings, while others help to maintain order and stability within the group. These bylaws or club rules are important tools in the struggle to keep singers from "backsliding" and for promoting group solidarity. While almost every Memphis quartet has a system of laws, some groups operate under casual, somewhat loose regulations. Others like the Harps of Melody and the Gospel Writers, have strict codes.

BYLAWS
For the Harps of Melody—Adopted Sept. 13, 1950.
I. Every member of the Harps of Melody must be a member of some church and in good standing with her church.
II. Every member of the Harps of Melody must show a spirit of unity and fellowship which means love and care towards each other and all on one accord.
III. Rehearsal time shall be from 8:00 to 10:45 pm. Every member is responsible for making sure that all meetings and rehearsals are strictly private as possible when meeting in the home, unless there is a prospective member involved.
IV. Each member of the Harps of Melody must be on time as much as possible for rehearsals and programs.
V. Any member interrupting while another member is talking in meetings or rehearsals shall be supervised.
VI. Every member of the Harps of Melody is asked not to smoke in public or on church property or any public place, or chew gum on program.
VII. Realizing that the public has its eye on the Harps of Melody every member must respect and obey officers on programs and in public places.
VIII. Any member discussing any business or secrets of the Harps of Melody with any other than the members of the group shall be suspended.

IX. Any member that creates a disturbance while on program or in rehearsal or humiliate the Harps of Melody in any way shall be dealt with as the group sees fit.

X. Every member must be clean and neat in appearance on all programs, and uniform must be becoming.

XI. Any member of the Harps of Melody using profanity in the meetings, programs, rehearsals or any public place shall be suspended.

XII. Whenever the Harps of Melody appear on program each member must always perform to the best of her skill and ability. We must always pray and ask the Spirit of God to dwell with us at all times.

XIII. Any member who misses 3 meetings and come in on the 4th meeting with a good reason will be heard by the group and do as the group see fit.

By-Laws for the Gospel Writers

I. Business Meeting and Rehearsal every Saturday at 5:00 PM.
   A. Order of the Meeting:
      1. Devotion by the Chaplain.
      2. Business meeting carried out by the President.
      3. Rehearsal under the supervision of the manager.

II. All members are under the direction of the manager at all times except during the business meeting.

III. Each member is required to pay weekly dues.

IV. Each member is required to meet on time at all of the group's engagements or meetings.

V. All members are to be uniformed.

VI. Each member is required to carry himself in such a manner, so as not to downgrade or disgrace this group in any way.

VII. Each member is required to fully support this group both spiritually and financially to the best of his ability.

These bylaws cover a multitude of problems and sins and allow the group to exert some leverage over members who break the rules. Although punishment for infractions is not explicitly covered, monetary fines determined by the president are most often levied. Serious offenses generally mean a higher fine, and if the affront is grievous enough, then a member can be suspended or dropped from the quartet. Along with internal order, quartets are also concerned with their public image, as is underscored by their rules related to public decorum and dress. The quartet singers have carefully shaped and cultivated a finely tuned image, that of respectful and forthright Christians who dress well, in the height of fashion.

It is difficult to ascertain precisely how the rules and club system evolved. The first of Memphis's black quartets to record, the I.C. Glee Club, consciously referred to itself as a "club." Many of the quartet veterans whose careers date back to the 1920s and 1930s—Elijah Ruffin, Clara Anderson, Luther McGill, and James Harvey—also frequently refer to older groups as clubs. In their heyday many quartets were closely or directly associated with neighborhood churches, local companies, or neighborhood groups—for example, the Jolly Sunshine Boosters Club Quartet, which was part of a well-known south Memphis civic club in the late 1940s. Such connections help to account for the quartets' formal rules, their internal structures, and their strict hierarchies.

Another aspect of the close-knit nature of this musical community is the way in which quartets are trained. Quartet training is very demanding, requiring extremely specialized skills. The process is critical because it involves the transmission of musical repertoire and style. By preserving certain musical traits, quartet trainers also provide a crucial link between one generation of musicians and another, as well as links between groups. At first glance the role of gospel quartet trainers appears quite simple—they teach songs. But their functions are actually far more detailed and complex. Trainers have long been regarded as specialists by quartet singers, who initially called upon them for several reasons. One was to help groups orient new members. Etherlene Beans of the Willing Four Softline Singers says that Elijah Jones was often asked to attend their rehearsals when new members were being trained. Groups also requested that trainers aid them in learning new songs or arrangements; thus the trainer assisted with the intricacies of vocal timbre, rhythm, and harmony—three of the key ingredients in gospel quartet singing. If a trainer developed a new arrangement that proved popular, other local groups often asked him to provide them with the same or similar arrangement.

Trainers have sometimes been asked to locate new singers for groups, though most groups recruit members themselves. For many years Elijah Jones served as the unofficial coordinator for quartets that needed new singers, and when Huddie Moore was forming the Memphis Spiritual Four in the middle 1930s, Jones did not wait to be asked but stepped forward and volunteered his services. Clara Anderson recalls that Jones's mentor, Gus Miller, offered to help the Busyline Soft Singers. Similar observations regarding the eagerness of quartet trainers to help groups have been made by many other Memphis singers, which suggests that the trainers saw themselves as providing a unique and invaluable service to the community as well as propagating the music they loved.

Although they were often very busy helping quartets and spent innumerable hours in this service, trainers were not motivated by the prospect of financial rewards. All of the Memphis trainers have been singers, though none of them forged a full-time living from gospel music. Gus Miller, for example, survived with the help of his family and a veteran's pension he received as the result of a severe wound sustained in World War I. Elijah Jones spent his entire life as a blue-collar worker. Some trainers may have been offered money for their services, but this was strictly a free-will offering. Etherlene Beans notes that Elijah Jones "never did get money from us. Now, in late days, we used to give him a little money, a little transportation money on his gas, but he never made money off us. He just likes singing . . . and he was always willing to assist us in singing."[11]

This observation provides the key to the motivation of quartet trainers. While some people were able organizers or willing to publicize events, these talented men loved harmony singing and their help was a gift to their fellow singers. George Rooks, who knew and sang with Elijah Jones off and on for nearly forty years, recalls that Jones stood at the nexus of the quartet community. Most weekends found him singing or attending a quartet program or a rehearsal. Trainers of Miller's and Jones's stature were also frequently asked to judge "quartet contests" (a performance event to be discussed shortly).

Being recognized by one's peers as a trainer denotes a special status within this musical community. Gospel quartet trainers are blessed with unusually perceptive ears and minds and the ability to communicate their knowledge. When groups regularly come to certain individuals asking for assistance, this acknowledges the community's respect for their talents. It is evident that Memphis trainers have enjoyed intuitive skills honed through practice and application rather than through formal education. Elijah Ruffin, who has worked with about a dozen local groups, considers his training ability a natural gift, albeit one shaped by nearly five decades of experience. Most quartet singers are self-taught or have learned through an apprenticeship system that has nothing to do with formally graded musical education. Some singers may aspire to become trainers, but first they must be accepted by their peers.

As I have already intimated, males have dominated quartet training in Memphis. Indeed, the singers I interviewed did not mention women in their discussions of training specialists, except for women such as Clara Anderson, who worked with the Harps of Melody and Golden Stars, who did train their own groups. One result of this male-dominated training system is that Memphis's female quartets almost always refer to their voices as bass, baritone, alto, and lead. It is at first startling to hear women's parts called baritone or bass, but this terminology is so commonplace in Memphis that it quickly loses its novelty. The practice is perhaps best explained by the fact that quartet trainers "give" people their voices; that is, they often assign each person to a vocal range. Thus the trainers designate the lowest female voice, like the lowest male voice, as bass.

The fundamental process of training quartets is itself relatively easy to describe—the trainer simply sings each part to all of the singers in turn and then the singers blend the parts in four-part harmony. Long-time Memphis trainer Jack Miller articulates the process: "The first thing is the voice. Check the voices out; see if the voice is fitted for a tenor, baritone, lead or bass. Then you go from there. You have to sing the four voices to get the pitch of the song, to teach it. Then you work on the time of the songs, how long you should go with it. Some people are quick to catch on, some are not. If they got the talent to catch on and the voice, then you train them in a couple months." [12] While the procedure sounds simple, it demands an unusual knowledge and skill. First, the trainer must be able to sing each of the four voices; in fact, trainers have often filled the role of "utility singers" in their own quartets. Second, the trainer intuitively conceives harmonies, rhythms, and tempos, a process that is refined and adjusted as the parts are taught to the group. Finally, the lack of a notation system means that the trainers work entirely through oral means, relying heavily upon tonal memory and sheer repetition. Training a quartet absolutely requires an immense amount of skill as well as a willingness to invest a great deal of time, concentration, and energy.

The most renowned and influential trainer in Memphis, Elijah Jones, worked with countless groups during his career. Etherlene Beans describes how Jones helped the Willing Four Softline Singers:

> He would train you how to control your voice, how to keep your voice with the next singer, not to get too loud for the next singer, not to get too loud for your music [instruments], not to get your music too loud for you. I have a loud voice and he always taught me to tone my voice down so that I wouldn't drown the other singers out. He always teach us to say our words distinctly, not to drag through them. He always teach you to sing words distinctly, and you cannot sing a song unless you know it. He helped us a whole lot. It was just remarkable what he could do with singers.[13]

Trainers also are noted for their suggestions regarding vocal and tonal qualities or techniques. For instance, a trainer might advise that the featured singer affect a more raspy tonal color or sing his or her part falsetto; a trainer could make the arrangement of a song distinctive by altering the tempo during the chorus or by having the background sung more staccato.

Groups would call upon the services of trainers for extended periods of time, as Leon Moody of the Jolly Sunshine Boosters Club Quartet recalls:

> For years and years we would go to Gus [Miller] and he would okay each of the songs that we'd rehearse. You can go so far with a group, after you stay together long enough, you can mighty near tell yourself when you are getting off at all. We got to the point where . . . if one fellow missed a note or key or something, it might take us 30 or 40 minutes or maybe an hour. But we would change it or correct it. After so long we would go back to Gus, maybe once or twice a month and he would . . . check us.[14]

The groups themselves utilized such basic ideas in their ongoing struggle to achieve "their own sound." The spark of creativity frequently began with the trainers, but suggestions from within the group often carried it forward. Radical changes in the styles of Memphis quartet singing, particularly prior to World War II, came slowly. When quartets began functioning in the realm of popular culture during the 1940s and 1950s, however, the local appearances of touring groups, records, and radio created an atmosphere for more rapid innovation.

Despite this ongoing emphasis on innovation among certain Memphis quartets, trainers never lost their prestige or influence within the local quartet community. Elijah Jones remained in demand as a trainer until his death in January 1980. Long after the "boom years" of quartet singing, many Memphis quartets still wished to learn the art of harmony singing from this acknowledged master. The other master trainer was Gus Miller, who spent his adult life confined to a wheelchair. His participation in World War I suggests a birthdate circa 1890 and possibly accounts for his disability. Elijah Jones recalled that Miller sang with and had trained the Harmony Four when they first met in the late 1920s. Gus Miller's half-brother, Frank (a former quartet singer now living in St. Louis), reports that during the 1920s and 1930s Gus shuttled back and forth between Memphis and St. Louis, where he had a married daughter. Little more is known of Miller's personal life except that he apparently died in Memphis around 1960.

We do know quite a lot about Miller's influential work with several local groups during the 1930s. Because of his infirmity, he was unable to sing for extended periods, though he was a member of at least one group, the legendary Middle Baptist Quartet, after the Harmony Four split up in the early 1930s. James Harvey recollects Miller's skill as a trainer: "Gus was almost as good as Elijah Jones. I think if Gus would have kept it up, he would have been as good as Elijah. He was dedicated to it. There is something about group work that you've got to hear a song . . . you just hear the tune and put it together. He was just that type person; he could do that. It seem like a talent he have [and] could share with somebody else." [15] Elijah Ruffin, Clara Anderson, and others active during the depression years also recall Gus Miller with great respect. They speak of a period when Miller, rather than Jones, was the busiest trainer in Memphis.

Due to increasingly ill health, Miller's work as a trainer greatly diminished during the years following World War II, and he was quickly replaced by his talented apprentice, Elijah Jones. Born in Millington, Tennessee, in 1906, Jones moved to Memphis with his family in 1924. The sound of harmony singing fascinated him and he soon became immersed in the quartet community. By 1928 he was working as a laborer and singing: "When we were around home, we were always singing around the house. I began to say

'I'm going to get to singing.' I picked up one or two fellows and we sat around and singed. I didn't know nothing about singing then, just picked it up. After I sang it, it comed to me more. So I got to where I could separate voices. Once I could separate voices, it give me a gift and then I could train voices. I got where I could sing all voices myself." [16]

Although considered a good singer, Elijah Jones's most important contribution to Memphis harmony singing was undoubtedly his role as a trainer. He started his own group, the Gospel Writers, in the late 1930s but was soon training another group for young women, the Gospel Writer Junior Girls. This group eventually became the Songbirds of the South, one of the most respected female groups in Memphis quartet history. A similar story can be told of the Gospel Writer Junior Boys, which changed its name to the Dixie Nightingales in the early 1950s and went on to enjoy an impressive career. It is difficult even to estimate how many groups Jones worked with during the peak of his career, but it must have been a score or more.

In the middle 1950s, for reasons unknown, Jones disbanded the Gospel Writers and absented himself from quartet singing for nearly twenty years. He still occasionally helped train groups but not nearly as readily as he once did. Equally enigmatic was his 1976 reemergence, which marked a revival of the Gospel Writers and his return to active quartet training. Perhaps this flurry of activity was a presentiment of his fatal heart attack in 1980. Whatever the reasons, his work between 1976 and 1980 helped to reactivate the groups stressing older, more conservative singing and performance styles.

Afro-American gospel quartets have always emphasized performance and communication with their audience. Hence, performance events provide a vital key to understanding this music and its importance to members of the black community in Memphis. Quartet programs are the most common medium for the public to hear and see these singers. Nearly every Sunday and on many Saturdays since the 1920s, Memphis gospel quartets have appeared in churches and auditoriums throughout the city. Although all quartets have some direct affiliation with churches, either as church-related groups or simply as members of a church, they have not always appeared as part of the worship service itself. In fact, congregational singing or choirs most often present the musical offering during regularly scheduled services.

Quartets in Memphis usually perform on special musical programs held during the afternoons or evenings, which often feature more than one ensemble. In a very real sense quartet programs constitute an extension of the Sunday morning worship service, the difference being the programs' emphasis on music as the instrument by which to worship God. Local quartet programs typically last between one and three hours. They are promoted within the black church community by way of placards, posters, notices in the church bulletins and newspapers, announcements from the pulpit, over the radio, and during other programs, and by word-of-mouth. If more than one group is involved, the guests sing first while the host quartet remains to finish the program and to assist in closing the church.

The other type of quartet program in Memphis involves out-of-town groups brought in especially to perform. Both programs are similar in the way they are promoted and the places in which they are held. There are, however, some very critical contextual differences. Although both local and out-of-town programs feature quartet singing, they are not truly analogous. The major programs held at the City Auditorium, the Mason's Temple, and the large churches in Memphis have been religious music events *and* popular entertainment. Especially during the fifteen years following the end of World War II, the popular professional quartets were prominent members of the greater black community and some were as well known as their secular counterparts. Attendance at programs and the frequency with which their records or live performances were heard over the radio confirmed certain groups' popularity. Personal appearances in Memphis by these quartets provided an occasion for religious worship in song and the opportunity to see "stars" perform.

This performance context is very different from a program by local groups like the Royal Harmony Four, the Keystone Masters of Harmony, or any one of a number of other Memphis quartets active during the postwar years. While the basic premise of praising the Lord in song is identical, the difference is more than simply the facile distinction between a local and a professional quartet. One group sings for a community of relatives, peers, and neighbors in a local church, while the other gospel quartet works in a larger, more spacious setting for an audience with whom they have had little, if any, direct personal contact.

Members of Memphis's quartet community are aware of this distinction. Because money and prestige are involved, a program headlined by a non-Memphis quartet such as the Five Blind Boys of Mississippi or the Dixie Hummingbirds is perceived as a special event. Singers from these quartets are considered specialists because they make at least part of their livelihood from music. Memphian Willie Neal speaks of the need to balance spiritual and material desires:

> That's what gospel quartet is all about—being a Christian. It don't mean perfect. . . . We [the Dixie Nightingales] had sung with the top groups of the decade—the Dixie Hummingbirds, the Mighty Clouds of Joy, the Five Blind Boys, the Spirit of Memphis, all those groups. Some of these groups have really made it big, but we are still the more humble gospel.
>
> It is my personal belief that salvation is free. I was singing gospel songs and I was singing from the heart; but in the back of my mind, I was also looking for that dollar. That doesn't mean that you can't do it [make money], but it's what's in your heart and that has to do with the spirit. The spirit is not the dollar.[17]

In fact, local quartet unions and promoters of major programs did use the money that they had raised from concerts in different ways—aptly illustrating Neal's point. A certain portion of this money always went back into the community, but the amounts differed greatly. The City Quartette Union, for instance, assisted people within Memphis neighborhoods and gave food to the needy at Christmas. The United Singing Union fulfilled much the same function during the 1950s. By contrast, the money raised by ticket sales for programs involving professional groups primarily went to cover a variety of expenses including hall rental, advertising, the promoters' percentage, and the groups' fee. A local church or group often cosponsored these programs, taking responsibility for some of the promotions and part of the other financial obligations in return for a percentage of the profits.

Despite these subtle though notable differences between the two types of programs, both performance events have many similarities. Specifically, they are cultural ceremonies by quartet singers with religious worship as the primary goal. These performances have always been regularly scheduled public events featuring highly trained and well-regarded singers. As cultural events, quartet programs are complex and are structured according to a clearly established format with three essential "players": the emcee (or master of ceremonies), the quartets, and the audience. The program itself opens with a well-known song led by the emcee, a minister, or a quartet member and performed by everyone in the audience. This helps to establish a feeling of fellowship among the participants. A prayer offered by one of the ministers then follows the opening song.

The role of an emcee is to assure that the quartets appear in the correct order, to keep the program moving on time, and to make proper introductions. The emcee also fills in the time between groups, while equipment is being changed and the quartets are getting set up, with announcements of future programs, light-hearted jokes, and brief testimonials (sometimes called "recognitions") for people attending the program. This person is clearly a specialist, often someone known within the community who has fulfilled this role before. Emcees are generally male and are often disc jockeys or in some way affiliated with the mass media. Occasionally an individual from outside this fraternity, such as "Doctor" Frost with the City Quartette Union, takes this role, but more often it is someone like Theo "Bless My Bones" Wade from WDIA or "Cousin" Eugene (Walton) of KWEM. For strictly local programs one of the group members or a clergyman frequently serves as the master of ceremonies.

Quartet programs generally start slowly and build in intensity. Much of the success of this type of cultural performance depends upon the interaction between the quartet and the audience. By the 1950s almost all Memphis quartets, and certainly each of the out-of-town groups, stressed stage presence with well-choreographed and well-planned performances. Quartet singing, particularly after the advent of touring professionals, also has been an emotional experience. The singers gesture to the audience and speak with them either directly or through sermonettes pioneered in the late 1940s by Silas Steele, and the audience responds in kind. This interaction is vividly recalled by Tommie Todd, who sang with the Gospel Writers following World War II:

> When we would go and render our programs, a lot of times we'd get converts. A lot of times people would join church on our singing. That's the reason I liked it, because there was something in it I could feel, that other people could feel. That's the reason it had such a pull. So many people would come to hear us because we would give them something that was a help to them. We would have our prayer service just like revival, then we'd go from there. When we got into our singing, people would be shouting. One time they got shouting so bad until a lady got hold to the wrong end of my tie and pulled . . . choked me! When we got singing like that they'd be shouting and throwing pocketbooks and things like that.[18]

Long before black popular singers such as Little Richard, Wilson Pickett, and James Brown gained the limelight, professional quartet singers like Silas Steele and "Jet" Bledsoe of the Spirit of Memphis were highly respected for their ability to "work" an audience. Their performances combined stage presence, singing, and visual techniques calculated to motivate and engage the crowd. Visual techniques included carefully rehearsed movements on stage, crawling along the floor, and walking on the benches among the audience, which was a distant cry from the descriptions of more sedate programs held during the 1920s and 1930s and bears the distinctive marks of the showmanship and bravado of professional quartet singers.

The frantic nature of post–World War II and professional quartets bothered older quartet singers like Leon Moody, who possessed a different sense of what quartet singing should be:

> These other guys went to using a guitar, maybe take a verse or two and then they would run the chorus 15 or 20 times. We sung a song, it lasted 3 or 4 minutes. Every song we sung, we tried to tell a message. We figured that in every song we sung, if we couldn't give them something to think about, that song wasn't worth singing.
>
> Some people just get up and go for a lot of Hallelujah. Most generally [those people] . . . go for guitars and a whole lot of noise. They do a lot of performing, a lot of show. I think if it is supposed to be a religious program it should be a service.[19]

It would be facile to simply dismiss certain stage techniques as stylized antics. Professionalism undeniably has changed the character of black gospel quartet performances, but the singers still draw inspiration from older role models. It is clear that some of these characteristics—dramatic body gestures, emotional vocal styles, and flamboyant behavior—can also be partially attributed to the Pentecostal movement and to African ritual. These aspects of black religious culture provide a model of emotional worship that has been present in Afro-American culture for many decades— the ring shout, the chanted sermon, and holy dancing.[20]

Along with singing and visual effects, quartet performances have also utilized other related verbal techniques. Perhaps the most affecting is the stage patter or speech that quartet singers use in addressing the audience. This mode of communicating is different from the everyday speech heard on the streets and contains many ornate phrases and biblical references; it is often formulaic as well. Although no one explicitly teaches quartet singers this way of speaking, the communicative mode, though not so long and cohesive, is reminiscent of the St. Vincent "sweet talking" documented by Roger Abrahams.[21] I am not aware of any term used by the quartet singers themselves to describe this phenomenon.

Singers employ this device when emotions are running high and the program has reached a fever pitch. Its very existence implies a two-way dialogue with an audience that responds with shouts of encouragement such as "Sing it!" or "I feel that spirit!" This powerful point in the performance involves both the audience and the quartets in a heated spiritual exchange called "getting happy," "shouting," or "feeling the spirit." Neither party is a mere recipient or a transitive agent; both take positive, forceful, and direct roles in this two-way line of communication. It is an intensely moving experience that helps sweep both the singers and their audience onto a more advanced emotional plane. Such a dialogue resembles the keen emotional lift that can be created in a tightly packed basketball arena as the crowd and the home team feed off one another.

The gospel quartet audience shows its approval and participates in other ways, too. The people often clap more loudly for specific quartets or request an encore. And because they are familiar with the quartets and their music, they frequently call out for certain musical selections and acknowledge some of the more impressive vocal techniques or choreography displayed on stage. These are just a few of the ways the audience becomes an indispensable part of the performance.

The three agents in these gospel events know their parts well, for such public performances have gone on in Memphis since the 1920s. The programs have evolved over the past sixty years into a standardized format, closing with a prayer offered by one of the ministers. This does not mean that the emotions and singing are not heartfelt or real, but the framing devices that signal the beginning and end of a gospel quartet program vary little among performances. Many people come to participate during the singing itself, for this is when everyone enjoys the spontaneity and spirituality. Along with the ritualized opening and closing ceremonies, mutual participation and an understanding of these well-mapped-out roles constitute the very heart of a gospel quartet performance.

The programs themselves, whether local, professional, or a mixture of the two, typically follow the format just described. However, there have been two types of closely related, specialized programs that are a little different in their intent. These are *quartet contests* and *song battles.* Quartet contests simply pit one group against another. Although little has been written on the subject, such contests have been reported in Birmingham, Alabama, and the Virginia Tidewater. During the 1930s and 1940s, churches primarily held the contests in Memphis. They were billed as quartet contests in order to build up greater interest in specific programs, a ploy that often worked. Each group would have to perform between four and six selections and the quartet giving the best performance was declared the victor.

Judges for these contests evaluated the finer aspects of singing and determined the winners by assigning points to each group. Although the criteria were subjective, they usually included rhythmic precision, enunciation of words, inventiveness, accuracy of harmony, and ability of the singers. Judges were almost always quartet singers who were not participating on the program. Elijah Jones, a veteran judge, trainer, and singer, explained the selection process: "I always liked judging 'cause so many folks didn't know singing. You got three judges that know singing, then you get fairly seeded. They would look for time, music, don't miss no minors or sharps. The one that makes the most points, that's the one that wins. During that particular time [1930s], we didn't have but four voices: leader, tenor, baritone, and bass. They would listen to each voice. We had judges all up into the late thirties and forties." [22]

Local sponsoring churches often held such contests to raise money. The winning group received a modest share of the donations collected at the door, but perhaps more important, the group members' performing ability was acknowledged by their peers. To be champion of a quartet contest meant prestige and greater respect for the group, which is one of the reasons why the contests were so popular. During the 1940s and 1950s quartet singing became even more fashionable, and a shift occurred in the format and style of these competitions: they became song battles and were frequently staged in large auditoriums.

In Memphis, many song battles took place in the Mason's Temple or the City Auditorium downtown. These performance events were a manifestation of popular culture and a logical evolution of the earlier contests. The audience's applause, rather than peers intimately familiar with quartet singing, decided the winner of the song battle. Elijah Jones observed, "we started having audiences judging in the '50s [and] then you just get out there hoopin' and hollerin', and if they like that, then you be the man." [23] His obvious disdain for the event reflected a clear movement from a program ruled by the quartets themselves to one dominated by popular opinion. That these competitions had changed is reinforced by Julius Readers: "It sort of worked like the group that get the most shouts or the most applause—you know what the favorite group was. You didn't need judges then because if you were tough, when you hit the floor you knowed who had it then, because two to one if you a favorite in that town, when they call your name, everybody just go wild! Then you get up there, their hands clap, and you know who was the winner." [24]

The fact that large auditoriums were the sites of so many song battles further underscores the movement away from community or neighborhood events and toward a more secular world, in which popular tastes prevailed. Regardless of the context or motivation, some singers did not approve of this emphasis on competitiveness and refused to participate in the song battles. They felt that quartets should work together in their musical ministry and not try to prove one quartet's superiority over others. In their view such performances violated the spirit of fellowship that bound singers together.[25] As interest in quartets dwindled nationwide, in the late 1950s, fewer people turned out for song battles and the number of these programs fell; today they are completely anachronistic.

The final context in which quartets can be observed is their regularly scheduled rehearsals, which are not open to the general public. Like the public programs, however, quartet rehearsals follow a format to which the group rigorously adheres. The opening cue is a prayer and scripture reading by a group member. Then the president calls the roll, reads the minutes from the previous meeting, and asks for discussion of old and new business. The treasurer covers financial matters and the secretary gives an account of upcoming programs. While such business and procedural matters seem mundane, they often take up about one-quarter of each rehearsal. These weekly gatherings, which usually rotate among the homes of each quartet member, provide an arena for the discussion of mutual concerns and are critical for the week-by-week operation of the group. Rehearsals are also important for polishing material, working on older songs, and introducing new tunes or arrangements. If the quartet has a musical advisor or trainer, most of these decisions are left to him. Nearly all of the rehearsals that I attended, however, were remarkably democratic. A spirit of cooperation prevailed, and members were able and often encouraged to volunteer their views regarding the music.

Different singers often have their "own" songs that feature the lead vocal. When rehearsing these numbers, the featured singer would most often make suggestions for changes in tempo, dynamics, or the timing of the background singers. Sometimes one singer would stop and alter the voicings if someone was not following the proper line or if they felt they could improve the harmony. Such alterations were always open to discussion, and in the absence of a recognized trainer the song leader's opinion had priority. The process of learning or reworking material is still an oral tradition and seems to have changed little since the era of Gus Miller and Elijah Jones. The rehearsals themselves last anywhere from one to three hours. When the quartet completes work on singing, the next step is to agree on the time and location for the next meeting. Then a closing prayer is offered and the rehearsal ends.

Quartets in Memphis retain their feeling of an extended family. As the family grows older, its members become more acutely aware of death reducing their numbers. Younger people join the community, permitting groups like the Gospel Writers, the Pattersonaires, and the Spirit of Memphis to thrive. As long as a singer such as the Spirit of Memphis's Earl Malone teaches young singers his distinctive bass lines and the group's repertoire, this unique community will continue to exist and evolve in new directions.[26]

NOTES

1. See Alan Merriam and Raymond Mack, "The Jazz Community," *Social Forces,* 38 (1960), pp. 200–219; Robert Stebbins, "The Jazz Community: The Sociology of a Musical Sub-Culture" (Ph.D. dissertation, University of Minnesota, 1964); Robert Stebbins, "A Theory of the Jazz Community," in *American Music: From Storyville to Woodstock,* ed. Charles Nanry (New Brunswick, N.J.: Transaction Books, 1972), pp. 115–34; William Ferris, *Blues from the Delta* (Garden City, N.Y.: Doubleday, 1979); and Raymond Allen, "Old-Time Music and the Urban Folk Revival," *New York Folklore,* 7 (1981), pp. 65–81.

2. Merriam and Mack, "Jazz Community," p. 211.

3. Ferris, *Blues from the Delta,* p. 22.

4. Doug Seroff, brochure notes, *"Bless My Bones": Memphis Gospel Radio—The 1950s,* Pea-Vine PLP-9051 (Tokyo, 1982), p. 1.

5. Huddie Moore, interviewed by Kip Lornell, February 2, 1983. Unless indicated otherwise, all interviews were conducted by the author in Memphis, Tennessee. A copy of the tapes and a transcript are deposited in the Mississippi Valley Collection, Brister Library, Memphis State University.

6. Mary Davis, interview, May 10, 1982.

7. Cleo Satterfield, interview, June 7, 1982.

8. Moore interview.

9. Etherlene Beans, interview, July 3, 1982.

10. Flozell Leland, interview, June 6, 1982.

11. Beans interview.

12. Jack Miller, interview, October 1980.

13. Beans interview.

14. Leon Moody, interview, February 8, 1981.

15. James Harvey, interview, June 19, 1981.

16. Elijah Jones, interview, October 1979.

17. Willie Neal, interview, April 14, 1981.

18. Tommie Todd, interview, August 11, 1982.

19. Moody interview.

20. For summaries of this concept see Lawrence Levine, *Black Culture and Black Consciousness* (New York: Oxford University Press, 1977), pp. 174–90; see also Portia K. Maultsby, *Afro-American Religious Music: A Study in Musical Diversity* (Springfield, Ohio: The Hymn Society of America, 1980).

21. Roger Abrahams, "The Training of Man-of-Words in Talking Sweet," in *The Man-of-Words in the West Indies* (Baltimore: Johns Hopkins University Press, 1984), pp. 109–21.

22. Jones interview.

23. Ibid.

24. Julius Readers, interview, May 28, 1982.

25. For a different perspective on song battles see Burt Feintuck, "A Noncommercial Black Gospel Group in Context: We Live the Life We Sing About," in *Black Music Research Journal*, 1 (1980), pp. 37–50.

26. Ray Allen discusses this aspect of the music, as well as gospel singing as a complex performance event, in "'Singing in the Spirit': An Ethnography of Gospel Performance in New York City's African American Community" (Ph.D. dissertation, University of Pennsylvania, 1987).

5

"The Forces That Shape Spiritual Quartet Singing"

Black gospel quartet singing in Memphis largely reflects the musical values of late-nineteenth- and early-twentieth-century religious beliefs and performance practices. Instead of following the route established in the 1880s by the Fisk University Jubilee Singers (the blending of traditional spirituals and black American vocal devices with more conventional, contemporary European choral techniques), the community-based Memphis groups worked within vernacular musical norms learned by the singers as they grew up in the Mid-South. Most African Americans living in Memphis during the early decades of the twentieth century attended churches where call-and-response, melismatic vocals, and striking rhythmic contrasts were heard regularly. The use of specially trained choirs, often singing large choral arrangements or compositions by Bach, Haydn, Gluck, Verdi, or other eighteenth- or nineteenth-century Europeans, as part of their worship service remains outside of most black Memphians' personal experiences. To members of pioneering Pentecostal churches, such a vocal ensemble would be contrary to their theological tenets.

This conflict within the black sacred musical community began in (mostly northern) urban churches early in the twentieth century and can be most simply characterized as a struggle between progressive and traditional forces. The progressive branch wished to throw aside the legacy of slavery by leaving the past behind while pushing for the adoption of Anglo-American hymns and recomposed Civil War spirituals. Progressive African-American church-goers viewed such regal performances as part of a larger mission to move their culture toward the perceived American norm. Their efforts to "mainstream" black Americans were part of a larger effort meant to obliterate older black worship styles and the music that had been part of the church service for decades. This attempt to assimilate with the dominant cultural norms met with intransigent opposition from traditionalists who wanted their Sunday music to remain familiar, just like the "Old Landmark" that Reverend Brewster referred to several decades later.[1] The progressive forces woefully underestimated the conservative nature of established black religious practices, especially music that, as Pearl Williams-Jones suggests, "retains the most noticeable African-derived aesthetic features" within the larger matrix of African-American culture.[2]

Gospel quartets, along with small "untrained" choirs and choruses who were occasionally joined by soloists, formed the core of traditional musical groups in Memphis's Protestant churches. Not surprisingly, these assemblies reflected the indigenous music found among African Americans born and raised in the Mid-South. Mary Davis, for example, began her sacred singing career at the "Do-Right" Baptist Church near Clarksdale, Mississippi, in the middle to late 1920s. Sumlin, Mississippi, lies in the heart of Delta cotton country, some hundred miles south of Memphis, and offered its black citizens no formal music education. Davis believes her abilities are a natural gift: "I was singing ever since I was three years old . . . it was just something in me."[3]

An earlier chapter, "A Family of Singers," demonstrates that traditional sacred singing was often a family or community affair, with the singers learning their performance practices from older friends and relatives. This background is further typified by the experiences of Etherlene Beans, who grew up in Fayette County, some fifty miles east of Memphis. Beans attended the Philadelphia Baptist Church of Rossville, Tennessee, during the 1920s; here she heard "old-time" gospel music, and her mother sang monthly solos while her young daughter sat in rapt attention. Much to the distress of progressive thinkers, such folk practices helped to ensure that the established rules for black vernacular sacred singing would be perpetuated.

While members of the Memphis gospel quartet community have shown an utter lack of concern regarding the use of folk practices in their singing, some members of the black intelligentsia felt deeply about this issue. In his introduction to "Utica Jubilee Spirituals: As Sung at the Utica Normal and Industrial Institute of Mississippi," C. W. Hyne underscored the importance of such traditional elements as "quarter-tones, slurrings, and unusual harmonies" that would lose their impact if they tried to "dress them up unduly."[4] Hyne argued that these traditional elements of sacred singing created something distinctive and unique, a cultural matrix of which they should be proud.

Memphis gospel quartet singers, in fact, have long reflected many elements of this aesthetic as naturally as they breathed, or, to paraphrase the Canadian novelist Robertson Davies, their approach to singing is "bred in the bone." And it is the singing itself that exemplifies most strikingly their roots in the "deep" Mid-South, which can be heard in contemporary quartets but which were first documented on the recordings of the I. C. Glee Club from 1928 to 1930. They largely performed according to many of the basic rules of "common practice" Western harmony, some of which are described in Chapter 2. But their singing is thoroughly spiced with distinctly African-American sensibilities: vocable-like moans that sometimes drop down an octave, such as the lead singer who closes "Chickasaw Train." A gruff or raspy vocal—made all the more taut by constricting one's throat—is one of the preferred styles of singing, especially by the lead singer. These quartet singers also display a tendency to hit a note a quarter or even a half tone sharp and slide down into the proper note, which can be heard on "Trouble Don't Last Always." The vocal technique used most often by bass singers (known locally as "pumping") employs a highly rhythmic ideophonic sound like "alankalanka, alankalanak," which Joyce Jackson suggests "adds tonal color, intensity, texture, and contrast."[5] A variant of this technique is used in "Panama to Chi." Such traditional elements of black vernacular singing occur frequently on the Illinois Central's recordings, just as they can be heard on contemporary Delta blues recordings by Charlie Patton and Son House.

Many of these older-style groups emphasized spiritual or spiritual-like songs at the core of their repertoire. Spirituals themselves have a very complex, complicated history. They originated in the eighteenth century and have roots in both black and white musical culture. The black spiritual tradition emerged as a distinctive body, which included hundreds of texts, in the very early nineteenth century. By Reconstruction these so-called slave songs had become well known to most black Americans, including those in the Mid-South. All of the Memphis singers grew up with these old familiar songs, and quartets incorporated them into their programs at churches and other community gatherings.

The classic form of the spirituals—a simple alternating line of text with a constant refrain—expedites learning these songs and also facilitates extemporization. A variation on this form, antiphony, is also found in spirituals. This call-and-response format can be heard in many other types of twentieth-century African-American vernacular popular music, such as soul, go-go, or funk. Many of the Memphis quartets emphasize simple repetition and blend these forms in their performances of spirituals. The Holy Ghost Spirituals, for example, use their lead singer to introduce a textual idea, which is immediately echoed by the background harmony singers. The first chorus of "Ninety-Nine and a Half Won't Do" illustrates how they accomplish this:

> Text: Lord, I'm running, Lord.
> Refrain: And I'm running Lord.
> Repeat
> Text: Said, I'm trying.
> Refrain: Trying to make a hundred
> Repeat
> Text: Ninety-Nine
> Refrain: Ninety Nine and a half won't do
> Repeat
> Text: Got to be
> Refrain: It got to be one hundred
> Repeat
> Text: Ninety-nine
> Refrain: Ninety-nine and a half won't do
> Repeat

Elijah Ruffin, bass singer and trainer for the Harmonizers, uses a similar technique in their version of "Roll, Jordan, Roll," a pre–Civil War spiritual. Lead singer Hershell McDonald opens with the phrase "Roll, Jordan, roll," which is immediately echoed by the rest of the group in beautifully phrased close harmony. At the beginning of the second stanza McDonald sings "Now brother, you ought to have been there," to which the harmony singers react with "Yes, my Lord." Such repetition of short phrases is also part of a related performance style, known as the "drive" section of a gospel song, which is discussed later in this chapter.

By the time of the next wave of commercial recordings that included several groups from Memphis occurred some twenty years later, the style of singing had not changed radically, but their repertoire had expanded to include more of the newly composed gospel songs. Lucie E. Campbell—who spent her entire adult life in Memphis, after being born in Duck Hill, Mississippi, in 1885—emerged as one of the earliest female gospel composers; certainly she was among the best gospel composers of her day. Her exceptional career as a composer stretched from 1919, when she copyrighted "Something Within" (the first gospel song published by a black American woman) through a final contribution, "Come, Lord Jesus, Abide with Me," in 1963. During one remarkable thirty-two-year stretch that ended in 1962, Campbell presented one new song to the National Baptist Convention each year. Not only is her longevity impressive, but the National Baptist Convention itself stands as the largest African-American Protestant denomination in the United States. Campbell did it all at the annual convention—composed sacred songs, directed musicales, oversaw daily performances, and coached singers—a herculean effort that belied her slight, almost petite, frame.

Her importance in gospel composing reached beyond live performance at the National Baptist Convention. Books printed between 1919 and 1923, such as *Gospel Pearls, Spiritual Triumphant Old and New,* and *Inspirational Melodies No. 2,* saw the initial publication of the influential Campbell compositions "Something Within," "The King's Highway," "Heavenly Sunshine," and "The Lord Is My Shepherd." Still in print, these three books remain a cornerstone for black American Protestant singers. Such songs clearly meant something to African-American listeners, many of whom were part of the "Great Migration" to the urban North or were touched by World War I. Luvenia George notes that "Campbell songs were popular with African churchgoers because her lyrics related to and reflected Black experience. She was oriented to biblical narratives and used imagery vividly to interpret and bring coherence to her own life and the life of her people."[6]

Lucie Campbell's gospel hymn publishing brought her national recognition, but she also worked within the black church community in Memphis. During the 1930s, for example, she often played the organ for Sunday services at Central Baptist Church. Some twenty years later Campbell assisted in the organization of the Bethesda Baptist Church. Her community involvement included the staging of large, elaborate sacred pageants. As early as 1932 she produced two major efforts "Memphis Bound" and "Ethiopia," which helped to lift the spirits of Memphians brought to their knees by the Depression. This African theme was utilized in later epic productions—"Ethiopia at the Bar of Justice" and "Ethiopia, Stretch Your Hands unto God." George has characterized these lavish pageants as "colorful" and "lively," and Campbell occasionally helped to mount these pageants in later years.[7]

All during the time she worked with churches in Memphis and mass choirs at the National Baptist Convention, Ms. Campbell continued to teach English and American History in Memphis and compose gospel songs. These songs not only saw print in the mass-produced hymnals, they were also sold at the annual conventions. Like the Chicago school of gospel songwriters, including Kenneth Morris, Thomas A. Dorsey, and Roberta Martin, individual copies of newly written individual songs were offered by the songwriters themselves. Armed with ten-cent copies of their latest efforts, the most popular songwriters could supplement their secular salaries by attending regional and national conventions.

Campbell's sacred music work kept her in the national limelight until her death on January 3, 1963. Luvenia George has characterized her importance in several fields:

She was a pioneer composer who "crossed over" from hymn writer to gospel song composer. She was instrumental in bringing to the national Baptist community the new gospel music through her position as music director. . . . [in] the early 1950s when the Clara Ward Singers, a flamboyant gospel group, were denied a place to sing on one of the programs . . . she promptly scheduled the group to appear. . . . Her music served as a model of the genre for composers and performers across the nation. She was a Black Memphis "breakthrough" in gospel music due to the appeal her songs had in the white community; Pat Boone and Lawrence Welk recorded "He Understands; He'll Say, 'Well Done.'"[8]

Some twenty years after Ms. Campbell began composing and publishing gospel songs, another Memphian, W. Herbert Brewster began his lengthy publishing career that in many respects paralleled the life of Lucie Campbell. Their musical training was largely formed during a time when the shape-note tradition was strong in Mississippi and western Tennessee. Both of them earned academic distinctions—Campbell as the valedictorian of her high school class and Brewster as an outstanding student at Roger Williams College in Nashville. They spent their lives associated with the Baptist Church, both with music and the religious pageants that were popular in the 1930s and 1940s.

Unlike his female counterpart, Brewster's compositions often drew not only upon the struggles of black Americans—most notably civil rights—but also from the Old Testament of the Bible. Brewster, who spent his entire adult life as a minister, also did not face the same sexism that kept Lucie Campbell from gaining a greater leadership role in her own Baptist Church. Finally, Brewster's career began late enough in the twentieth century that innovative gospel compositions were usually sought after, rather than shunned, even by the conservative members of African-American Protestant churches.

Reverend Brewster's impact as a gospel music composer, in fact, began to be felt most strongly in the 1940s, more than a decade after he began to write songs. Approximately fifteen years passed from the time that Reverend Brewster wrote his first song until he finally published one for general consumption. Brewster remained an active composer for nearly forty years, eventually publishing some two hundred songs. Because so many of Brewster's songs were written for his religious pageants, local artists were the only ones performing the sacred songs that flowed from his pen. Consequently, most were initially transmitted aurally to the members of his East Trigg Baptist Church who participated in these grand events.

The pageants, so important in Memphis, did not originate in the Bluff City. As long ago as the early 1920s, black-authored passion plays began to be performed at national religious conventions. Since both Campbell and Brewster regularly attended annual conventions, their participation in this genre is hardly surprising. While Ms. Campbell primarily composed songs for pageants, Reverend

Brewster became involved in all facets of these productions. William Wiggins observed that "it is Brewster, more than any other gospel composer-playwright, who was able to fashion a new Black religious drama tradition that used individually written gospel songs instead of the group-composed spiritual for the plot, symbols, and action of a church drama."[9] Reverend Brewster began in 1941 with a historical plot, "From Auction Block to Glory," and went on to write several plays, including the social commentary about drugs, "Deep Dark Waters." The concept of religious dramas has sometimes reached beyond the sphere of the church itself and into the popular realm. Langston Hughes wrote half a dozen such plays, and in earlier years James Weldon Johnson's "God's Trombone" had successful runs on the secular stage.

The nearly twenty-year period between 1941 and 1958 marked the watershed years for Reverend Brewster's composing and publishing. These years coincided not only with Brewster's own flowering as a writer, but as an important era for the professionalization of the gospel music industry and gospel quartets in particular. Moreover, this era can now be viewed as the early years of the civil rights movement, a fact that did not escape Reverend Brewster:

> The fight for rights here in Memphis was pretty rough on the Black church. The lily white, the black, and the tan were locking horns; and the idea struck me and I wrote that song, "Move on up a Little Higher." We'll have to move in the field of education. Move into the professions and move into politics. Move in anything that any other race has to have to survive. That was a protest idea and inspiration. I was trying to inspire Black people to move up higher. Don't be satisfied with the mediocre. Don't be satisfied. That was my doctrine. Before the freedom fights started, before the Martin Luther King days, I had to lead a lot of protest meetings. In order to get my message over, there were things that were almost dangerous to say, but you sing it.[10]

Why were these songs so meaningful to members of the black religious community in Memphis? For many vocalists the words brought a spiritual message of hope or of Christian salvation to them and to anyone who would listen. The older songs, some of which have a lineage that dates back to the nineteenth century, reminded them of the struggle for freedom from slavery crossing the River of Jordan in "Roll, Jordan, Roll" into a saner land where skin color was scarcely given a second thought. Or they could sing about and lament over the tribulations of Blind Bartimus, who "stood on the road and cried," just as they sometimes lamented their own lives. These messages of understanding and transformation required quite a leap of faith, one they could make only because of their firm belief in the salvation and hope offered by God. Despite their relative antiquity, spirituals and other traditional religious songs remained in the repertoire of some of the quartets into the 1990s. The retention of these older songs is hardly surprising given the inherently conservative nature of religious music in Memphis during this time.

But the newly composed lyrics and music of Brewster and Campbell, along with other important contemporary writers like Thomas A. Dorsey, Sallie Martin, and Kenneth Morris, also captured the hearts and spirits of Memphis quartets. Not only was the message spiritual, it was up-to-date, thus allowing them to remain both firmly respectable and on the cutting edge. James Shells began his career with the Independent Quartet in 1933 and followed a pattern typical of many of the city's community-based groups. Around the close of World War II the group went through a major renovation; they became the Campbellaires. Shells recalled that "we took on kind of a new look and began to sing some songs that were more meaningful. By working with Miss Lucie Campbell, we used her songs, and she had some very touching songs. She had a very beautiful song, 'Touch Me, Lord Jesus' . . . [and] I think her type of singing helped us to become more known. Wherever she recommended us, wherever her name was, we were recognized."[11]

Even more quartets and other vocal ensembles affiliated themselves with Reverend Brewster, possibly because of his closer ties to the mass media—particularly WDIA. Nina Jai Daugherty, for instance, became involved with Reverend Brewster's music in the middle 1930s, when she began to attend the East Trigg Avenue Baptist Church. She eventually became the church secretary, in addition to singing with the Brewster Ensemble, a gender-mixed group utilizing five or six voices that featured the compositions of Reverend Brewster. In 1943 the Brewsteraires came together, formed out of the Mt. Pisgah Gospel Singers. They, too, featured Brewster songs and had their own program over WDIA for nearly twenty-five years. In addition to gospel singing, all of the members of the Brewsteraires remained active in other kinds of church work: preaching, teaching Sunday school, or serving as a deacons. Despite the fact that the group was named for another Memphis minister, the Pat-tersonaires closely allied themselves with Reverend Brewster. Willie Gordon recalls these strong ties. "At first we were coached by Mrs. Nina Jai Daugherty from the East Trigg Baptist Church and by Reverend Brewster. Our best songs were written by Reverend Brewster and I'm really thankful to him for his music."[12]

The most dynamic Memphis singer involved with Reverend Brewster was Queen C. Anderson. Long a member of the all-female Brewster Singers, Anderson had the kind of voice that brought down the house and kept the audience hollering for more. Nathaniel Peck, a member of the Brewsteraires, declares that "Queen C. Anderson was one of the most spiritual gospel singers that I ever heard. She was dedicated, and . . . when she sang, she put everything in her singing. And to tell the truth, you couldn't sit near Queen C. Anderson without shedding tears. . . . She was one of America's best singers."[13]

Singers and vocal ensembles from outside of Memphis also per-formed the songs of Reverend Brewster. When Mason's Temple played host to a major program in the 1940s or 1950s, the chances were good that one of the groups would pay homage to the local master by performing one of his songs. Several of the biggest names in postwar gospel music—most notably Mahalia Jackson and Clara Ward—recorded Brewster compositions early in their careers. Cer-tainly "Move on up a Little Higher" by Mahalia Jackson and the Ward Singers' version of "Surely God Is Able" remain stellar examples of gospel singing from the decade following the close of World War II.

The principal reason for the popularity of both Reverend Brew-ster and Ms. Campbell is clear and simple: both writers could turn a phrase and leave even the most lax member of the church a true believer. As newly composed gospel songs became more widely dis-tributed and performed across the United States, the creative and spiritual nature of their intellect and strong belief became better known. With the passing years and the further publication of their own songs, it became clear that their lyrics appealed to many black Christians.

One of Ms. Campbell's early compositions, "Heavenly Sunshine," carries a simple message of hope that is reinforced by some of the nature-related metaphorical language found in the chorus. These words emphasized a theme to which black Christians could relate:

Yes, there is sunshine in the shadows . . .
sunshine in the rain. Sunshine when we're
burdened, sunshine when we pray. . . .
Heavenly sunshine, blessed sunshine all
the way.

Another of her well-known selections, "Just to Behold His Face," offered an even more dramatic central idea—ascension to Heaven and then seeing the face of Jesus. Campbell utilizes a simple, but effective, device in order to create tension and move this song toward its conclusion. The song suggests that it's not enough to "kneel with the angels, nor to see loved ones who're gone"; and concludes that "all I will want up in heaven, is just to behold his face."

Brewster, too, wrote songs that appealed to many of the same Christians who purchased the latest edition of *Gospel Pearls,* attended Baptist or Methodist churches, and thought of themselves as progressive. His songs always urged movement and change in the realm of social and Christian concerns. Not only do the titles themselves, most notably "Move on up a Little Higher," "I'm Climbing Higher and Higher," or "Packing Up," suggest movement, but also an important transformation. Memphis singers recognized the impact of these songs. Willie Neal, for instance, observed that "there's songs that Dr. Brewster wrote about having a little urge, pulling you to go on; when you wake up and don't feel like going on. The next thing you know, you've got that little urge that make you want to get up and go. Once you get there, you say that you're glad that you went."[14] Brewster himself, of course, knew that these changes come through Christian faith. In a song like "Our God Is Able," Brewster made it clear that transfiguration and salvation could be attained only through a journey in which we trust God, who "knows the road." This same song also contains an Old Testament reference to the trials by fire of Shadrach, Meshach, and Abednego; such biblical references were often found in Brewster compositions. Many of the popular jubilee quartets from the 1940s and 1950s—especially the Golden Gate Quartet—strongly favored songs with such references.

The words and phrases that flowed from Reverend Brewster's fertile imagination attracted the attention of singers from Memphis, through the rest of the Mid-South, and across the United States. Despite the fact that many of his best pieces were written with a specific passion play in mind, the songs themselves stand alone as triumphant works apart from their place in a pageant. Anthony Heilbut has observed that "if there is any one reason why we honor Brewster today, it is because of the social and political message implicit in his music. . . . During a period when civil rights became the dominant national issue, Brewster managed to insinuate themes of social progress and political struggle into his songs without turning them into watered-down propaganda, or gospel agitprop."[15]

Newly composed gospel songs slowly began to gain favor among local harmony singers during the 1920s, and the songs by these two composers were performed by many of the post-Depression quartet singers in Memphis for several reasons. First, the very concept of black Americans composing and then distributing sacred songs for their fellow Christians began to gain momentum starting with the early efforts of Reverend C. A. Tindley around the turn of the century. Second, the songs' direct message of hope in dealing with the world's vagaries through the promise of ultimate salvation had slowly increased in popularity among the general population of Protestant Christians. Third, the musical and compositional relationship of gospel with other forms of black popular music—especially blues—helped to promote its acceptance. Finally, Memphis singers were proud of Campbell's and Brewster's success and wanted to perform the compositions of local writers.

Brewster himself ultimately emphasized the publication of his musical compositions so that they could be disseminated beyond the rather limited world of black Christians in Memphis. Most of these compositions were initially taught aurally. Queen C. Anderson, for instance, could not read music, but her exceptionally sophisticated ear permitted this talented singer to learn the song after a single hearing. Brewster used this process to teach Anderson many of the songs that she performed during her regrettably brief career (she died in 1959 at the age of forty-six). Ironically, Brewster ultimately used a similar technique to sow his spiritual message across the United States. Horace Boyer notes that "he would create his composition, teach it to his group, and they would sing it for someone, a music scribe, who in a kind of shorthand system would transcribe the music and Brewster would have it published."[16]

Even though Campbell and Brewster were viewed as progressive thinkers and writers, their work remained an interesting blend of the traditional and innovative. The classic gospel compositions of Thomas A. Dorsey from the 1920s and 1930s informed both writers, though Brewster in particular more often relied upon the so-called gospel blues form. Beginning with "Lord, I've Tried" and continuing such important compositions as "Thank You, Lord" and "Just over the Hill," Brewster utilized the gospel blues model. Black Christians in Memphis, including quartet singers, heard these songs in church and eventually on phonograph records and over the radio. Memphis, of course, has long been known as a town for blues, but what is the musical relationship between blues and gospel blues? Horace Boyer points out three similarities between these forms of black American music:

1. Secular blues is based on a constant harmonic scheme, as is gospel blues.
2. Secular blues is composed of a three-line poem with the rhyme scheme of *aab,* while gospel blues is composed of a four-line poem with a rhyme scheme of *aaba.*
3. Secular blues requires three units (three four-bar phrases) of musical time to express its poetry, while gospel blues requires four units of musical time (a different middle and closing section are incorporated into gospel blues).[17]

The vamp, a harmonically static section, is another musical device incorporated into many of Brewster's songs and, during the 1940s, became a standard springboard for improvisation among gospel singers, including quartet singers who call it the "drive" section of a performance. This particular device relies upon repetition with minor variations as a way to emphasize and then reemphasize a particular point in a song. It's a rhetorical tool found in African-American oral culture, used by Martin Luther King, Jr., in his "I Have a Dream" speech, and heard in many of today's rap songs. This technique has also been used as a vehicle for instrumental extemporization by jazz musicians, especially after the bebop era. Beginning in the early 1960s, some "free" jazz players, such as guitarist Sonny Greenwich or saxophone player Albert Ayler, performed extended modal compositions based on a vamp.

Memphis quartets used such vamps during their own live performances in churches and other venues. Not surprisingly, the Pattersonaires, who specialize in Brewster songs, utilize this device.

Toward the close of the Brewster composition "He's Worthy," the lead/tenor singer James Shelton utilizes the vamp as the foundation for his vocal gymnastics. With the other harmony singers urging him on, Shelton "works" this section for more than sixteen bars of improvised singing.[18] In a live performance this section would almost certainly have lasted longer. Similarly, the Holy Ghost Spirituals (a female quartet) follow a similar musical path in their performance of Dr. Brewster's "Old Landmark." Lead singer Juanita Wilson extemporizes her vocal on the section that begins "Let's go back, to the Old Landmark."

During their performance of "Swing Down, Chariot," lead vocalist "Jet" Bledsoe of the Spirit of Memphis utilizes two of his favorite vocal devices during the brief (about four bars) drive section that begins after the second repetition of the chorus:

> Background singers: Swing, Swing, swing! Swing, swing, swing!
> Bledsoe: Well, well, well, well-well-well-well.

First, he delays his entrance, retarding it just enough to create some tension between his singing and that of the chorus, which further emphasizes the syncopation of the background chorus. After Bledsoe begins singing "well, well" in the same range as the background singers, he suddenly and dramatically leaps an octave and then increases the tempo of his singing to keep pace with the others.

The fact that vamp sections are heard in so many of Brewster's 1940s compositions may be related to the role Memphis has played in Pentecostal religion. As the home of the Church of God in Christ—the largest African-American Pentecostal sect—Brewster was exposed to the religious tenets and musical practices of these "holiness" groups. Although neither Brewster nor any of the scholars who have written about him directly address this point, the early recordings of Mid-South Pentecostal singers provide evidence by way of their use of vamps on these pioneering recordings. The late 1920s records by the Memphis Sanctified Singers and other Bessie Johnson–led groups, often use this device, albeit limited by the constrictions of three-minute recordings. Moreover, the piano playing of Arizona Dranes (a sanctified Texan, who came to Memphis in order to attend the annual fall conventions of the Church of God in Christ) also employs it in her recordings for the OKeh label.[19]

Ray Allen discusses the use of a vamp section in performances by New York City gospel quartet singers during the late 1980s. In New York City the singers referred to it as the "drive" or "working" part of a song, which demonstrates great parallels with its Memphis counterpart. Allen describes the phenomenon: "A drive section begins when the instrumentalists stall on one chord while the background singers repeat a single vocal line over and over. At this point the lead singer begins to ad-lib, switching from his or her regular singing voice into a tense, high pitched rhythmically repetitive chant or singing chant. . . . a second lead singer may join the first and throw improvised phrases back and forth in a tight call-and-response format."[20] Allen further characterizes the drive section as consisting of "short repetitive words and phrases."[21] It is here that the lead singer "speaks" to the other Christians in the audience, asking if they feel sanctified, too.

Memphis quartet singers practice a similar technique, particularly the "newer" groups, the ones with closer ties to more contemporary performances practices and conventions. Although the older, jubilee style groups—such as the Harmonizers—occasionally utilized a drive section during their live performances in a church, the hard-edged quartets with roots in the 1950s almost always did so. Some of this attitude can be heard in the Gospel Writers' "New Born Soul," which group leader George Rooks introduced to the group. Rooks learned the song around 1955 when he sang with the Jordan Wonders, a local quartet that included Reverend Raymond Conley. In many instances toward the middle and end of this selection, Rooks and the other harmony singers build off one another antiphonally. Here is a short section from near the end of "New Born Soul" that illustrates this type of interplay.

> Rooks: "All I know"
> Response: "All I know"
> Repeated
> Rooks: "One Tuesday evening"
> Response: "All I know"
> Rooks: "Lord, head got wet"
> Response: "All I know"

The interplay illustrated by this brief passage underscores the fact that Memphis quartets are engaged in spiritual singing, an act that holds meaning for the singers and the audience beyond the singing itself. The primary meaning is an expression of Christian values. Although many contemporary quartet performances are not always part of Sunday morning worship services, the singers are still "preaching" a message extolling, among other things, the salvation and peace found when one embraces Christ. The songs often refer to events found in the Bible—the word of God set in print that is the guiding light for all Christians—including songs about some of the more dramatic events depicted in this book. The story of Noah is well known to many people, but one favorite of "jubilee" groups is the story of Blind Bartimus. The Harps of Melody relate this dramatic parable about transformation brought about by this most public acceptance of Christ:

> In my God's Bible, in the Book of James,
> Christ were healing the crippled and the lame.
> He went to the poor in the need of bread,
> Healing the sick and raising the dead.
> He passed by a man that could not see.
> The man was blind; he was blind from birth,
> Tell me that his name was Blind Bartimus.
> Chorus:
> Well, old Blind Bartimus stood on the way.
> Well, Blind Bartimus stood on the way.
> Well, old Blind Bartimus stood on the way,
>
> Crying, "Oh Lord, have mercy on me."
> When Bartimus saw that the Lord was nigh
> Fell on his knees and began to cry.
> "Oh thou Man of Galilee,"
> Crying "Great God almighty, have mercy on me."
> Cried "Oh Lord, Mary's baby.
> Oh Lord, Son of David.
> Oh, Lord, bleeding lamb.
> Oh my Lord, oh Bethlehem."
> Chorus:
> Then my God, he stopped, he looked around.
> Then he saw Blind Bartimus on the ground.
> Then he touched his eyes with the palm of his hand.
> Blind Bartimus saw like a natural man.
> He cried "Thank God, Mary's baby.
> Thank God, Son of David.

Thank God, bleeding lamb.
Oh, thank God, oh Bethlehem."
Chorus:

Other songs performed by Memphis quartets simply praised God; his wisdom, goodness, forgiveness, and glory, among other themes. The song that begins each program by the Harps of Melody, "Sing and Make Melody Unto the Lord," exemplifies this theme among quartet singers. Lead singer Clara Anderson boldly states the song's motif in her first line, "I'm going to sing, sing and make melody unto the Lord."

Quite a few of the songs performed by quartets also underscore their belief in the importance of being a dedicated and hard-working Christian. The Holy Ghost Spirituals reinforce this attitude in "Ninety-Nine and a Half Won't Do." From their perspective, anything less than 100 percent is not good enough, because you are still falling short of attaining your goal: "You got to make one hundred; ninety-nine and a half won't do." But the striving to achieve is not always enough; you must sometimes fight for what you believe is right and proper. Lucie Campbell takes a militaristic and forceful stance by stating, "I'm a soldier in the army of the lord," in the chorus of her traditionally based hymn "I'm a Soldier."

These words and this music proved popular enough in the post–World War II era that quartets sometimes appeared in distinctly secular settings. Not only did they sing outside of churches, quartets were sometimes used to actually sell a church. Tommie Todd, for instance, recalls how Wallace Johnson (founder of Holiday Inns and a local builder) hired local favorites, the Gospel Writers, to sing on the back of a flatbed truck in order to draw a crowd and help sell newly built churches: "[Johnson] used to build churches out in the country, on the plantations . . . and the Gospel Writers they would go and he would furnish the car and the driver, and take us to the church. We would sing at the church and they would take in a lot of members. A lot of times we would carry along a minister; sometimes the minister would take the church, you know and that's how they started."[22]

Even more dramatic were the numerous appearances by quartets at the WDIA "Goodwill Revues," a charity fund-raiser that began in 1949 and continued into the 1960s. The 1956 revue (the program for which is reproduced in the middle section of photographs) included performances by the Brewsteraires, the Sons of Jehovah, the Dixie Nightingales, the Reed Singers, and the Friendly Echoes. Listed among the headliners, not surprisingly, were the Spirit of Memphis as well as Reverend Cleophus Robinson and the Happyland Blind Boys. This particular revue, with each nightly performance clearly divided between "Part One: A Pilgrimage to the Holy Land" and "Part Two: Early American Rock 'n' Roll, Blues and Pop Stars," featured such well-known popular musicians as Ray Charles, the Magnificents, the Moonglows, and B. B. King. Interestingly, the 1956 Goodwill Revue also included a minstrelesque sketch with WDIA staff announcers appearing as Native Americans in an epic about intergenerational conflicts revolving around rock 'n' roll.

Despite these notable exceptions, Memphis's black American gospel quartet singing has taken part in largely sacred contexts and adhered to certain cultural norms developed over years of performances. Sunday church services occasionally included quartets; however, choirs and soloists usually provided the musical sustenance. Quartets most often performed during public programs held on Saturday afternoon or evening. As Ray Allen observed, "A quartet singing program is, in many ways, an extension of the Sunday morning worship service—an opportunity for people to 'have church' . . . with the quartet singer, rather than the preacher, taking center stage."[23]

Programs were most always held at local churches, often in the predominantly black sections of Memphis: Orange Mound, North Memphis, or Whitehaven. Advertising came through word of mouth, in church programs, or on placards posted in public places. Occasionally, programs were held in private homes, usually by groups just beginning to sing together. Huddie Moore describes the early appearances by the Spiritual Four in the late 1930s—"When you first getting started, you be a little shy about going out and facing the public. We would rehearse and set up programs at different one's houses. Just say you gonna have a program, we invite other groups and set up chairs, and sing in the house. We would get ready to get out on the stage at the church. We used to have a nice time at a house program."[24]

At a quartet program in post–World War II Memphis, the singers themselves served as the primary organizing force. Since most of the quartet singers were devoutly religious, their intent was clear:

to provide the other program participants—singers and audience alike—with a Protestant Christian message through words and songs. Joyce Jackson has written about the roles shared by quartet singers and the preacher alike, and noticed that "quartet musicians share the expressive role occupied by the preacher, because they both function to deliver the word of God in a performance style that is sanctioned by the black community. The singer sings of familiar biblical and human situations and dilemmas just the same as a minister would preach about them."[25]

Memphis quartet singers also frequently fulfilled this role. While they did not fancy themselves to be proper preachers, the singers knew their message of Christian salvation paralleled that of their minister. Hershell McDonald of the Harmonizers observed that "we believe that we carry the gospel in a number of ways. One is direct teaching of principles, which we carry through songs. In our singing, our work is twofold—to edify and serve as inspiration for those who are members of the body and as a source of inspiration and a way to draw those who are not members of the church."[26] Their work, in fact, reinforced the preacher's Sunday morning message, though their medium was song not sermon. But it proved to be quite effective at swaying people and committing them to remaining with the church, be it Methodist, Baptist, or AME. The singers appreciated this power, and some, such as Tommie Todd, proudly recalled that "a lot of times people would join church on our singing."[27] The ability to motivate fellow Christians proved to be important to other Memphis quartet singers. Among them was Etherlene Beans of the Willing Four Soft Singers, who simply commented that "we just would go where we thought the spirit was needed."[28]

The very titles of songs performed by Memphis quartets reinforce the spiritual nature of their work. One favorite from the late 1940s, "Touch Me, Lord Jesus," came from the pen of Lucie Campbell and suggests the underlying need for change and transformation. Another of Campbell's compositions, "In the Upper Room with My Lord," also indicates the need to look upward, to a higher spiritual realm striven for by Christians interested in the afterlife. Early in Campbell's career (1923) she wrote the optimistic "Heavenly Sunshine," which includes the lines "There is sunshine when we're burdened / . . . yes, heavenly sunshine when we pray." These are words and sentiments to which her peers could relate, which underscores the reasons for her popularity among African-American Christians. During the midst of the Depression, Campbell wrote the hopeful "He Understands; He'll Say 'Well Done,'" and in 1946 she published "Praise Ye the Lord." Memphis quartets also performed similarly titled and equally inspiring songs written by the other great Memphis gospel composer, Reverend Brewster. As recently as 1984 the Pattersonaires recorded his "I Feel Something Drawing Me On," which appears on High Water LP 1004.

Not only is it important for singers to enunciate clearly so that the listeners could understand the lyrics, they also had to sing with spirit. As the quartet movement gained momentum among the population in general, it appeared that programs simply provided a greater number of black American Christians who wished to hear the latest in harmony singing. The fifteen- to-thirty-minute segments typically granted to each quartet during an evening's program allowed them to introduce church members and other attendees to higher states of spiritual ecstasy. I have heard both singers and members of the audience refer to this transcendent process as "shouting the church," "moving on up higher," "feeling the spirit," even "wreck the house" or "get the church on fire." These vigorous, almost violent, metaphors underscore the radical transformation that can occur during a quartet performance.

The increased acceptance of the ecstatic behavior found in the numerous local holiness churches proved to be another factor in this aesthetic/sacred shift. In writing about the post-Thomas A. Dorsey era, Jeremiah Wright observed that "gospel music [now] induced the sort of 'frenzy' and 'fist and heel' religion that had come to be associated with Holiness and Pentecostal churches which engaged in such activities as holy dancing and speaking in tongues."[29] With the proliferation of Pentecostal churches in Memphis beginning in the second decade of the this century—the Church of God in Christ in particular, but many small "storefront" churches as well-local black Americans gradually became more accustomed to seeing people in states of spiritual possession as these churches came to be viewed as more mainstream. Furthermore, the newly composed gospel songs favored by quartets—for example, Brewster's "He's Worthy"—tended to be similar in feeling and spiritual intent to the more spontaneous praise songs of the holiness church. Parallels between postwar gospel quartet singing, including the process of learning new material and the African-American time sense found in performances, and Pentecostal church services also exist. As Michael Hayes observed:

> Improvisatory in nature and simple in structure, these songs of praise are rendered differently each time they are sung. Black Pentecostals sing their praise songs in a way similar to the way jazz musicians play their instruments. Just as jazz musicians have an inventory of jazz riffs and chord progressions to call upon, so have the Pentecostal praise leaders an inventory of familiar calls at their disposal. . . . Black Pentecostals learn their praise songs by rote via the medium of oral transmission, and it is the spiritual mood of the moment that determines what is sung or played.[30]

While such states of spiritual happiness are often associated with Pentecostal churches, most Memphis quartets have been and continue to be affiliated with Baptist and Methodist churches. Despite the fact that it is home to the Church of God in Christ and that quartet singers certainly know people who belong to holiness churches, the direct musical interaction between these two strains of Protestant churches in Memphis itself has proven to be rare. Their musical traditions are certainly different; musicians associated with the Church of God in Christ, for example, rarely sang in four-part harmony. They usually sang in unison or some what rough heterophony; beginning around 1910 and continuing through the 1940s holiness singers often performed with the accompaniment of guitars, pianos, washboards, and other instruments. Furthermore, members of Pentecostal churches believe in direct communication with God, and many members of the congregation join in the music making, rather than utilizing a specific musical organization like a quartet.

Despite the lack of direct musical interaction within Memphis itself, holiness worship practices have clearly influenced gospel quartet practices after World War II. In fact, what might be described as an inclination toward "commercialism" by quartets seems to be partially a result of this trend. The physical movements on stage, dramatic posturing, and dynamic vocal styles of a "soul killer" such as Silas Steele of the Spirit of Memphis would have been considered normal during a service of the Church of God in Christ of the 1940s. As one of the lead vocalists of a major quartet, Steele was considered an innovator in the late 1940s, but as part of a powerful new fashion in singing that was gaining acceptance by the middle 1950s. In the 1990s, after forty years of this performance practice, the quartet audience has come to expect theatrical and emotional behavior during the course of a program. Its absence is often viewed as a deficit on the part of the singers or simply that the holy spirit is not with the quartet during their portion of this particular program.

In "A Family of Singers," I describe, among other things, the shape and order of quartet programs held in Memphis during the 1940s and 1950s. A quartet performance typically contains three complex elements—physical movement, personalization of the event, and the singing itself—which help to facilitate the spiritual nature of this service.[31] First is the physical presence and activity of quartet singers during their performances. Because the lead singers in a quartet serve a function similar to that of a preacher, they usually come to the forefront. The principal vocalist during a quartet performance not only sings about the healing and saving power of Christ, she or he also adds dramatic action or movement that reinforces their intent to "move the spirit." Lead vocalists may sometimes clench their fists, close their eyes, or get down on their knees during a performance. The other harmony singers occasionally engage in similar physical movement: some of it is spontaneous, while other gestures are well planned and rehearsed. For example, during the refrain for "Up Above My Head I Hear Music in the Air," the Gospel Writers would all look upward.

Occasionally they dance when the power of the Holy Ghost enters their spirit, which often happens during the portion known as the "drive section." A drive section almost always occurs during the performance of a hard gospel song, such as Reverend Brewster's "He's Worthy," which the Pattersonaires have been singing for over thirty years. During this song lead singers James Shelton and Willie Neal typically swap the principal vocals, but the "drive" most often happens when Neal comes to the fore. Neal improvises, usually with a mixture of falsetto and growling voices, while the other singers harmonize on the chorus, repeating it while the leader is feeling the spirit. A drive section can last for between a minute and ten minutes or more, if the spirit is strong and the audience receptive. These rhythmic refrains often utilize the types of chants (a mixture of speech and singing) frequently heard during sermons and oral formulas that implore the listeners to participate directly: "Can you feel the spirit," "Ain't God real!" or "Pray with me, brothers and sisters."

But among quartet singers in Memphis some controversy regarding such performance practices clearly exists. While most quartet singers under the age of sixty accept dramatic gestures, the extended drive section, and spiritual ecstasy as part of every program, some of the veteran singers or groups that sing with older jubilee-style groups question the sincerity of what they view as "antics" on stage. George Rooks, who came up under the direct guidance of master trainer Elijah Jones, believes in the power of pure harmony singing to reinforce the ecclesiastical power of their message. When asked about younger quartets, he remarked, "They'll start off in spiritual and end up in the rock, you see. In other words, if they can't get the crowd to come one way, they change over. You get 'em to jumping; they think they doing a good thing! I never liked it and Jones never liked it."[32]

Another aspect of quartet performance is the personalization of the spiritual message that each group attempts to transmit. Because many of the quartet singers and members of the congregation know each other well, a convivial air often pervades these performances. Before and after the program many people greet each other by first name or nickname, and other pleasantries—especially inquiries about absent family members and mutual friends or sick relatives—are exchanged. The ambiance reminds one of a cooperative country supper that includes friends and neighbors.

Once the quartets begin singing, a down-home atmosphere continues as the groups attempt to draw everyone into this devout milieu. The emcee often "recognizes" people in the congregation, or the lead singer might incorporate a friend's name into an introduction or a speech. At one of the programs that I attended, Clara Anderson quietly but deliberately called attention to several people by invoking their names to testify near the beginning of a performance by the Harps of Melody. Anderson did this because she knew they had the extra burden of critically ill relatives. Quartet singers who were also good at this kind of verbal banter are sought after because they can put the congregation at ease. Ray Allen writes that "such greetings assist the singers in establishing rapport with the congregation and are a catalyst for additional artist/audience interaction. Furthermore, they provide yet another vehicle for singers to affirm their spiritual intent and the religious nature of the program."[33] In Memphis, Silas Steele of the Spirit of Memphis, Jack Franklin of the Southern Wonders, and Floyd Wiley of the Southern Jubilees were well regarded as among the best talkers of the post–World War II era.

This personal touch, along with the fellowship and the harmony singing itself, have become important and expected ingredients in a quartet program. Singers often refer to such speech as sermonettes; they usually punctuate the performances before a song begins and also permit the speaker to interject more of themselves into the program. Sermonettes are another way of reinforcing the sincerity of the singers and helping to erase any doubts of their intent. And members of the congregation often respond with their own interjections of encouragement. This give-and-take helps to prepare the congregation, and singers have told me that it can create a more spiritual atmosphere.

In his research with New York City quartets Ray Allen also noted the importance of such speech, which usually occurred during the opening narrative, and offered several examples of singers telling of the miraculous power of God.[34] According to Joyce Jackson, quartet singers in Baton Rouge, Louisiana, "strive to bring their own religious conviction and experiences to the performance arena and to dramatize the message of their songs in a unique personal way."[35] In each case all of these experiences, conflicts, and troubles are seen to resolve through their Christian faith. This message of personal involvement with Jesus helps everyone at the program to understand that salvation comes through spiritual involvement, which is relayed not only through quartet singing but their own experiences.

Certain components of the singing itself also help to reinforce the emotional nature of a quartet program. In some ways this is an extension of the personalization of the program, for the singers are striving to put their own stamp on their fifteen-minute to half-hour public display. Many quartets have their own signature numbers; for example, the Harps of Melody almost always open with "Sing and Make Melody unto the Lord," and in the 1940s the Rock Island Quartet often began their set with a gospel train song "Rock Island Line." Gospel quartet performances are not fixed entities, and the African-American musical aesthetic, whether secular or sacred, calls for variation and improvisation. No matter how well a song has been rehearsed or how often it has been sung, no two performances are identical.

The song provides the outline or a basic framework for the singers—in hard gospel it's usually the lead singer—who work in their own personal approach. And the congregation and singers substantially agree on the aesthetics or about what makes a performance move beyond the mundane. A sudden, unexpected growl or the dramatic leap of an octave often evokes shouts of approval or awe from singers and fans alike. Silas Steele stands out as one of the most revered lead vocalists among Memphis singers, but other, now almost totally forgotten singers, also touched many of the audience members. Because they never recorded, these names usually remain in the minds of singers or as images on old photographs and are recollected during interviews. Avery Savage, for example, recalled that South Memphis singer "James Arthur Brown . . . was one of the best. You might have thought Silas Steele was good, but he'd run a ring around Steele!"[36]

Throughout this book I refer to programs featuring more than one quartet; these were usually part of an anniversary or else occurred when an out-of-town group headlined with local groups who completed the show. Each of these events lasted from two to four hours, with each group occupying a time slot of between fifteen minutes to half an hour. Etherlene Beans remarked that her 1983 anniversary program involved "about ten groups," including quartets such as the Mighty Kings of Harmony, the Millerette Singers, and the Christian Harmonizers. In Memphis the number of quartets at an anniversary typically swelled according to the popularity and activity of the host quartet. Beans observed, "You work the year through, and you sing and support the other groups that are having theirs. Ours is the third Sunday in June every year, and the groups we supported during their anniversaries, they come and help us. You really call it an appreciation program."[37] In recalling major programs from the early 1950s with crowd-pleasing, out-of-town groups such as the Pilgrim Travelers and Dixie Hummingbirds, Ford Nelson of WDIA stated, "There was a little rivalry on stage for the sake of the audience; during those concerts they would sing one song maybe fifteen, twenty or even thirty minutes . . . that live sound of people happy and shouting, the applause—it was extremely exciting!"[38]

These elements point to a flexible sense of time, which is part of a larger black aesthetic in culture and music. Jazz musicians highly regard this ability to improvise with relatively few time restraints. One prime example is Duke Ellington's 1956 Newport Jazz Festival concert, which was recorded by Columbia Records. Ellington was scheduled to perform for approximately one hour, but during "Diminuendo and Crescendo in Blue" tenor sax player Paul Gonsalves got hot, brought the audience to its feet, and extended the performance for nearly twenty minutes beyond its normal length. No one complained that Ellington's set lasted some 33 percent longer than scheduled. It would be hard to imagine a well-planned two-hour concert by the Berlin Philharmonic or the National Symphony Orchestra running this long over its advertised time without lots of raised eyebrows. For this to occur at a gospel concert or jazz performance, however, would cause no pause.

Temporal tolerance is part of the gospel aesthetic because of the interior-driven and inspirational nature of this art form. It's music moved by the spirit, not dictated by the hands of a clock. Mellonee Burnim asserts that a gospel musician "exercises his or her creative abilities and understanding of a Black concept of time by extending the length or notes at climactic points, repeating phrases or sections of a song, signaling instruments to temporarily 'drop out,' or even adding a reprise at the end of the song that has been especially well received. Any one of these possibilities may occur . . . at any given moment [and] such aspects of performance are not rehearsed."[39] In her study of black gospel quartets, Joyce Jackson notes that the gestures required in "extending the length or notes, repeating phrases, or signaling instruments to drop out is done through outer time," but "the coordination of these actions is determined by internal consciousness [or] inner time."[40]

As part of the black American musical aesthetic, Memphis gospel quartets exploit such elasticity as a license to improvise. This is especially true for hard gospel groups, which developed after World War II, and less true for older-style a cappella groups. Elijah Ruffin trained the Harmonizers to be a "harmony group, make harmony music";[41] as a result these four men sang in the older jubilee style without instrumental accompaniment. Except for some improvisation on the part of the lead singer, this style emphasized control and closely following set arrangement. Their versions of spirituals such as "Go, Tell It on the Mountain," "Glory to His Name," or "Nearer My God to Thee" changed in very subtle ways; once Ruffin was satisfied with their arrangement, he usually directed only a slight change in harmony or an alteration in tempo. Significantly, the length of these songs varied little from performance to performance. When asked about hard gospel, Ruffin replied, "See, I don't like no gang of hollering, there's no music in it. . . . I don't like people to get up and sing two or three numbers in one-half hour—it gets people tired."[42]

Hard gospel quartets, on the other hand, take a greater license with time. Jackson notes that "it is in the [hard] gospel quartet style that . . . one can really hear 'black meter' operating fully."[43] This expansion of time does not occur in each performance during a program, but most often when the singers feel happy and move into a transcendent state during the drive section.

It is at the point when the Holy Spirit takes control that the relationship between performer and audience shifts into an altered sense of time. Such a dramatic shift consists of both spiritual ecstasy, which singers claim is beyond their ability to control, and learned behavior, for which they know the rules of the game. On one hand, the participants wish to remain in an ecstatic state, for it moves them beyond their daily routine and into a desired spiritual realm. At the same time, they all know the tactics for altering time well enough that they've agreed which rituals are acceptable. It then becomes the quartet singer's choice—whether you believe it is conscious or unconscious—regarding which techniques to use in order to continue in this spirit-induced state.

The quartets that best balanced these factors became the most in demand. The elastic time sense had been fully embraced by the early 1950s as the length of quartet performances grew and the strategies for "building a program" became more formalized. In Memphis this was due to two factors found within the commercial ranks of gospel quartets. First, out-of-town groups, most notably the Soul Stirrers and Dixie Hummingbirds, became known as "soul killers," and people came to expect their extended performance tactics. Second, local groups—especially the Spirit of Memphis—

began to host longer, less rigidly controlled and planned programs. Robert Reed recalls a technique that one of their lead singers, Silas Steele, used on "I'll Tell It," which inevitably included one of Steele's popular sermonettes: "That was his keynote! That and 'Day is Past and Gone.' Man, that guy turned the house out . . . he'd turn around and ask the police [who were guarding the stage] 'Do you love the Lord' and they'd holler!"[44]

Indeed, the Memphis quartet singers who came of musical age following World War II sensed the shifts of interest and momentum of their audience in order to respond to the spiritual mood of a program. They altered the time frame in a number of ways. If the spirit is strong and the house is rocking with the excitement of mutual emotional participation, the drive section becomes more intense as the lead singer invokes the power of the Holy Spirit. The 1980s version of the Gospel Writers often performed "New Born Soul" near the close of their portion of the program, for its fitting refrain that could be exploited for its drive section: "I've got a new born soul, since the Holy Ghost took control." George Rooks himself takes control and heightens the spirit through a gradual increase in tempo from about M.M. 75 to over 100, and through the repetition of "new born soul," over which he interjects a series of scatted moans, falsetto cries, and other wordless improvisations. While Rooks sometimes moves around the stage, he rarely testifies. Through the use of these performance strategies, Rooks himself, in conjunction with the power of the Holy Spirit, has taken control of time.

The length of the performance becomes flexible and continues so long as the Spirit is present. The song builds, the audience responds, and the power of the Holy Ghost takes control. Members of the audience can help to manipulate time, too. They encourage the devotional ecstasy and lengthen the performance by "falling out" (when they are possessed by the Holy Ghost) or entreating the vocalist to "tell the truth" or "sing it right." Typically, they also clap or join with the harmony singers in repeating the chorus, for they, too, feel the power of "a new born soul." Such a dramatic performance continues so long as the spirit is present; with its departure, Rooks, the rest of the Gospel Writers, and the audience itself quickly wind down.

Among Memphis quartets, the Gospel Writers is nearly anomalous. Most groups perform in the hard gospel style, though a handful reflect the repertoires and performance techniques popular in the 1920s and 1930s. The Gospel Writers is one of the few groups that feel comfortable in both camps. Their leader, George Rooks, initially sang with the Veteran Jubilees, a "hard quartet" based in Memphis during the middle 1950s. With the Veteran Jubilees, Rooks remained relatively unconcerned with the elements of harmony singing because they knew their audience wanted performances with a "fast beat" where "you can cut loose." He slowly became more fascinated with harmony singing when the "old" Gospel Writers sometimes appeared with the Veteran Jubilees: "I kind of got into it right after I got into the Veteran Jubilees because they had Elijah Jones and them on their programs. . . . They could sing harmony and I would sit there and listen to them, and I would start to do that with the Veteran Jubilees, I would get a little of that in."[45]

This division between the attitudes toward performance practices, singing styles, and repertoire displayed by jubilee and hard gospel quartets is not unique to Memphis. Ray Allen uncovered a similar schism among quartets in New York City:

> Many of the older groups tend to shy away from what they consider to be flamboyant theatrics—the preached song introductions, extended drive sections, choreographed dance, and rhythmic jam sessions. But the middle-aged and younger groups who were reared on the postwar hard gospel sound make use of the full range of strategies. For them, these stylized behaviors form a repertoire of expressive components that, in various combinations, produce an aesthetically pleasing and spiritually fulfilling performance."[46]

Aesthetic tensions within black American culture have helped to shape black gospel quartet singing in Memphis. Beginning with the post-Reconstruction struggle between black Americans who wished to follow their down-home performance practices and those who wanted to incorporate European-oriented singing styles, these conflicts reflect the apparent oppositions between "old" and "new" values. Our current perspective suggests these changes are more evolutionary than revolutionary, although it is important to underscore how controversial they appeared at the time. These contentious issues are often generational and can be seen in oppositions beginning during the early part of the twentieth century (the use of spirituals versus newly composed gospel songs) and continuing to the present decade (the performance styles of traditional versus contemporary gospel quartets). The fact is that the values displayed by Memphis's black American gospel quartets—their repertoire, approaches to vocalizing, shape of their program, etc.—reflect elements of a unique musical community that is informed not only by individual talent and experiences but by African-American culture in general.

NOTES

1. In Chapter 1 of *The Rise of Gospel Blues: The Music of Thomas Andrew Dorsey in the Urban Church* (New York: Oxford University Press, 1992), Michael Harris views this conflict in terms of "assimilationists" versus "traditionalists" and further suggests that the early gospel composers—especially Dorsey—helped to bridge this gap.

2. Pearl Williams-Jones, "Afro-American Gospel Music: A Crystallization of the Black Aesthetic," *Ethnomusicology,* 19 (1975), p. 373.

3. Mary Davis, interview, May 10, 1982.

4. C. W. Hyne, "Utica Jubilee Spirituals: As Sung at the Utica Normal and Industrial Institute of Mississippi" (n.d., n.p.).

5. Joyce Jackson, "The Performing Black Sacred Quartet: An Expression of Cultural Values and Aesthetics" (Ph.D. Dissertation, Indiana University, 1988), p. 182.

6. Luvenia George, "Lucie Campbell: Her Nurturing and Expansion of Gospel Music in the National Baptist Convention, U.S.A., Inc.," in *We'll Understand It Better By and By,* ed. Bernice Johnson Reagon (Washington, D.C.: Smithsonian Institution Press, 1992), p. 115. Ms. George's essay informs this entire section about Lucie Campbell.

7. Ibid., p. 117.

8. Ibid., pp. 118–19.

9. William H. Wiggins, "William Herbert Brewster: Pioneer of the Sacred Pageant," in *We'll Understand It Better By and By,* p. 249. Wiggins has also written on other aspects of black folk religious drama in "In the Rapture," *Festival of American Folklife Program Booklet* (Washington, D.C.: Smithsonian Institution Press, 1976), pp. 5–7.

10. Bernice Johnson Reagon, ed. "William Herbert Brewster: Rememberings," in *We'll Understand It Better By and By,* p. 201.

11. James Shells, interview, May 20, 1982.

12. Willie Gordon, interview, April 14, 1981.

13. Nathaniel Peck, interview, January 31, 1981.

14. Willie Neal, interview, April 14, 1981.

15. Anthony Heilbut, "'If I Fail, You Tell The World I Tried': William Herbert Brewster on Records," in *We'll Understand It Better By and By,* p. 234.

16. Horace Boyer, "Herbert W. Brewster: The Eloquent Poet," in *We'll Understand It Better By and By,* p. 212-13.

17. Ibid., p. 214.

18. Boyer discusses this technique in "Herbert W. Brewster: The Eloquent Poet," in *We'll Understand It Better By and By,* pp. 214 and 217.

These performances by Memphis quartets can be heard on "Happy in the Service of the Lord: Memphis Gospel Quartet Heritage—the 1980s," High Water LP 1002.

19. These selections by Dranes and Johnson are detailed in Godrich and Dixon, *Blues and Gospel Records 1902-1943* (Essex: Storyville Publications, Ltd. 1982).

20. Ray Allen, *Singing in the Spirit: African-American Sacred Quartets in New York City* (Philadelphia: University of Pennsylvania Press, 1991), p. 119.

21. Ibid., p. 120.

22. Tommie Todd, interview, August 11, 1982.

23. Ray Allen, Singing in the Spirit, p. 77.

24. Huddie Moore, interview, February 2, 1983.

25. Joyce Jackson, "The Performing Black Sacred Quartet," p. 167.

26. Harmonizers Rehearsal, February 22, 1982.

27. Todd interview.

28. Beans interview.

29. Jeremiah A. Wright, Jr., "Music as Cultural Expression in Black Church Theology and Worship," *The Journal of Black Sacred Music,* 3 (Spring 1989), p. 4.

30. Michael G. Hayes, "The Theology of the Black Pentecostal Praise Song," *Black Sacred Music: A Journal of Theomusicology,* 4 (Fall 1990), pp. 31-32.

31. Ray Allen, *Singing in the Spirit,* Chapter 4, "Shouting the Church: Quartet Performance Strategies," details these processes among New York City quartet singers. My own viewpoint on Memphis quartet performances has been sharpened by and filtered through Allen's work.

32. George Rooks, interview, November 27, 1982.

33. Ray Allen, *Singing in the Spirit,* p. 103.

34. Ibid., pp. 104-6.

35. Joyce Jackson, "The Performing Sacred Quartet," p. 167.

36. Avery Savage, interview, March 22, 1982.

37. Beans interview.

38. Ford Nelson, interview, June 6, 1982.

39. Mellonee Burnim, "The Black Music Quartet Tradition: Symbol of Tradition" (Ph.D. dissertation, Indiana University, 1980), p. 161.

40. Joyce Jackson, "The Performing Sacred Quartet," p. 170.

41. Harmonizers Rehearsal.

42. Elijah Ruffin, interview, March 2, 1981.

43. Joyce Jackson, "The Performing Sacred Quartet," p. 171.

44. Robert Reed interview with Doug Seroff, Memphis, Tennessee, June 1979.

45. All of the quotations in this paragraph come from the George Rooks interview.

46. Ray Allen, *Singing in the Spirit,* p. 125.

6

"On Records and over the Airwaves"

Commercial radio stations and record companies always try to give their audiences what they think is or will be in line with popular tastes. But popular tastes are notoriously fickle. The commercial success of most musicians is fleeting at best, which is why the mass media are always looking for something new.

Until the post–World War II years, most of Memphis's black gospel quartets sang in neighborhood churches and remained closely allied with the folk community. This situation changed quickly after the war, however, when thousands of fans regularly packed the Mason's Temple and the City Auditorium for programs featuring professional quartets. As the popularity of black gospel quartet music grew in Memphis, the relationships among local groups, radio stations, and record companies became stronger. This symbiotic association reached its zenith between 1950 and 1955, when Peacock/Duke Records was recording the most popular Memphis quartets and radio stations like WDIA broadcast "live" performances by many Memphis groups. However, such business affiliations actually began some twenty-five years earlier.

Near the turn of the century the commercial recording of traditional music in America began with companies like Victor and Columbia issuing performances of indigenous folk and ethnic musicians. Not until the early 1920s did the recorded documentation of American folk music reach significant proportions. During that decade and the next, thousands of black jazz bands, hillbilly singers, gospel groups, blues musicians, and string bands made records.[1] Memphis gospel quartets also played a small part in the pre–World War II recording boom.

The first and only local group documented during this era was the I.C. Glee Club, which OKeh Records brought into its temporary Memphis studio on February 16, 1928. Employees of the Illinois Central Railroad founded this group—one of at least three Memphis area quartets to bear the initials "I.C." Although OKeh did not release a single song from this initial session (possibly because of technical problems), the group traveled to Atlanta a year later to record six more sides for the company, all of which were issued. The group continued to record for OKeh until their final session in 1930 in New York City, which yielded four records.[2]

Such spatial variation in recording sites was not unusual, because OKeh and other record companies regularly sent portable field units to cities across the South, where they remained for several days to three weeks. Memphis, Atlanta, New Orleans, San Antonio, and St. Louis were just some of the locations in which OKeh recorded during the late 1920s. In addition to the I.C. Glee Club, the company recorded only one other Mid-South quartet while in Memphis in 1928; the Invincible Quartet of Rust College, located about fifty miles southeast of Memphis in Holly Springs, Mississippi. OKeh also documented blues singers during this session, two of whom, Lonnie Johnson and John Hurt, were to become well-known.

These field recording sessions were always arranged in advance. Some of the musicians had previously recorded, but the companies were always seeking new talent. Sometimes they followed the advice of their own record dealers; in other cases they relied on the expertise of local singers. Two black bandleaders in Memphis, Will Shade and Fess Williams, were intimately familiar with local blues and jazz performers and almost certainly "scouted" for previously unrecorded talent, asking them to attend the sessions.[3]

After this early OKeh session with the I.C. Glee Club, no other Memphis gospel quartet recorded for nearly twenty years. There are two probable reasons for this long hiatus. First, the Great Depression pushed most record companies into or near bankruptcy. A very few companies, like Columbia, that went bankrupt were quickly reorganized and struggled through the 1930s. They never recorded any Memphis quartets, however, preferring instead to stay with predepression artists like Charley Patton, Willie McTell, Rev. J. M. Gates, and the Norfolk Jubilee Quartet. The inherently conservative nature of these companies, which became even more evident as the industry began recovering during the mid- to late 1930s, also hindered the chances for Memphis groups to record. The quartets that did record during the few years prior to World War II—the Heavenly Gospel Singers, the Golden Gate Quartet, and Mitchell's Christian Singers—tended to be either well established or groups whose initial records sold well. The other major reason that no Memphis quartets made records during this period was that few companies conducted field recording sessions after 1930 and almost none were held in the Mid-South. The American Record Corporation, for instance, held the only Memphis field session in 1939 and they recorded no black religious music.

After World War II the very nature of the record industry changed. Between 1942 and late 1944 shortages of the shellac necessary to press records, along with a recording ban called by the American Federation of Musicians, very effectively shut down the entire industry. As the war finally ground to a close and America's economy began to recover, a new spirit of entrepreneurship in the record business became evident. Columbia and Victor and their related companies tended to dominate the industry prior to 1945, but the late 1940s witnessed a rapid proliferation of small record companies that were willing to take a risk on local or regional talent of every conceivable description.

There are many obscure and important examples of this phenomenon from all over the country. In New York City, Atlantic Records and Apollo Records each entered the market and made a significant impact by issuing a wide variety of folk, popular, and jazz discs. Chicago was home base for the Aristocrat/Chess complex of labels, while Los Angeles served as headquarters for Imperial Records. In Memphis, Sam Phillips's Sun label became a critical force in recording rockabilly and rhythm 'n' blues music but had little impact on religious music.[4] There were scores of other companies located in smaller cities and rural areas across the United States, though many released only a few records before folding. The fact is that although literally hundreds of independent record companies formed after 1945, only a minute fraction of them became successful business enterprises. Yet they did record numerous fascinating and important examples of American music. And as a result of this trend, more Memphis groups finally gained access to the recording studios.

The first local group to get into the studio during this entrepreneurial period was the Spirit of Memphis. The group's experience clearly illustrates how these new record companies operated and also demonstrates the importance of professionalism among quartets, another important aspect of gospel singing during the immediate postwar years. Throughout the 1940s the Spirit of Memphis was perhaps the most popular quartet in the Mid-South. Although each of the singers maintained a full-time job, the group sang nearly every weekend and on local programs during the week. The weekend engagements frequently carried the group far from Memphis, and it was at one of these out-of-town programs that the group got its break.

The year was 1948 and the Spirit of Memphis had been engaged to sing in Birmingham, Alabama, on a major program. Robert Reed recalls the trip:

> We sang this song, "Happy in the Service of the Lord." And the audience, I don't know what happened, but they . . . acted like they hadn't heard a song like that before. It just went over big! So this guy, this nice white guy, so he said, "How would you guys like to record that song for me?" We said, "Okay," you know. He was the director of this radio station. . . . It was in Bessemer, a very popular station there. We sang this song down there at the auditorium and the promoter was a guy named Polk. So when we got the engagement there, then he, Mr. Polk, asked us how would we like to record "Happy in the Service of the Lord?" And do you know that we recorded that record and we couldn't keep 'em there in Birmingham![5]

It is not clear exactly what company first issued the record. The entry for the selection in Cedrick Hayes and Robert Laughton's discography credits the issue to De Luxe,[6] an independent company based in New Jersey. There is an advertisement in the June 14, 1949, *Memphis World*, however, listing the Spirit of Memphis as Hallelujah Record Company artists. Quartet members Robert Reed and Earl Malone recall selling the record locally before it was available on De Luxe.[7] Thus it appears that Hallelujah was probably a "one-shot" label that Polk produced and the group marketed;

later a deal was worked out with De Luxe, and by late 1949 the New Jersey-based company was marketing the disc. In any event, this recording of "I'm Happy in the Service of the Lord" set the local gospel community ablaze. Besides capturing a fine performance, the record symbolized the acceptance of Memphis quartet singing by a larger and more far-flung audience. It was almost certainly on the strength of this record and its well-deserved local and regional reputation that the Spirit of Memphis reached an agreement with King Records—one of the larger and more important independent companies.

King Records is an archetype for all postwar independent enterprises. Formed by Syd Nathan in 1943, King built a strong, diverse catalog that included hillbilly artists like the Delmore Brothers and the Brown's Ferry Four, as well as popular black artists like Tiny Bradshaw and the Swan Silvertone Singers. Nathan seemed especially drawn to black gospel music and the money it brought to his company. By late 1949 the Spirit of Memphis had signed an exclusive agreement with King Records and remained with the company until the close of 1952—halcyon years when their base of popularity was solid. The group's live performances were outstanding, with a lineup that featured the powerful, often breathtaking alternating leads by Wilbur "Little Ax" Broadnax, Silas Steele, and Jethroe Bledsoe.

"Jet" Bledsoe, an early member of the Spirit of Memphis, still lives in Memphis. He vividly recalls when the quartet was on top:

"Days Past and Gone" was the record that really introduced us on King Records. Silas Steele was preaching on that record. Nobody had ever heard anything like that! We got that record out there . . . and that's what sold us throughout the country. Silas was a great singer and a showman. He was second lead and he would "brace" me anytime we would get in tight 'cause he could talk. That's when we had some of them talking records. They criticized me for letting him do that type of thing on a record, 'cause nobody wasn't doing no preaching when I made the record "Lord, Jesus." They [King Records] caught it in the auditorium [the Mason's Temple]. He [Syd Nathan] put that thing out and that record went out all over everywhere! We made all kinds of money and that's the way we got to go on the road and make appearances. We would pack every auditorium everywhere! Sometimes I look at the map up there [of the United States] and I say, "Well, which states haven't I been in?"[8]

Besides the aforementioned "preaching" records, the Spirit of Memphis recorded quite a few jubilee-style arrangements of traditional songs like "I'm on the Battlefield" and "Everytime I Feel the Spirit." The group also delved into more contemporary gospel material. One of the best examples of this is "The Atomic Telephone," which incorporates the once-popular "atomic age" motif with the somewhat more traditional theme of communicating with Jesus by way of the telephone. Such vivid imagery, a wonderful example of popular songwriting, apparently came from the pen of Syd Nathan. "The Atomic Telephone" is not an anomaly; several artists, including other religious singers, recorded songs using this theme.[9]

Although its King recordings sold well, the Spirit of Memphis soon grew dissatisfied with the financial arrangements. According to Earl Malone, a lack of accountability and perhaps honesty were the prime reasons the quartet and King Records parted ways late in 1952: ". . . he'd [Nathan] give us an advance, an advance royalty. And . . . that was the size of it. He'd give us maybe $400 or $500 . . . to cut a session. We never did get no statement."[10] Shortly thereafter the Spirit of Memphis signed with the aggressive and tough Don Robey of Peacock Records, thus beginning an association that lasted until the late 1960s.

Earl Malone recalls that Robey offered the group a respectable financial arrangement and even traveled to Memphis from Houston to sign the contract. By contrast, record companies in postwar Memphis all but ignored local quartets. Even Sam Phillips, the city's most talented record entrepreneur, whose reputation as a hustler with an eye for talent was well deserved, evidently believed that such groups did not have enough commercial potential—or maybe he was too busy trying to deal with the likes of Carl Perkins, Elvis Presley, Rufus Thomas, Joe Hill Louis, Jr. Parker, and Jerry Lee Lewis. Phillips did record four local quartets—the Gospel Tones, the Brewsteraires, the Gospel Travelers, and the Southern Jubilees—but he released virtually none of their sides. Chess picked up and issued one Brewsteraires disc, and Sun released one record each by Brother James Anderson and the Jones Brothers (the latter two are stylistically removed from the quartet tradition). For the most part, however, companies outside the Mid-South provided Memphis quartets with recording opportunities. Robey was in charge of the Peacock and Duke labels, which recorded the majority of Memphis gospel quartet sides (fifty-two of ninety) during the 1950s. He had the Spirit of Memphis under contract between 1953 and 1968, while the Sunset Travelers and the Southern Wonders had much briefer, though earlier associations with his companies. (According to matrix numbers assigned for the Southern Wonders' initial session, it was the first group to record for Robey.)

He certainly made money with gospel quartets or he would not have recorded so many of them. Because Duke/Peacock was a very small operation with only a handful of people involved in its day-to-day business operations, the singers themselves had extensive personal contact with Robey. Their opinions of him vary, but by all accounts he was an extremely demanding person, a perfectionist with a clear vision of what he wanted. Grover Blake, founder and manager of the Sunset Travelers, perhaps best describes Robey: "If you trying to get *his* ideas, he was 100 percent with you."[11]

If Blake and the Sunset Travelers were wary and respectful of Don Robey, the same could not be said for Jack Franklin and the Southern Wonders. Robey's suggestion that the Southern Wonders sing popular music in addition to religious songs antagonized the quartet. Ernest Moore, a group member between 1952 and 1957, reflects on the increasingly hostile situation: Robey "was an uncooperative man. He knew what would sell, he wouldn't let us record it. First thing he wanted us to sing pop and we wouldn't sing it. What was the song, 'Lovie Dovie'? That's what he wanted us to sing. When it came to gospel music, he thought he could lure you over to sing what he wanted you to sing."[12] The Southern Wonders' manager and founder, Jack Franklin, echoes Moore's observations: "He dragged me out to see his fishing boat and that's where he wanted to talk all that stuff [singing secular music]. What Robey cared about gospel music and religion wasn't nothing! He was a millionaire and he was making money. At that time pop would sell fast. He was trying to get Blair and McKinney . . . have Blair play pop and have McKinney sing 'em."[13]

This bickering and Robey's attempt to factionalize the Southern Wonders escalated to such a level that the group attempted to break their contract with him. This proved impossible because Robey's hold over them included more than juat a recording relationship: he was also the owner of the Buffalo Booking Agency of Houston, Texas, the exclusive agent for live performance dates by

Peacock/Duke artists. In addition to refusing to release the Southern Wonders from their recording contract, Robey also placed a
stranglehold on their touring schedule. Jack Franklin explains:

> One thing we did, we refused to take any more bookings. We just
> stopped and told Evelyn [Johnson, secretary of the Buffalo Booking
> Agency] that if she didn't book the places closer together, we just
> weren't gonna do it! She had us booked in Pensacola, and had us
> jumping from Florida to Grand Rapids, Michigan! She had started
> booking them close together, 100 to 200 miles apart, but that trip
> was a little too far apart.[14]

The Southern Wonders made no more recordings after their final
Peacock session in mid-1953, yet they did stay together as a full-
time professional quartet until late 1957, when they finally came
off the road to resettle in Memphis. Unquestionably, some bitterness toward Don Robey remains in the hearts of at least several of
the group members, but this is tempered by an understanding of
his importance in furthering their careers.

Although Grover Blake staunchly maintains that he and the Sunset Travelers kept on Don Robey's good side, there appears to have
been some ill-will between them regarding singer O. V. Wright.
During the early 1950s Wright was a high school student in sub-
urban Germantown, Tennessee, when Blake recruited him. Wright
was one of the superb quartet singers of the 1950s and performed
with the Sunset Travelers for several years. In 1956 he left Blake's
group to join the ever-popular Spirit of Memphis. Two years later
Wright left gospel music altogether, lured by Don Robey's prom-
ises of a career in pop music. Wright never returned to religious
singing, a fact that seemed to upset Grover Blake, though he never
directly stated it.

A similar situation occurred with Joe Hinton at roughly the
same time. Hinton was a dynamic lead singer with the Spirit of
Memphis in 1957 and 1958, but he left the group after listening to
Robey's popular music pitch. Earl Malone relates:

> He was with us for a good while until Robey, you know, talked to
> him about everything he could do with the pop field. Robey talked
> him into it, you know what I mean. He and I was roommates . . . out
> on the road. And he talked to me about it. I said, "Well, if you think
> you can do better—do it!" So he decided he'd better get started . . .

Robey was interested in him . . . thought he would make another Sam Cooke.[15]

At the root of these conflicts seems to have been the need to reconcile religious convictions with the more lucrative financial rewards offered in the popular music field. Gospel quartet singers frequently were torn between serving the Lord through song and the prospects of more comfortable circumstances in the popular sector. But despite the temptation, the overwhelming majority of singers and quartets in Memphis remained with religious music. Former gospel disc jockey and quartet singer Eugene Walton has very strong opinions on this subject:

> I'm a firm believer that to be successful, you have to pick which way you want to go and go that way. Our [the Gospel Travelers'] determination was to stick with gospel. In the black audience, they won't tolerate it here in Memphis—you singing blues and gospel all at the same time. They won't accept it. We didn't go [into pop music] because we would have been committing suicide in gospel. Above that, my religious belief is that . . . whatever you going to do, you do it. But don't straddle the fence.[16]

Regardless of these webs of conflict and the problems between Robey and the Memphis quartet singers, his documentation of this music is unparalleled. Whether some other regional record entrepreneur, such as Johnny Vincent of Ace Records in Jackson, Mississippi, would have taken the initiative to record these Memphis quartets remains pure speculation. David Clark, who worked as a producer and an artists and repertoire (A&R) man for Peacock/Duke Records between 1953 and 1970, provides an inside view of Robey and the way he ran his business.[17] Clark, who today does A&R work for Malaco Records in Jackson, Mississippi, produced dozens of jazz, blues, gospel, and pop sessions for Robey and, along with his boss and Evelyn Johnson, was at the heart of the company's operation in Houston and later in New York City.

> I think Robey was one of the most controversial guys ever been in the business. I worked with Robey for eighteen years. For eighteen years I got my money on time. . . . He did some great things for me and some great things for the groups. A lot of the groups, I'm going to tell you what happened, especially with gospel groups. They'd go down to Houston; they'd go to Robey's office. "We need a

car." Robey would buy them a car. "We need $10,000 for uniforms." Robey would buy them uniforms. Robey would have them sign for their money. This was Robey's money, it wasn't theirs! Robey would have them sign a promissory note. Now when royalty time come, and time to collect his money, the groups would freeze up because they figure they shouldn't have to pay it all at once. They wanted royalties, but they had gotten their money up front, and Robey was going to get his. It was that simple.[18]

Robey was, according to Clark, an extremely shrewd business-man, with the record company and booking agency being only two of his many ventures. Although he kept himself well informed and was intimately involved with the daily operation of his musical entreprises, Robey was also deeply embroiled in financial matters totally unrelated to music:

> Most of the time Robey was watching his horses—his other invest-ment. Robey had a lot of investments. Robey also had about thirty or forty of his own racehorses. What made him so controversial, no-body ever knew what he was doing. A lot of them rock and roll groups that was appearing across the country . . . part of the bank-roll was from Robey. Alan Freed did a lot of things with Robey's money. He could go through a lot of money. Robey was a gambler. Robey was the only gambler, I think the only man I knew, could walk around with a million dollars in his pocket and nobody would rob him![19]

One of the more interesting recordings from this era, "God's Chariot" (Parts 1 and 2), indirectly involves Don Robey. The year was 1952 and the Gospel Travelers were singing regularly over WDIA. David Mattis, one of the station administrators, decided that the time was right to enter the growing field of independent record companies. He heard the group sing a topical song one day, quickly decided that this song had commercial potential, and chose it to kick off his new Duke label: "They had a great tornado that went through the Mid-South and this bunch called the Gospel Travelers came up and they wanted to cut it and we cut it as a two-sided record and I cut the wind behind it and 'God's Chariot' was the tornado. It was a really exciting gospel thing. . . . It was excit-ing with the wind and the tornado came and God came roaring across the field."[20]

Because he was new in the business, Mattis was soon seeking a partner with more savvy and record industry connections. After sifting through his options, he signed a contract with Don Robey in the fall of 1952. Like so many people before and after him, Mattis soon had ill feelings about his new business associate; not surprisingly, money was involved. When Mattis confronted Robey, the Houston businessman pulled out a .45-caliber revolver and placed in on the desk. After a prolonged negotiation that involved many dollars in legal fees and a good deal of bitterness, the two men reached a settlement. In the end Mattis got some cash, copyright agreements, and future royalties, while Robey ended up with some fine master tapes, which would eventually make money for him, as well as rights to the Duke label.[21]

Of course, Robey did not record all of the best quartets in Memphis or even all of the "commercial" groups, but his impact was the most profound. Nashboro Records in Nashville, Tennessee, recorded many regional black gospel groups, though they were involved with only two Memphis quartets: the Dixie Nightingales and the Sons of Jehovah. This brief association occurred in 1959 and 1960, at the end of the period when quartets were popular. As a result of this neglect, gospel quartets in Memphis largely turned to "vanity" record labels. Such companies provide local quartets, or anyone else with enough money, with a 45-rpm disc or an LP album they can sell. The group pays a set fee for the studio time and the cost of labels, sleeves, and pressing; and the studio owner turns over the 500 or 1,000 records to the group, whose responsibility it is to market them. The profit for studio owners comes from their role as middlemen: they generally bill their clients about 25 percent above costs.

Style Wooten's Designer, Good News, and Golden Rule imprints comprise the most active vanity labels used by Memphis gospel groups since the late 1960s. Although Wooten has been in the record business only since 1968, precise information regarding his various labels is difficult to obtain. It appears, however, that he has recorded at least two local quartets—the Harps of Melody and the Royal Harmony Four. One of the first groups with which Wooten worked in the late 1960s was the Harps of Melody, and since this was also one of the Designer label's first releases, he recalls the session vividly: "It was like this . . . it was something new. If you gonna be in the record business, you have to adapt. I adapted. You gotta get in there and work with it. I used Charles Bourne [on piano] . . . to try and hold them on key and give them something for the station to play. I didn't know whether the station would play it or not. It was a new experience trying to work with them, to be the best possible, always keeping in mind airplay."[22]

Several other local quartets that generally sang a cappella also experienced an augmentation of their ranks when they went into the studio. Flozell Leland of the Millerettes recalls that her group did a session with J & W Records, a very obscure Memphis company that issued a handful of records in the mid-1960s before going out of business: "I felt like . . . we could do the job without music [instruments], but they felt that we couldn't do the job without music. This led us to . . . believe that they knew what they were doing. Maybe they did and maybe they didn't; anyway, they stuck this music to us."[23]

Most recently, High Water Records, which is affiliated with Memphis State University, entered the field of black gospel quartet music. In 1983 the company issued two 45-rpm discs by two male quartets and a long-playing anthology of Memphis quartets (see the comprehensive Memphis Gospel Quartet Audiography). More recently the same label has released two albums by local harmony groups, the Pattersonaires and the venerable Spirit of Memphis. It remains to be seen whether specialist labels like High Water will continue to document this music or whether private entrepreneurs in this spirit of Don Robey will move back into this field of recording.

Several Memphis radio stations have provided a significant forum for black gospel quartets equal in importance to the role that the record companies played. Although quartet performances on local radio can be documented as early as 1929, they did not assume a prominent role until the late 1940s when KWEM and WDIA featured regularly scheduled "live" broadcasts. The importance of these broadcasts for Memphis quartets cannot be overstated. They served the dual purpose of promoting the group's musical ministry and the quartet itself. Radio instantly provided quartets with a larger and more far-flung audience than they could possibly hope to reach at any local church. Singers quickly recognized the importance of radio and, as Huddie Moore of the Spiritual Four explains, its almost magical power to expand their audience: "It was pretty important. . . . [Say] you was going to have a program on Sunday evening; when you do your broadcast, you announce where you going to be, name of the church and who's going to be on your program to help you. It will help to sell your crowd for the program."[24]

Like many Memphis quartets, the Spiritual Four, which Moore founded in the late 1930s, sang over at least three local radio stations between the late 1940s and the mid-1960s. The group had a regular weekly program on WDIA during the early 1950s, followed by a similar stint on KWAM, and completed its radio career with broadcasts on WLOK in 1964. This pattern is typical of quartet radio work and represents a trend that began near the dawn of radio broadcasting in Memphis.

As well as being the first Memphis group to record, the I.C. Glee Club holds a similar distinction in the field of broadcasting. Probably because of OKeh's interest, WREC invited the group to their studios. The *Memphis Press-Scimitar* of February 1, 1929, offers the following information: "The feature from WREC, 'Voice of Memphis Station,' Friday-night will be the singing of the I.C. Glee Club Negro quartet. These harmony singers have been heard in many leading cities in the North and East, and have made numerous tours. They will be on the air from 8 to 9:00 PM."[25] According to officials of the Illinois Central Gulf Railroad, this was the quartet's second appearance on WREC; the theme of their program "was built around an imaginary trip on ICRR's Memphis-St. Louis 'Chickasaw' passenger train."[26] From this description it would appear that OKeh Records recorded the theme song either under the title "Panama to Chi" or "I'm Going Home on the Chickasaw Train."

According to interviews with local quartet singers, we know that at least the following groups had radio programs: the Spirit of Memphis, the Gospel Travelers, the Four Stars of Harmony, the I.C. Hummingbirds, and the Independent Quartet. These live shows were heard over WHBQ, WMPS, WMC, and WNRB (which is no longer in business). And there were certainly other gospel quartets performing on Memphis radio stations during the depression years.

The increased number of black quartet appearances on Memphis radio clearly parallels popular interest in this music and its documentation by record companies. Many more Memphis quartets broadcast regularly during the 1940s and 1950s than during the 1930s. Unquestionably, two stations (WDIA and KWEM) played the paramount role in promoting and disseminating quartet music over the Mid-South's airwaves. KWEM began serving the area from West Memphis, Arkansas, in 1946 with a format that blended secular and religious music, news, and talk shows, most of which were oriented toward a white audience. The sizable Afro-American population in Memphis was clearly underserved by the mass media, however, and by 1949 KWEM had altered its policies in an attempt to reach this market. Their strategy was to add a few black disc jockeys and to expand their programming of black secular and sacred music. Several very important rhythm 'n' blues artists of the 1950s and 1960s broadcast over this station early in their careers: Jr. Parker, James Cotton, and Howlin' Wolf (Chester Burnett). Howlin' Wolf, for example, had a weekly program on KWEM in 1952, just about the time his recordings for RPM and Chess hit the market. Black gospel music also entered the station's format at about the same time.

Although KWEM programmed black gospel music throughout the day, the station confined this music primarily to Sunday morning. Before KWEM moved its studios to Memphis and altered its call letters to KWAM in 1953, many local quartets traveled across the Mississippi River Bridge to perform on these Sunday morning broadcasts. Walter Stewart, a black man who served as a liaison between the station and the groups, was the first emcee for the Sunday morning broadcasts. The quartets that appeared are known to include the Jollyaires (to which Stewart belonged), the Southern Jubilees, the Evening Doves, the Harps of Melody, the Gospel Travelers, and the Keystone Masters of Harmony.

The only change made when these Sunday morning programs moved to Memphis was that "Cousin" Eugene Walton took over Walter Stewart's position. Cousin Eugene, of the Gospel Travelers, maintained his dual role as disc jockey and quartet singer until his group disbanded in the middle 1960s. He continued to work at the station, however, until his retirement in 1982, after nearly thirty years of service. Walton's retirement resulted from policy disagreements with management and a format shift that relegated gospel music to a much less prominent role.

Cousin Eugene's affiliation with local quartets was most important during the 1950s when the station regularly played and heavily promoted this music:

> Mostly on Sunday mornings the various groups had broadcasts on the station. I was the only one they chose to be the emcee on the air. The station's responsibility was for booking the groups and, of course, it was my responsibility to see that they got on the air on time. I made the various announcements and made sure everything went right. The groups started coming on at 7:00 A.M. . . . right up until 10:00 or 10:30 A.M. Most likely they had a 15-minute program each, but every once in a while some had a 30-minute show. Mostly, the groups sponsored their own selves. I don't think many of them had an outside sponsor.[27]

The cost of airtime during the early 1950s was about twelve dollars per quarter hour, and most quartets willingly paid this fee because of the publicity the broadcasts brought to them. Only a very small percentage of the Memphis groups had records available, making radio their most important medium for exposure. Walton relates:

> Well, they wanted to be heard. Some of the groups think they sing very well and the people didn't know about them. That was their way of getting heard . . . getting on the air so people could hear them. And by the same token, the people listened to them on the air. That's how they got established. If you weren't on the air, you had a pretty rough go with trying to get programs. That was why it was vitally important to be on the air.[28]

After a half-year of experience with these live Sunday broadcasts, Cousin Eugene slowly began to accept more duties at KWAM. He soon hosted a two-hour Saturday afternoon shift featuring records by the Trumpeteers, the Jubilaires, the Golden Gate Quartet, the Dixie Hummingbirds, and other popular quartets. Within a year after his first air-shift, Walton was a full-time employee of KWAM.

KWAM's weekly schedule featured live quartet programming until the late 1950s; by 1960 it had entirely ceased. This radical shift occurred for two major reasons. First, popular tastes moved away from the quartets and toward other forms of black gospel music. Second, KWAM's management changed its financial and managerial policies. Walton recalls that "the gospel format opened up and we began to take in church services, so that kind of narrowed the time for quartets because church services mostly want a whole hour. We had so many demands for church services that it limited the time for quartets. The church naturally had their listening audiences . . . [and] could also pay more money."[29]

KWAM's switch to other programming enabled WDIA to become an even more consequential outlet for Memphis gospel music and quartets. WDIA began as a low-power daytime operation in 1948, and from its inception the station oriented itself toward a black audience. During its first few years, WDIA programmed much religious music. Rev. W. Herbert Brewster's renowned "Camp Meeting of the Air," a show that spotlighted many local gospel singers like Queen C. Anderson and the Brewsteraires, was broadcast live on WDIA. In fact, many of the best local black religious groups sang on this station at one time.[30]

The impact and critical importance of WDIA increased dramatically in July 1954 when the station boosted its power to the maximum permissible output of 50,000 watts and began around-the-clock programming. Prior to this time the station served only Memphis and the immediate surrounding counties. The changes meant that WDIA virtually blanketed the Mid-South, as well as many other sections of the country after sundown. Thus WDIA instantly became the primary outlet for ambitious black quartets because they now could reach hundreds of thousands of people.

Even before this power increase, however, WDIA had been a potent force within the community of black musicians in Memphis. Doug Seroff states:

WDIA was Memphis' premier black music radio station during the legendary years of the early 1950s when the Memphis music scene was exploding with creative energy. At the time the station featured a great deal of live music from their studio. Along with the gospel artists many well known blues and R & B stars, including B. B. King, Johnny Ace and Joe Hill Louis, had regular fifteen-minute programs on WDIA, either weekly or daily. Some of these programs were commercially sponsored, others sponsored by the groups themselves.[31]

There were several notable local and national sponsors for Memphis quartets who broadcast over WDIA. Locally, the Littlejohn Taxi Company was one of the Spirit of Memphis's first sponsors;

General Mills later underwrote this group, while the Pet Milk Company sponsored the Southern Wonders. According to Ford Nelson, an employee of WDIA from 1949 through 1984:

> . . . as far as sponsors are concerned, that would always originate with our sales department. A lot of people didn't know that. We never charged groups to be on the air. If we thought enough of them to put them on the air, we treated them in a special way. If they carved out a big chunk of audience, the sales people would say, "These guys are pretty good." We would cut an audition with a group, say a 15-minute audition with the Dixie Nightingales with my voice on it . . . [if we were] trying to sell it to a sponsor. That made it more professional, rather than a group coming in with Joe's Shine Parlor or something like that. It always gave the station a lot of class.[32]

At the very heart of this activity were two long-time WDIA employees, Theo "Bless My Bones" Wade and Ford Nelson. Wade, who died in 1980, was for many years associated with the Spirit of Memphis prior to joining WDIA's staff and, because of his various affiliations, was one of the key figures in the city's gospel community. Wade did not simply confine himself to his job with WDIA, which began in 1952; he also booked, promoted, and emceed gospel shows. But even more important, members of local quartets had a strong regard for Wade, who seemed to get along with everyone. Nina Jai Daugherty of the Brewster Singers remembers: "Brother Wade was a marvelous person. He was a friend to those quartet singers, gospel singers. He was a good friend to them. He tried to help publicize wherever they were going to be and invite you to be with them. He was simply a great personality."[33]

Theo Wade remained with WDIA until his death. Throughout a nearly thirty-year tenure at the station, his principal role was with religious music. During the week he and Ford Nelson divided a two-hour evening shift entitled "Hallelujah Jubilee," a program devoted to all forms of black gospel music. Each afternoon Nelson had his own show, "The Gospel Train," which also spotlighted the recordings of black gospel groups. The popularity of quartets was such that in 1954 the King Cotton and Nat Buren Packing companies underwrote a daily fifteen-minute program featuring the records of the Golden Gate Quartet.

Interspersed throughout the radio programming day were fifteen- and thirty-minute blocks of live music. Naturally, gospel quartets played a prominent role on these shows. For example, during June 1952, WDIA's daily format included live broadcasts by the Spirit of Memphis (10:00 A.M.–10:15 A.M., sponsored by Gold Medal Flour) and the Songbirds of the South (noon–12:15 P.M., sponsored by the Ballard Company). The same month's Sunday lineup featured a fifteen-minute show by the Gospel Travelers. Such live presentations continued throughout the 1950s, and in 1955 WDIA added a Saturday night program: "Brother Wade had a Saturday-night slot which was something else, which really became an opportunity to showcase a lot of local talent. I wasn't on Saturday nights; he had the whole thing from 7 to 9. It was called 'Hallelujah Jubilee,' . . . [and] about 80 percent to 90 percent was . . . quartets."[34] It was partially through this important program that groups like the Dixie Nightingales, the Sons of Jehovah, the Jordan Wonders, the Jubilee Hummingbirds, the Dixie Wonders, and other "hard" gospel quartets became so popular in the Mid-South.

Another of the quartet-related activities in which WDIA participated was the promotion of concerts throughout the Mid-South. Ford Nelson or Theo Wade emceed many of these programs, which featured groups heard on WDIA. Even more important than these gospel shows were the programs promoted by the station itself. The best known of these was named after one of WDIA's most popular weekly events, "Hallelujah Jubilee Caravan." This name provided a direct connection with WDIA, which helped to attract audiences to the programs. Ford Nelson recalls:

> The station would lease a bus. They would do this about once a month and make contact with some well-known auditorium or . . . hall, maybe down in Mississippi or up in Tennessee. The prime groups would perform on these live shows. We would pick them up and take them on the bus. We would fix up a box of barbecue and have lots of fun! Wade and I would go down and emcee this live show. They would tape it sometimes and bring it back and play it on the air. The shows were . . . very popular with the community.[35]

One of the most widely traveled veterans of Memphis quartet singing, James Darling, thought that Theo Wade was one of the finest emcees in the business:

He turned out to be one of the best in the country, everybody liked him. He was funny, you know . . . had a way of handling his audience. When we were going someplace and the audience seemed to be a little dry . . . he'd walk out casually, unconcerned like. He'd say "I'll tell you what I'd like you to do with me children. We gonna pull a train. I want you to put your hands together. Everytime I do this [claps his hands together], I want you to do it." Like a locomotive. He'd do . . . this and they started faster and faster. At the end he'd say "You sure do burn me out!" That would get the house, you know. We'd have lots of fun off Wade.[36]

The "Star-lite Revue" and the "Goodwill Revue," both WDIA-sponsored, comprised a second type of program. The station produced these programs twice a year—once in the spring and again in the fall—to raise money for crippled black children in Memphis. During the 1950s these revues were divided into two distinct segments: one that featured religious music and another that highlighted popular music. The "Goodwill Revue" of December 4, 1954, provides an example of the caliber of talent these shows attracted. Two of the leading blues performers of the day, Eddie Boyd and Little Walter, headlined the pop music portion. The gospel segment spotlighted two local, albeit very talented, groups—the Spirit of Memphis and the Southern Wonders. Ellis Auditorium was the site for this program and, according to the December 7, 1954, edition of the *Tri-State Defender,* the station raised nearly $7,000.

It is evident from all the primary data that WDIA worked extensively with four or five local quartets, much to the benefit of all parties. While the quartets received the exposure that only this powerful station could provide, WDIA gained community support and added advertising revenues. The support of WDIA ultimately brought the Southern Wonders, the Spirit of Memphis, the Dixie Nightingales, the Songbirds of the South, and the Sunset Travelers all the work they could handle, but ironically it also caused conflicts with the groups' radio broadcasts. Some of them responded by dropping their radio commitments; others reduced the number of broadcasts. Most stations turned to transcriptions, which were prerecorded programs on discs. Doug Seroff observes that the stations routinely recorded transcriptions for broadcast at the appropriate times: "While the artists were in the studio the disc jockeys and engineers sometimes recorded ten-inch vinyl dubs of their most popular numbers, which were played on the air between 'live' broadcasts. Some of the songs on these dubs became better known around Memphis than the artists' recordings." [37] These transcriptions, in fact, are the only sound documents that remain of some quartets. For example, the highly regarded Songbirds of the South never recorded commercially, but several of their 1952 and 1953 transcriptions from WDIA have survived. [38]

As I noted earlier, general interest in black gospel quartets began to wane in the middle 1950s, a trend that accelerated as the decade closed, and that was reflected in the gospel programming by local commercial stations. By the early 1960s, gospel quartets rarely performed live on either KWAM or WDIA. As long as quartets remained popular, drew crowds, and sold records, they were generally heard over Memphis's airways; but as their popularity diminished, so did their airtime. Today quartet harmony singing is very hard to find on Memphis stations. As far as the local commercial radio programmers are concerned, it is an anachronism. WLOK and WDIA occasionally program records by local hard gospel quartets like the Spirit of Memphis or nationally recognized groups such as the Sensational Nightingales or the Mighty Clouds of Joy. Airtime for gospel quartets has largely shifted to noncommercial and public radio stations, most notably WSMS (operated by Memphis State University) and community radio station WEVL. Their eclectic programming, especially on WEVL, invites its listeners to sample all sorts of local music, including a wide range of quartets. Such enlightened programming has opened the ears of mostly younger, white listeners to this music. Nonetheless, the quartet audience largely consists of middle-aged and elderly black residents of Memphis. Because the industry is so heavily oriented toward music that attracts a mass audience, rich gospel harmony singing is not likely to return to Memphis's high-power commercial radio outlets anytime soon. [39]

NOTES

1. Useful information on this era is found in Ronald C. Foreman, Jr., "Jazz and Race Records, 1920–1932" (Ph.D. dissertation, University of Illinois, 1968); Robert M. W. Dixon and John Godrich, *Recording the Blues* (New York: Stein and Day, 1970); and Bill C. Malone and Judith McCulloh, eds., *Stars of Country Music* (Urbana: University of Illinois Press, 1975).

2. For discographical information on the I.C. Glee Club and all other Memphis groups, see Appendix I.

3. This aspect of field recording in Memphis is covered in Kip Lornell, "The Field Recording of American Folk Music: A Case Study from Tennessee in 1928," *Tennessee Folklore Society Bulletin,* no. 4 (Winter 1981), pp. 153–59; reprinted in *The Sounds of People and Places: Readings in the Geography of American Folk and Popular Music,* ed. George Carney (Washington, D.C.: University Press of America, 1987), pp. 91–101.

4. For further information see Colin Escott and Martin Hawkins, *Sun Records: The Brief History of the Legendary Record Label* (New York: Quick Fox Press, 1980).

5. Robert Reed, interviewed by Doug Seroff in Memphis, Tennessee, June 1979; transcript in the author's possession.

6. Cedrick Hayes and Robert Laughton, *Gospel Records 1943-1969: A Black Music Discography* (London: Record Information Services, 1992).

7. Earl Malone, interviewed by Kip Lornell in Memphis, Tennessee, October 11, 1980. Unless indicated otherwise, all interviews were conducted by the author in Memphis; tape and transcript copies are deposited in the Mississippi Valley Collection, Brister Library, Memphis State University.

8. Jethroe Bledsoe, interview, May 21, 1982.

9. Rounder Records, *The Atomic Cafe,* 1982.

10. Earl Malone, interviewed by Doug Seroff in Memphis, Tennessee, August 5, 1979; transcript in the author's possession.

11. Grover Blake, interview, July 10, 1982.

12. Ernest Moore, interview, May 21, 1982.

13. Jack Franklin, interview, May 21, 1982.

14. Ibid.

15. Malone interview, August 5, 1979.

16. Eugene Walton, interview, February 2, 1982.

17. David Clark, interviewed by Kip Lornell in Jackson, Mississippi, February 25, 1982.

18. Ibid.

19. Ibid.

20. Roger Meeden and George Moonoogian, "Duke Records—The Early Years, An Interview with David J. Mattis," *Whiskey, Women, and . . . ,* no. 1 (June 1984), p. 18.

21. Ibid., pp. 18–26.

22. Style Wooten, interview, July 17, 1982.

23. Flozell Leland, interview, June 14, 1982.

24. Huddie Moore, interview, February 2, 1983.

25. *Memphis Press-Scimitar,* February 1, 1929, p. 20.

26. Personal correspondence, Robert W. O'Brien to Kip Lornell, July 27, 1982.

27. Eugene Walton, interview, March 14, 1981.

28. Ibid., February 5, 1983.

29. Ibid., March 14, 1981.

30. Doug Seroff, liner notes, *"Bless My Bones: Memphis Gospel Radio—The 1950s,* Pea-Vine PLP 9051 (Tokyo, 1981), and Rounder 2063 (Boston, 1989).

31. Ibid., p. 1.

32. Ford Nelson, interview, June 2, 1982.

33. Nina Jai Daugherty, interview, May 21, 1981.

34. Nelson interview.

35. Ibid.

36. James Darling, interview, August 2, 1983.

37. Seroff, *"Bless My Bones,"* p. 2.

38. Ibid. The record contains transcriptions by the Southern Wonders, the Sunset Travelers, the Dixie Nightingales, the Brewsteraires, and the Spirit of Memphis.

39. For more about WDIA's history, please refer to Louis Cantor, *Wheelin' on Beale* (New York, Pharos Books, 1992).

"Blessed Are the Dead"

Black religious quartet singing has been a significant part of American folk and popular music since at least the turn of the twentieth century. This book examines quartet singing in Memphis, Tennessee, over a sixty-year period during which nationally recognized groups like the Spirit of Memphis and locally influential artists like the Middle Baptist Quartet, the Harps of Melody, and the Gospel Writers helped to create a unique musical culture. The continuous interaction between folk and popular culture that has characterized Afro-American quartet singing since Reconstruction is one of the recurring themes in this book. Between 1945 and 1955 black American gospel quartets became a highly visible and influential part of popular musical culture. Such peaks, which also occurred less dramatically during the 1920s, resulted when quartet singing was "discovered" by the printed and electronic agents of popular culture.

Similar cycles of popularity mark the history of many types of Afro-American vernacular music. Another example can be found in jazz, when the big "swing" bands of the late 1930s and early 1940s made millions aware of the genius of Duke Ellington, Cab Calloway, Count Basie, and Jimmie Lunceford. Jazz took another, albeit smaller, leap into general popularity in the late 1950s, propelled by artists such as Dave Brubeck, Thelonius Monk, and Miles Davis. The "blues revival" of the 1960s brought the music of Robert

Johnson, Skip James, Muddy Waters, B. B. King, John Hurt, and Gary Davis into homes across the country. A more striking example is the early 1970s ragtime revival when the movie *The Sting* focused widespread attention on this long-moribund musical genre. Yet the popularization of these genres simply could not be sustained. The very nature of popular culture is ephemeral, as exemplified by the boogie-woogie fad of the late 1930s when Pete Johnson, Meade Lux Lewis, and Albert Ammons were accepted by a large audience. Just as a small, loyal audience for boogie-woogie still exists, black gospel quartets have retained a following in their community.

Black American quartet singing has also been characterized by the tension between secular and sacred ambitions. This theme recurs throughout its history as groups and individuals have debated whether to stay with God or join the world of popular music. As far back as the turn of the century, groups such as the Dinwiddie Colored Quartet were abandoning their sacred roots for pop music careers. And as the stakes grew larger, the temptations increased. During the 1940s college groups such as the Hampton Institute Quartet and church groups such as the Golden Gate Quartet turned to secular music and gained an even greater multiracial audience. The more conservative church members objected to this trend and tended to ostracize those who favored "worldly" gain over spiritual wealth. (This secular-sacred phenomenon is not limited to quartets. Aretha Franklin and "Little" Richard Penniman, for instance, have moved back and forth between these two worlds; and gospel quartets have supplied more than their share of great singers, like Sam Cooke and Lou Rawls, to secular music.)

The support of a white audience is also noteworthy in the development of religious quartet singing. The Fisk Jubilee Singers prospered partly because of the interest shown in them by multiracial supporters in the United States but also around the world. Other institutional quartets in later years were careful to go after the money found in the pockets of white listeners and record company executives. Following World War II, the Golden Gate Quartet's movement into Café Society and their eventual expatriation underscores the importance they placed on pleasing white audiences. Anglo-American interest in quartets has taken an upward turn in recent years, though not in terms of popular support for the music. The fact is that nearly all of the historical and discographical research related to black American gospel quartets has been done by whites, a trend with parallels in other fields of Afro-American music such as blues and jazz.

"Happy in the Service of the Lord" brings to light three points specifically related to quartet singing in Memphis. First, the fact that at least eighty black gospel quartets were active in Memphis clearly demonstrates the importance of this style as an expression of religious music. Second, Memphis has been a center for quartet singing in the Mid-South and, arguably, the entire country. The number of local semiprofessional and professional quartets, the frequent programs held in the Mason's Temple, and the importance of performances by Memphis's community quartets outside of the city, all support this point. Finally, the quartet tradition in Memphis is not extinct. The a cappella groups that sing in local churches still retain a traditional repertoire and performance style, while the popularity of more modern quartets like the Spirit of Memphis indicates that quartets will be part of the city's religious music for many years to come.

Quartet singing is not Memphis's only form of black religious musical expression. The music of Pentecostal or "holiness" worshipers, for example, is also quite strong. The headquarters for one of the largest black Pentecostal sects, the Church of God in Christ, is located in Memphis. The works of important black gospel composers such as Thomas A. Dorsey and Rev. Charles Tindley, which are often performed by choral groups or choirs, have also been important in the local Baptist and Methodist churches since the 1930s. Such religious traditions and other secular musical styles such as blues are related in different ways to the Memphis quartet tradition. But each has forged its own unique heritage that demands separate, book-length treatment. To include these and other types of black religious music in this book would have obscured my tight focus on quartets.

Let me suggest some other unexplored avenues for research in local religious music. Along with the musical traditions of the Church of God in Christ, Memphis has bred two nationally recognized gospel composers, Lucie E. Campbell and Rev. W. Herbert

The Sons of Jehovah, circa 1962, were a premier "hard gospel" quartet in Memphis, beginning in about 1955: Fred Newsome, Frank Perkins, Arthur Saunders, Frank Black. *Author's collection.*

Formed about 1930, the Royal Harmony Four was still active in 1980: James Randolph, Jr., Eddie Crawford, Tony Bobbins, John Friday, Jack Miller. *Author's collection.*

The Evening Doves continued a capella harmony singing into the middle 1960s: (*top*) Florence Wiley, Mary Alice (?), Louise Pegues, Mary Jones, Marie Walton; (*bottom*) Floyd Wiley. *Courtesy of Marie Walton.*

The Brewsteraires sang together for nearly twenty-five years before breaking up in the early 1970s. *Author's collection.*

In August 1983 the Harps of Melody sang at the Gospel Quartet Heritage Program: Clara Anderson, Mabel Robinson, Hazel Young, Elizabeth Morris. *Photo by Lynn Abbott.*

The Pattersonaires performing at the August 1983 Gospel Quartet Heritage Program: Willie Neal, Jimmie Mountain, Ernest Donaldson, Roy Neal, Alphonzo Davis, James Shelton. *Photo by Lynn Abbott.*

The Spirit of Memphis on stage at the Gospel Quartet Heritage Program, August 1983: Melvin Mosley, Robert Reed, James Darling, Earl Malone. *Photo by Lynn Abbott.*

James Darling, August 1983. *Photograph by Lynn Abbott.*

Jack Steptoe & Melvin Mosley (*standing*) rehearse with Robert Reed, Earl Malone, and James Darling prior to the August 1983 Gospel Quartet Heritage Program. *Photo by Lynn Abbott.*

Brewster. The Smithsonian Institution conducted symposia on both Campbell (1983) and Brewster (1982), but these discussions by no means exhausted their subjects. Also, the influence of black gospel music in Memphis on the local soul, rockabilly, and blues tradition should be examined. Elvis Presley, among others, listened to black gospel music while growing up in Memphis. A critical exploration of this interaction would be a valuable addition to our knowledge of American popular music.

Outside of Memphis there are numerous research topics. Basic information regarding the Fisk Jubilee Singers and the Hampton University groups lies buried in poorly financed, underorganized archives—which is probably the fate of much information on other institutionally affiliated quartets. But the jubilee singing movement must be studied for it is fundamental to an understanding of quartet history; moreover, it is of critical importance to our general understanding of black American cultural, economic, social, and musical history.

Although much of the quartet research has focused on groups that made commercial recordings, the recorded groups in cities like Chicago, St. Louis, and Baltimore basically remain enigmas. The same is true for entire states such as South Carolina and Kentucky. Intensive local histories or statewide surveys are vital not only for their musical information but also for their cultural implications. A modular, interdisciplinary approach to the study of black culture and music is needed because the two offer a microcosm that can readily be fit into a larger picture.

Perhaps the most pressing concern is the decided lack of research on community quartets, which are the backbone of the gospel quartet tradition. Such groups are the least glamorous to research—most of them did not make commercial recordings, never traveled extensively, nor had a nationwide following. However, community quartets have had a strong local and regional impact, tend to reflect regional styles of singing, and are the wellspring for nearly all of the commercially successful groups.

Unfortunately these research topics are not often promoted in our universities due to their interdisciplinary nature. Such musical communities are usually below the scrutiny of most historians, while sociologists generally do not document musical activity. The worst offenders are most music departments, which woefully neglect or totally ignore American music, or else relegate it to second- or third-class status. No literature or history curricula in the United States downplay indigenous topics to the same degree as do departments of music. This pejorative observation applies to *all* types of American music, not just vernacular black religious music.

The present study underscores the interdisciplinary path that music research can take. Scholars may wish to pay closer attention to the spatial aspects of music. It is undeniable that perspectives from cultural geography can be rewarding and exciting because they present a discipline sadly overlooked by students of American music. Studies of black gospel music should closely examine the unique communities from which these styles spring. The importance of performance practices and community studies serves to reinforce the role that anthropology can play in any examination of music.

The narrow research focus on historical and discographical matters makes it impossible, in this book, to offer cross-regional comparisons. From a cultural point of view, for example, how do the roles taken by Memphis quartet trainers relate to those in other cities? Is quartet training always a male domain? What of the written bylaws utilized by some Memphis groups? Do quartets across the country adhere to the same standards or do they even formalize such rules?

Geographical research, which included plotting the performance migration patterns of the Spirit of Memphis, raised questions regarding the routes taken by other groups. Was the Spirit of Memphis's travel pattern unusual or did the group follow the same patterns as other professional quartets? Furthermore, how do social networks influence performance travel patterns in other sections of the country? These and many other tantalizing questions await future researchers.

Another area of serious concern for scholars in American music is the marked dearth of published discographies. In black religious music, for instance, there is no comprehensive listing. *Blues and Gospel Records 1902–1943* is the most authoritative, but it neglects important groups like the Fisk University Quartet and covers only a specific time period. There is *no* published listing available for the years following 1969, which is a terrible handicap because of the importance of the record industry in disseminating repertoire, vocal techniques, and other related matters. The compilation of such a discography is a difficult task; however, the accomplishment of this and the other research areas that I have outlined would represent a significant step forward in our comprehensive understanding of black American music.

I

Memphis Quartet Listing

This is an exhaustive list of Afro-American gospel quartets active in Memphis between the mid-1920s and 1987. The groups are divided into three categories—professional, semiprofessional, and community—according to their status. A few groups like the Southern Wonders are found in more than one category because their status changed over the years. The approximate dates each group was active as a harmony quartet are given in parentheses. Several groups—the Gableaires, the Jubilee Hummingbirds, and the Southern Jubilees—are still active but now perform more modern gospel music.

Professional
Southern Wonders (1952–57)
Spirit of Memphis (1950–62)
Sunset Travelers (1953–60)

Semiprofessional
Dixie Nightingales (1952–62)
Gableaires (1955–61)
Jones Brothers Quartet
  (1954–64)
Jordan Wonders (1953–60)
Jubilee Hummingbirds
  (1954–62)
Sons of Jehovah (1953–63)
Spirit of Memphis (1945–50,
  1962–present)
Spiritual Travelers (1954–65)
Sunset Travelers (1960–present)

Community
Bells of Harmony (1948–54)
Brewsteraires (1947–72)
Busyline Soft Singers (1931–38)
Campbellaires (1947–59)
Conner Gee Singers (1938–47)
Delta Friendly Four of Memphis
  (1946–49)
Dixie Wonders (1954–63)
Drifting Clouds Quartet
  (1947–50)
E. and S. (Construction Company)
  Quartet (1932–36)
Evening Doves (1950–60)
Fitch Brothers Quartet
  (1942–48)
Friendly Echoes (1951–60)
Golden Echoes (1948–51)

Golden Stars (1939–47)
Gospel Tones (1948–52)
Gospel Travelers (1939–62)
Gospel Writer Junior Boys
(1947–52)
Gospel Writer Junior Girls
(1939–49)
Gospel Writers (1937–55,
1976–present)
Harmonious Spirituals (1941–45)
Harmonizers (1976–present)
Harmony Four (1927–32)
Harps of Melody (1950–present)
Hiawatha Glee Club (1931–35)
Hollywood Specials (1930–40)
Holy Ghost Spirituals
(1976–present)
I.C. Glee Club (1927–38)
I.C. Harmony Boys (1932–39)
I.C. Hummingbirds (1934–41)
I.C. Quartet #2 (1930–40)
Independent Quartet (1932–46)
Jollyaires (1947–52)
Keystone Masters of Harmony
(1947–53)
L. C. and I. Singers (1952–56)
Lake Grove Quartet (1941–48)
Loving Junior Girls (1942–46)
M. and N. Junior Girls (1939–43)
M. and N. Singers (1937–48)
Majestic Soft Singers (1945–55)
Memphis Spiritual Four
(1936–70)
Middle Baptist Quartet
(1933–40)
Missouri-Pacific Lines Booster
Quartet (1927–35)
Mount Olive Wonders (1927–33)
Mount Pisgah Glee Singers
(1941–52)
National Christian Singers
(1941–51)

New Gospel Writers
(1986–present)
Old Red Rose Quartet (1925–30)
Orange Mound Harmonizers
(1932–35)
Orange Mound Specials
(1934–39)
Pattersonaires (1953–64)
Rock Island Quartet (1941–50)
Royal Harmony Four
(1931–present)
S. and W. (Construction Com-
pany) Quartet (1928–30)
Songbirds of the South
(1948–56)
Southern Bells (1947–53)
Southern Harmony Boys
(1937–45)
Southern Jubilees (1945–65)
Southern Wonders (1941–52)
Spirit of Memphis Junior Quartette
(1933–39)
Spirit of Memphis Quartette
(1930–45)
Spiritual Pilgrims (1943–68)
Sunshine Jolly Boosters Club
Quartet (1941–54)
T. M. and S. Quartet (1927–30)
True Friends Gospel Singers
(1939–50)
Union Soft Singers (1938–46)
United Specials (1975–present)
Vance Ensemble (1974–present)
Veteran Jubilees (1952–59)
Walker Specials (1951–55)
Wells Spirituals (1949–60)
Willing Four Soft Singers
(1946–present)
Zion Glee Singers (1938–42)
Zion Hill Spirituals (1937–78)

II

Jethroe Bledsoe's 1952 Travel Diary for the Spirit of Memphis

April 3—Hutchison, Kansas
April 6—Davenport, Iowa
April 7—Omaha, Nebraska
April 8—Des Moines, Iowa
April 10—Youngstown, Ohio
April 11—Cleveland, Ohio
April 13—Newark, New Jersey,
    and Philadelphia, Pennsylvania
April 14—Pittsburgh, Pennsylvania
April 17—Humbolt, Tennessee
April 20—Atlanta, Georgia
April 21—Memphis, Tennessee
April 22—Memphis, Tennessee
April 23—Memphis, Tennessee
April 24—Memphis, Tennessee
April 25—Oxford, Mississippi
April 27—Memphis, Tennessee

May 4—Austin, Texas
May 18—El Dorado, Arkansas
May 19—Gladwater, Texas
May 21—Shreveport, Louisiana
May 22—Wichita Falls, Texas
May 23—Sherman, Texas
May 26—San Antonio, Texas
May 28—Tyler, Texas

May 29—Greenville, Texas
May 30—Dallas, Texas

June 6—Fort Worth, Texas
June 9—Monroe City, Texas
June 13—Pensacola, Florida
June 14—Birmingham, Alabama
June 15—Birmingham, Alabama
June 16—Montgomery, Alabama
June 20—Memphis, Tennessee
June 21—Oxford, Mississippi
June 22—Durham, North Carolina
June 23—Durham, North Carolina
June 24—Durham, North Carolina
June 25—Durham, North Carolina
June 29—Oxford, Mississippi

July 1—Washington, D.C.
July 6—Buffalo, New York
July 7—Buffalo, New York
July 8—Buffalo, New York
July 11—Cincinnati, Ohio
July 13—Detroit, Michigan
July 14—Detroit, Michigan
July 15—Detroit, Michigan
July 16—Detroit, Michigan

July 18—Dayton, Ohio
July 19—Welch, West Virginia
July 20—Beckley, West Virginia, and Charleston, West Virginia
July 22—Lambert, Mississippi
July 27—New Orleans, Louisiana
July 28—Mobile, Alabama

August 1—Memphis, Tennessee
August 3—Topeka, Kansas
August 4—Topeka, Kansas
August 6—El Paso, Texas
August 7—Tucson, Arizona
August 8—Phoenix, Arizona
August 10—Oakland, California
August 11—San Francisco, California
August 12—Los Angeles, California
August 22—Pine Bluff, Arkansas
August 24—Houston, Texas

August 28—Lambert, Mississippi
August 31—Memphis, Tennessee

September 8—Albany, Georgia
September 14—New Orleans, Louisiana
September 15—Baton Rouge, Louisiana
September 16—Gladstone, Texas
September 17—Newton, Texas
September 19—San Antonio, Texas
September 21—Mexa, Texas
September 22—Longview, Texas
September 24—Stanton, Oklahoma
September 25—Tulsa, Oklahoma
September 28—Topeka, Kansas
September 30—Arlington, Tennessee

Comprehensive Memphis Gospel Quartet Audiography

This is a comprehensive listing of the commercial and noncommercial recordings by Memphis gospel quartets and other closely related groups between 1928 and 1987. The serious gaps found in this audiography fall between 1960 and 1980, when several Memphis quartets were recorded by local companies whose files are nonexistent. The High Water Record files include so many unissued songs that for clarity's sake only that label's issued performances are listed. The selections designated "Perkins Disc" are home recordings done by Frank Perkins, founder of the Sons of Jehovah. The format for this audiography is adapted from Godrich and Dixon, *Blues and Gospel Records 1902-1943,* and includes more complete details (recording date and location and personnel) than the Selected Audiography. Long-playing reissues of older material are also included because many of the original 78-rpm and 45-rpm issues are very difficult to locate. Reissues are italicized to differentiate them from original issues. Finally, I wish to acknowledge the assistance of Cedric Hayes and Bob Laughton, whose *Gospel Records 1943–1969: A Black Music Discography* (London: Record Information Services, 1992) proved invaluable in updating the discography from the first edition.

Rev. William Herbert Brewster
Brewster Singers: Queen C. Anderson and Gurice Malone (lead vocals), Dorothy Ford (tenor and piano-1), Hessie Ford (alto), Nancy Jerome (alto) Brewsteraires: Odell Rice (baritone), Nathaniel Peck (tenor), Henry Reed (bass), Solomon Alston (tenor), unknown organ (a), unknown drums and piano (b)
Memphis or Philadelphia, circa mid-1950 to early 1952

BS 1	I'll Go (a)	Gotham G644
BS 2	Want the Lord to Smile on Me (b and b)	Gotham G644
BS 3	Hope of This World Is Jesus (a)	Gotham G672
BS 4	When I Shall Meet Him Face to Face (1)	Gotham G672
BS 5	Give Me That Old Time Religion (a and b)	Gotham G687 and Roberta 2687
BS 6	So Glad I've Got Good Religion (b and c)	Gotham G687, Roberta 2687, and *Rounder* 2063
BS11	These Are They (b)	Gotham G709
BS12	Jesus Is the Perfect Answer (b)	Gotham G709

The above session is quite confusing. BS 3, 5, and 6, for example, seem to involve all of the singers, while BS 4 appears to include only members of the Brewsteraires. The following label attributions should help to clarify the situation: BS 1/2 issued as "Brewster Singers Of Memphis"; BS 3/5/6 issued as "Rev. W. H. Brewster and His Camp Meeting of the Air"; BS 4 issued as "The Brewsteraires of Memphis"; BS 11/12 issued as "Queen C. Anderson and the Brewster Singers"; BS 5 and 6 have a narration by Rev. Brewster then vocals. Roberta 2687 may not have been issued.

Queen C. Anderson and the Brewster Singers

Queen C. Anderson (lead), Dorothy Ford (tenor), Ella Clark Williams (vocal), Nina Jai Daugherty (vocal), Dorothy Ford (organ).
Memphis, June 9, 1956

Bank in the Sky	Rounder 2063
Walk thru the Water	Rounder 2063

Rev. W. Herbert Brewster with the Brewster Singers

Dorothy Ford (tenor), Hessie Ford and Nancy Jerome (altos), Queen C. Anderson (lead-1), Nina Jai Daugherty (lead-2), Dorothy Ford (piano)
Memphis, circa 1954

Speak to Me Jesus (2)	Tan Town unnumbered
Jesus, the Perfect Answer (1)	Tan Town unnumbered and *Rounder* 2063

Brewsteraires

Odell Rice (baritone), Nathaniel Peck (tenor and lead-1), Henry Reed (bass), Solomon Alston (tenor and lead)

Memphis, Dec. 26, 1951

F-1008	Where Shall I Be When That First Trumpet Sounds	Chess 1502 and *Sunbox* 105
F-1009	(The Lord Gave Me) Wings for My Soul	Chess 1502 and *Sunbox* 105
	(I Heard a Voice) in the Middle of the Night	Chess unissued

Memphis, circa 1953

	Hold On Dot	1132
	That's Enough (1)	Dot 1132
	Jasper Walls	Dot 1133
	More of Jesus, Less of Me	Dot 1133

Memphis, circa 1953

Add D. K. Rodgers (baritone and lead-2)

	King's Highway (1 and 2)	Pea-Vine PLP 9051 and Rounder 2063

Add Melvin Lee (guitar)

	Wait until My Change Comes	Pea-Vine PLP 9051 and Rounder 2063
	Bye and Bye I will See Jesus	WDIA Test
	Tredding [sic] the Wine Press Alone	WDIA Test
	On My Way to Glory Land	WDIA Test
	It's Amazing	WDIA Test
	Anywhere	WDIA Test

Memphis, Apr. 28, 1955

	So Glad (Got Good Religion)	WDIA test

Memphis, 1972

James Irby (lead) replaces Henry Reed; add Jimmy Bessler (piano) and [?] Bogart (electric bass)

	Book of the Seven Seals, Part 1	Sariron 5172 and *Rounder* 2063
	Book of the Seven Seals, Part 2	Sariron 5172 and *Rounder* 2063

Dixie Nightingales

Ollie Hoskins (lead), Willie Neal (baritone), Roy Neal (tenor), Willie Davis (bass), Nelson Lesure (guitar), unknown piano
Memphis, circa 1954

	In my Savior's Care	Rounder 2063
	Living for my Jesus	WDIA Test
	I'm Pressing On	WDIA Test
	Music in the Air	WDIA Test

Memphis, circa 1958
Willie Horner replaces Nelson Lesure; add unknown bass guitar

	I've Been Lifted	Pepper 910
	I've Got a New Home	Pepper 910

Memphis, circa 1958

	In My Saviour's Care	Pea-Vine PLP · 9051

Nashville, circa 1961

	My Destiny	Nashboro 728
	Now I Lay Me Down to Sleep	Nashboro 728
	I Would Not Be a Sinner	Nashboro 764
	I'll Go with You	Nashboro 764

Nashville, circa 1962

	Pleading for Me	Nashboro 808
	Death Is Riding	Nashboro 808

Memphis, circa 1965

CHA-9404	Assassination	Chalice C-102, *ZuZazz ZCD 2019, Stax CD SXD 086*
CHA-9405	Hush Hush	Chalice C-102, *ZuZazz ZCD 2019, Stax CD SXD 086*
	I Don't Know	Chalice C-103, *Stax CD SXD 086*
	Keep on Trying	Chalice C-103
	Forgive These Fools	Chalice C-105, *Stax CD SXD 086*
	There's Not a Friend	Chalice C-105, *Stax CD SXD 086*
	Nail Print	*Stax CD SXD 086*
	All I Need Is Some Sunshine in My Life	*Stax CD SXD 086*

This Is Our Prayer	*Stax CD SXD 086*
It Comes at the End of a Prayer	*Stax CD SXD 086*

Dixie Wonders

Male vocal group, unknown guitar, bass guitar, drums, piano (a)
Memphis or Houston, circa 1969

LRS11180	I Signed	Song Bird 1083
LRS11181	Almighty God	Song Bird 1083
LRS11309	Waiting for Me	Song Bird 1141
LRS11310	Search Me Lord	Song Bird 1141
LRS11332	Out Here on Your Word (a)	Song Bird 1153
LRS11333	Nobody But You Lord (a)	Song Bird 1153

Memphis, circa 1974
Presumably as above

Praise His Name (featuring Cleophas Mabone)	Designer PAG 7149
When They Get Old (featuring Perry Maples)	Designer PAG 7149

This record was issued as the "Dixie Wonders of Memphis, Tennessee."

Gospel Tones

Jack Stepter (lead), G. T. Widdington (lead), Tim Allen (baritone), C. D. Davidson (tenor), Cicero Lewis (bass)
Memphis, Dec. 10, 1951

Noah	Sun unissued
Get Away Jordan	Sun unissued
Rock My Soul	Sun unissued
Motherless Children	Sun unissued
Lord Be Near Me—Hear Me	Sun unissued

Gospel Trainers

John Spencer (baritone), Troy Yarborough (bass), Ray Hurley (tenor and guitar), Eugene Walton (tenor and lead)
Memphis, Spring 1952

God's Chariot, Part 1	Duke G-1 and *Krazy Kat* 7424
God's Chariot, Part 2	Duke G-1 and *Krazy Kat* 7424

Houston, Summer 1952
An unknown number of unissued titles for Duke Records
Memphis, circa 1955

TR-21	Man at the Door	Chariot 30
TR-22	Praying Time	Chariot 30

Gospel Writers

George Rooks (tenor and lead-1), David Ward (fifth), Willie Wilson
(tenor and lead-2), Jesse Allen (bass), Jimmy Allen (baritone and lead-3)
Memphis, June 28, 1982

Oh, My Lordy Lord (2 and 3)	High Water 420

Memphis, Oct. 29, 1982

Blind Barnabas (1)	High Water 420

Memphis, Feb. 24, 1983
Kevin Lott replaces Jimmy Allen

New Born Soul (1)	High Water 1002

Memphis, May 23, 1983
Roy Neal replaces David Ward; George Rooks dropped

Gospel Writer Boys Are We (2)	High Water 1002
Up above My Head I Hear Music in the Air (2)	High Water 1002

Harmonizers

Elijah Ruffin (bass and lead-1), McClendon Cox (tenor and lead-2), Julius
Guy (baritone), Hershell McDonald (tenor and lead-3)
Memphis, June 14, 1982

I'll Be Satisfied (1)	High Water 419

Memphis, June 28, 1982

Trampin' (3)	High Water 419

Memphis, Feb. 17, 1983

Roll, Jordan, Roll (3)	High Water 1002

Memphis, Feb. 24, 1983

My Lord Is Writing (1)	High Water 1002
I'm Leaning on the Everlasting Arm (1 and 2)	High Water 1002

Harps of Melody

Clara Anderson (tenor and lead), Mabel Robinson (tenor), Hazel Young
(baritone), Elizabeth Morris (bass), unknown piano and bass

Memphis, circa 1968
| 012 | Lord Bless the Weary Soldier in Vietnam | Philwood G-207 |
| 013 | King Jesus Will Roll All My Burdens Away | Philwood G-207 |

Memphis, 1971
| | Two Little Fish and Five Loaves of Bread | Designer 45-6925 |
| | He Took My Sins Away | Designer 45-6925 |

Memphis, Feb. 17, 1983
Joe Dysen replaces Hazel Young; instruments dropped
| | I'm Going to Sing and Make Melody unto the Lord | High Water 1002 |

Memphis, May 2, 1983
Hazel Young replaces Joe Dysen
| | Blind Bartimus | High Water 1002 |

Holy Ghost Spirituals

Gladys West (baritone and lead-1), Sylvia Smith (alto and lead-2), Juanita Wilson (baritone and lead-3), Armeta Nixon (tenor), Lorine Henry (tenor)
Memphis, May 3, 1983
Armeta Nixon dropped
| | Old Landmark (3) | High Water 1002 |

Lorine Henry dropped
| | Ninety-nine and a Half (2) | High Water 1002 |
| | Talk to the Man Upstairs (1) | High Water 1002 |

I. C. Colored Glee Club

C. H. Evans (first tenor), R. S. Saunders (second tenor), E. L. Rhodes (baritone), L. S. Brown (bass)
Memphis, Feb. 16, 1928
400252-B	Don't You Hear the Bells A-Ringing	OKeh unissued
400253-B	If I Get Inside	OKeh unissued
400254-B	Four and Twenty Elders on Their Knees	OKeh unissued
400255-B	God Told the Widow to Cook All She Had	OKeh unissued

Atlanta, Mar. 18, 1929
I. C. Glee Quartet, presumably the same personnel
| 402347-B | So Glad Trouble Don't Last Always | OKeh 8681 |

402348-B	He Pardoned Me	OKeh 8726
402349-B	Come On, Don't You Want to Go	OKeh 8726
402350-B	I'm Going Home on the Chickasaw Train	OKeh 8710
402351-B	God Told the Poor Widow to Cook All She Had	OKeh 8710
402352-A	When They Ring Dem Golden Bells	OKeh 8710

New York City, Oct. 23, 1930
Unknown piano (a)

404495-B	Riding on the Seminole	OKeh 8929
404496-A	All My Sins Taken Away	OKeh 8837
404497-B	Panama to Chi	OKeh 8929
404498-B	When the Leaves Turn Red and Fall	OKeh 8848
404499-B	Church Meeting	OKeh unissued
404500-C	Gambler, You Can't Ride This Train	OKeh 8848
404501-B	Sermon Revelation Fifth Chapter	OKeh unissued
404502-A	I Shall Not Be Removed (a)	OKeh 8872

New York City, Oct. 24, 1930

404503-B	If I Could Hear My Mother Pray Again	OKeh 8837
404504-B	Lord Have Mercy When I Come to Die	OKeh 8872

Jubilee Humming Birds

Male vocal group with Rev. Whitker (lead-1), Rev. Banks (lead-2), others
unknown, with guitar, bass guitar
Probably Memphis, circa 1964

Always Treat a Stranger Right (2)	Mayo 403
Stepped Out Just in Time (1)	Mayo 403

Probably Memphis, circa 1965
Presumably as above

Our Freedom Song (Free at Last)	Chalice C-106, *Stax CD SXD 086*
Press My Dying Pillow	Chalice C-106, *Stax CD SXD 086*
He's a Friend of Mine	*Stax CD SXD 086*
Stop Laughing at Your Fellow Man	*Stax CD SXD 086*
Jesus Will Fix It	*Stax CD SXD 086*
Give Me One More Chance	*Stax CD SXD 086*

Memphis, circa 1968
Probably as above

I'm Gonna Live Again Pt. 1	Sound of Memphis 1221
I'm Gonna Live Again Pt. 2	Sound of Memphis 1221

Rev. Whitker's correct name is "Rev. E. L. Whittaker."

Pattersonaires

James Shelton (lead), Charles Turner (tenor), Ernest Donaldson (baritone),
Jimmie Mountain (vocals), Willie Gordon (piano), unknown organ, bass,
drums
Memphis, May 6, 1965

Why Not Try My God	Chalice C-101
How Long, Oh Lord, How Long	Chalice C-101
God's Promise	Chalice C-107, *Stax CD SXD 086*
He's Worthy	Chalice C-107, *Stax CD SXD 086*
I Asked the Lord	Stax unissued
I Know That It Was Jesus	Stax unissued
I'm Saved	Stax unissued
Have Faith in God	Stax unissued
By Faith	Stax unissued
I Shall See Him Face to Face	Stax unissued
It Was for Me	Stax unissued
I Learned to Pray	*Stax CD SXD 086*
A Child of God	*Stax CD SXD 086*
Till Jesus Comes	*Stax CD SXD 086*

Memphis, May 23, 1983
Ernest Donaldson (baritone and lead-1), Roy Neal (tenor and lead-2),
Willie Neal (tenor and lead-3), James Shelton (lead-4), Willie Gordon
(piano and lead-5).

He's Worthy (4)	High Water 1002

Why Not Try My God? (3 and 4)	High Water 1002

Memphis, Nov. 6, 1983
Derrick Jackson (organ on all tracks), Aubrey Williams (bass guitar on all tracks except side 2, track 1), Squire Marshall (bass guitar on side 2, track 1), Alphonzo Davis (background and lead-6), Jimmie Mountain (tenor-7), William Fletcher (drums on all tracks)

I Shall See Him Face to Face (6)	High Water 1004
Old Landmark (2)	High Water 1004

Memphis, Jan. 8, 1984

Call Me (Here I Am) (4 and 7)	High Water 1004
Book of the Seven Seals (1, 5, 6, and 7)	High Water 1004

Memphis, Jan. 17, 1984

I Waited for an Answer (4 and 7)	High Water 1004
I Feel Something Drawing and Pulling Me (4)	High Water 1004
How Great Thou Art (4)	High Water 1004
I'm His, He's Mine (3 and 7)	High Water 1004

Memphis, Mar. 19, 1984

Faith Moves Mountains (2, 4, and 6)	High Water 1004

Rev. Cleophus Robinson

Vocal with unknown piano, organ (organ only-1), drums, and the Spirit Of Memphis (Jethroe Bledsoe, Silas Steele, Wilbur Broadnax, Earl Malone, Robert Reed, Fred Howard-2)
Probably Houston, July 1953

ACA2605	In the Sweet By and By (2)	Peacock 1719 and *Song Bird SBLP240*
ACA2606	When I Can Read my Title Clear (1)	Peacock 1719
ACA2607	He's a Wonder	Peacock 1724
ACA2609	I'm Holding On	Peacock 1724

Probably Houston, Texas, March 1954

Vocal with the Spirit of Memphis (vocal group as last), unknown piano, organ, drums

| ACA2761 | A Charge to Keep I Have | Peacock 1733 |
| ACA2764 | Jesus I Can't Live Without You | Peacock 1733 |

Probably Houston, Texas, April 1955
Willie Jefferson replaces Wilbur Broadnax and Silas Steele.

ACA3123	I Am Determined	Peacock 1741
ACA3125	Going Home to Jesus	Peacock 1741
	I've Got a New Born Soul	Peacock 1758
	Room, Room	Peacock 1758

See the Spirit of Memphis for further recordings by this group. Broadnax's first name is spelled both *Wilbur* and *Willmer*.

Silvertones

Unknown male quartet
Memphis, Apr. 2, 1950

| Beautiful City | Perkins Disc |
| Something within Me | Perkins Disc |

Memphis, circa 1952–54

Good Morning to Heaven	Perkins Disc
My Life Is in God's Hands	Perkins Disc
Something within Me	Perkins Disc
Beautiful City	Perkins Disc
Shadrack	Perkins Disc

Songbirds of the South

Cassietta Baker (lead), Elizabeth Darling (bass), Mary Louise Thomas (tenor), Irma Lee Jefferson (tenor), Elizabeth Darling (piano-1)
Memphis, July 24, 1952

| Ninety Nine and a Half Won't Do | Pea-Vine PLP 9051 and Rounder 2063 |
| Where Could I Go (1) | Pea-Vine PLP 9051 and Rounder 2063 |

Mary Louise Reddick (1st lead), Cassietta Baker (2nd lead), Elizabeth Darling (bass and piano-1); Ernestine Whitehead (tenor)
Memphis, June 20, 1953

| Jesus Met the Woman at the Well | Pea-Vine PLP 9051 and Rounder 2063 |
| He Is Able (1) | Rounder 2063 |

Cassietta Baker is Cassietta George; Mary Louise Thomas and Mary Louise Reddick are presumably the same person.

Sons of Jehovah

Frank Perkins (vocals), others unknown
Memphis, Apr. 10, 1952

Rock My Soul	Perkins Disc

Memphis, Mar. 28, 1956

WDIA Saturday Song	Perkins Disc
Teach Me (Our Prayer)	Perkins Disc

Memphis, Apr. 5, 1957
Add unknown guitar and Brother Rodgers (lead)

He Will Understand	Perkins Disc
You Must Be Born	Perkins Disc

Memphis, circa 1950–58
Unknown instruments and vocalists

If Jesus Holds My Hand, I Believe	Perkins Disc
I'll Go	Perkins Disc
Go and Tell the Reds We're Gonna Win	Perkins Disc

Unknown drums and guitar

On Calvary	Perkins Disc
John the Revelator	Perkins Disc

Unknown guitar

I'm Waiting and Watching	Perkins Disc
On an Island	Perkins Disc
What Could I Do?	Perkins Disc
Something Within	Perkins Disc
I John Saw	Perkins Disc

Unknown drums and guitar

WDIA, Part 2	Perkins Disc

Nashville, 1957–60
Frank Perkins (lead-1), Melvin Rodgers (lead-2), Willie Harrison (bass), Aubrey Lee Smith (baritone), Jessie Macklin (tenor), William Ferris (guitar), unknown piano, bass, and drums on most tracks.

High Cost of Living (1)	Nashboro 610
Teach Me Jesus (2)	Nashboro 610
Keep and Teach Me (1 and 2)	Nashboro 626
The Holy Bible (1)	Nashboro 626
Waiting for Me (1)	Nashboro 645
Jesus Hear My Plea (2)	Nashboro 645
It's Me Lord (2)	Nashboro 669
We Are Blessed (1)	Nashboro 669
A Servant of God (1)	Nashboro 709

Let My People Go (1)	Nashboro 709
Gonna Travel On (1)	Nashboro 737
Our Troubles of Today (1)	Nashboro 737
Judgement Day Is Coming (1)	Nashboro 763
You Gotta Live Right (1)	Nashboro 763
The Story of Noah (1)	Nashboro 792
Left All Alone (1)	Nashboro 792
Pleading for God (1)	Nashboro 817
Story of the Hebrew Children (1)	Nashboro 817

Southern Jubilee Singers

Joe Lee (tenor and lead-1), Dan Taylor (tenor), James Sanders (baritone); Eddie Henderson (bass and lead-2), Lavorne Smith (tenor and lead-3) Memphis, Dec. 19, 1951

Forgive Me Lord (3)	Sun Box 105
He Never Left Me Alone (1)	Sun Box 105
There's a Man in Jerusalem (2)	Sun Box 105 and Charley CR3012
Blessed Be the Name	Sun Box 105 and Sun 1062

Southern Wonders

Rev. Ernest McKinney (lead-1), R. L. Weaver (lead-2), Artis Yancey (bass), Ernest Moore (baritone), James Darling (lead-3), Henry Jack Franklin (tenor), L. T. Blair (guitar), unknown drums (a)
Houston, circa 1952

ACA2170	How Much More Can I Bear? (1)	Peacock 1725
ACA2171	Come on over Here (2)	Peacock 1702
ACA2172	Gambling Man (1 and a)	Peacock 1711
ACA2173	Who Is That Knocking? (1 and 2)	Peacock 1702
ACA2174	There Is No Rest for the Weary (1, 3, and a)	Peacock 1711
ACA2175	Jesus Died for You and Me	Peacock unissued

Memphis, Feb. 17, 1953

Thank You, Jesus (1 and 2)	Pea-Vine PLP 9051 and Rounder 2063
More Like Jesus	WDIA Test

Houston, May 1953

ACA2452	I'll Fly Away (1 and 2)	Peacock 1725

Memphis, Sept. 1, 1953

Anyhow	WDIA Test

	Lord Stand by Me (1 and 2)	Pea-Vine PLP 9051 and Rounder 2063

Houston, June 1955

ACA3164	My Jesus Is All (1, 2, and a)	Peacock 1750
ACA3165	I Was a Sinner (2)	Peacock 1750

Houston, Aug. 1955

ACA3217	The Chapel (2)	Peacock 1751
ACA3218	As an Eagle Stirreth Her Nest (1, 2, and a)	Peacock 1751

Spirit of Memphis Quartet

(Memphis Gospel Singers) Jethroe Bledsoe (lead-1), Silas Steele (lead-2), Earl Malone (bass and lead-3), James Darling (baritone)
Birmingham, Ala., May 1949

Twx-1	Happy in the Service of the Lord	Hallelujah Spiritual Twx-1
Twx-2	How Many Times (1)	Hallelujah Spiritual Twx-2
874	I'm Happy in the Service of the Lord (1)	De Luxe 3221 and *Pea-Vine PLP 9051*
875	My Life Is in His Hands (2)	De Luxe 3221

Memphis, Autumn 1949
Willmer M. Broadnax (tenor and lead-4)

	Joshua Fit the Battle of Jericho (1)	Gospel Jubilee RF-1404
	Mother Gone On (2 and 4)	Gospel Jubilee RF-1404
	Swing Down Chariot (1)	Gospel Jubilee RF-1404
	Freedom (1 and 2)	Gospel Jubilee RF-1404
	Ezekiel Saw the Wheel a 'Rollin' (2)	Gospel Jubilee RF-1404

The above are from a radio station WDIA (Memphis) program.
Cincinnati, Dec. 12, 1949
Wilbur Broadnax (lead-4)

K5812-2	On the Battlefield (1)	King 4358 and *King K-5020*
K4513	Days Passed and Gone (1 and 2)	King 4340 and *King K-5020*
K4514-3	He Never Left Me Alone (2)	King 4371 and *King K-5020*

K5815	Blessed Are the Dead (1)	King 4340 and *Gospel Jubilee RF-1404*
K5816	If Jesus Had to Pray (2 and 4)	King 4371 and *King K-5020*
K5817-2	Jesus, Jesus (2 and 4)	King 4358

Cincinnati, Apr. 1950

K5899-2	I'll Never Forget (1 and 4)	King 4407
K5900-1	Calvary (2 and 4)	King 4392 and *King K-5020*
K5901-2	Make More Room for Jesus (1 and 4)	King 4392

Cincinnati, Dec. 9, 1950
James Keele replaces Earl Malone

K5995-2	Automobile to Glory (1 and 2)	King 4429
K5996	If You Make a Start to Heaven (1, 2, and 4)	King 4440
K5997	God's Got His Eye on You (1 and 2)	King 4440 and *King K-5020*
K5998-2	I'll Go	King 4429 and *King K-5020*

Cincinnati, May 5, 1951
Earl Malone replaces James Keele; unknown organ (a)

K9041-1	Every Day and Every Hour (1 and 4)	King 4463 and *Gospel Jubilee RF-1404*
K9042	Everytime I Feel the Spirit (1, 2, and 4)	King 4471
K9043-1	World Prayer (1, 2, and a)	King 4463 and *Gospel Jubilee RF-1404*
K9044	Sign of Judgement (2)	King 4471 and *King K-5020*

Cincinnati, Aug. 14, 1951
Unknown organ and piano (b)

K9074-1	That Awful Day (1 and 2)	King 4538 and *King K-5020*
K9075	Tell Heaven I'm Coming (1 and 3)	King 4500 and *King K-5020*
K9076-1	Ease My Troubled Mind (1 and 3)	King 4538 and *King K-5020*

K9077	He Never Let Go My Hand (1 and 4)	King 4521 and *King K-5020*
K9078	The Ten Commandments (1, 2, and b)	*King 4500*
K9079	The Atomic Telephone (1 and 2)	*King 4521 and Gospel Jubilee RF-1404*

Cincinnati, Aug. 10, 1952
Fred Howard replaces James Darling

K9160	Toll the Bell Easy (1 and 2)	King 4575 and *King K-5020*
K9161	Jesus Brought Me Here (1 and 2)	King 4562 and *King K-5020*
K9162-1	There's No Sorrow (1)	King 4614 and *Gospel Jubilee RF-1404*
K9163-1	Workin' till the Day Is Done (1)	King 4614 and *King K-5020*
K9164	God's Amazing Grace (1 and 2)	King 4575
K9165	Just to Behold His Face	King 4562 and *King K-5020*

Memphis, Oct. 7, 1952

| K9179-1 | Lord Jesus, Part 1 (1) | King 4576 and *Folklyric 9045* |
| K9180-1 | Lord Jesus, Part 2 (1) | King 4576 and *Folklyric 9045* |

The Spirit of Memphis's King recordings have been reissued many times on the following albums: Audio Lab EP 7, EP 8, EP 9, EP 19, and EP20; King LP 573, LP 577, LP 942, and LP 954; Parlo PMD 1070 and PMD 1085; Polydor 657126; and Vogue V115, V116, V117, V120, V122, V124, and V149. It is so difficult to determine which issues are in print as of November 1994 that all of these issues are listed.

Houston, June 1953
Spirit of Memphis and unknown drums

ACA2374	God Save America (3 and 4)	Peacock 1710
ACA2375	Surely, Surely, Amen (1)	Peacock 1710 *and Gospel Jubilee RF-1404*
ACA2412	Since Jesus Came into My Heart (1)	Peacock 1717

ACA2413   I Will Trust in the Lord (1)   Peacock 1717
ACA2415   What Could I Do?   Peacock 1734
Houston, Feb. 1954
Unknown trombone (c), piano and drums (d)
ACA2711   When Mother's Gone (1 and c)   Peacock 1730
and *Gospel Jubilee RF-1404*   RBF RFS
ACA2756   I'll Tell It (2 and d)   Peacock 1754
ACA2757   He's a Friend of Mine (1, 4, and d)   Peacock 1730
ACA2758   Sweet Hour of Prayer (1 and a)   Peacock 1734
Memphis, circa 1954–55
                  Honey in the Rock   Perkins Disc
                  He Walks with Me   Perkins Disc
                  On Calvary   Perkins Disc
                  I'll Be Satisfied   Perkins Disc
                  Search Me, Lord   Perkins Disc
Houston, June 1955
Willie Jefferson (2) replaces Silas Steele and Wilbur Broadnax; L. T. Blair
(guitar); unknown drums (3)
ACA3128   Home in the Sky (1 and a)   Peacock 1746
ACA3129   Standing by the Bedside (2, 3, and d)*   Peacock 1746
ACA3130   Sinner Make a Change (2 and e)   Peacock 1805
ACA3131   He'll Never Let Me Fall   Peacock 1754
*Piano on this cut may be Napoleon Brown.
Memphis, Feb. 15, 1956
Joe Hinton (lead-5), Fred Howard (baritone and lead-6), Bobby Mack (lead-7)
                  Two Little Fishes and Five Loaves of Bread
                  (1 and 7)   WDIA Test
                  Blessed Are the Poor in Spirit (1)   WDIA Test
Memphis, June 4, 1956
                  Milky White Way (5 and 6)   Pea-Vine PLP
                                                                             9051 and
                                                                             Rounder 2063

                  Yes, He Will (The Lord Will Make a Way)   Rounder 2063
Memphis, late 1956
                  Sending up Material   WDIA Test
                  Walk of Life   WDIA Test
                  I Don't Know Why   WDIA Test
                  Savior, Don't Pass Me By   WDIA Test
Houston, late 1956
ACA3439   I Found Something (1)   Peacock 1769
FR2024   I Need Thee (5)   Peacock 1766
                                                                             and *Gospel*

		Jubilee
		RF-1404
FR2025	Come and Go with me	Peacock 1766
		Peacock 1769
ACA3438	If It Ain't One Thing (It's Another)	Peacock PLP190 and Peacock PLP 140

Houston, circa 1957–58
Bobby Mack (tenor and lead-7) replaces Fred Howard; Joe Johnson replaces L. T. Blair

FR2030	Lost in Sin (5)	Peacock 1766
FR2031	When (5)	Peacock 1779
FR2042	Story of Jesus (2)	Peacock 1779
FR2043	The Lord Loves Me (1 and 5)	Peacock 1785
FR2070	The Great Love (5)	Peacock 1785
FR2071	In the Garden (1)	Peacock 1798
FR2086	It Won't Be Long Now (1 and 3)	Peacock 1805
FR2087	Sinner Make a Change (see ACA3130)	Peacock 1805

Houston, circa 1959–60

FR8010	Doctor Jesus (1)	Peacock 1815
FR8011	'Twill Be Glory (1)	Peacock 1815

Unknown drums added

	Further Up the Road	Peacock 1828
	What Are You Doing in Your Town (1 and 5)	Peacock 1828
	If I Should Miss Heaven (1)	Peacock 1847
	Why? (3)	Peacock 1847 and Peacock PLP109
	Storm of Life (1)	Peacock PLP109
	Take Your Burden to the Lord (1)	Peacock PLP109
	Somebody Here Lord (4 and 7)	Peacock PLP109
	Ease My Troubling Mind (7)	Peacock PLP109
	Singing Won't Be in Vain (1)	Peacock PLP109

Walking with Jesus (1)	Peacock PLP109
Jesus Loves Me (1)	Peacock PLP109

Memphis, circa 1967

LRS 8428 Pay Day (1 and 2)	Peacock 3096
LRS 8429 My Explanation (1 and 2)	Peacock 3096

Houston, circa 1967

William Dixon replaces Joe Johnson; add Brown Berry (electric bass), unknown drummer, and William Walton (second lead-2)

LRS 8496 My Old Home Town (1)	Peacock 3117
LRS 8497 I'm in His Care (1 and 2)	Peacock 3117

Houston, circa 1968

LRS 8590 In the Water (1)	Peacock 3150
LRS 8591 Go Get Water (1)	Peacock 3150
LRS 8651 Christian's Chain Gang (1 and 2)	Peacock 3173
LRS 8652 Voo-doo-ism (1)	Peacock 3173

Memphis, Dec. 8, 1971

Unknown personnel

See What the End Will Do	Home Boy
Swing Down	Home Boy

Memphis, circa early 1970s

Unknown personnel, but presumably with Joe Hinton on lead since the record is billed as Joe Hinton with the Spirit of Memphis

41158-A See What the End Will Be	Gospel Express
41158-B Swing Down	Gospel Express

Nashville, 1972

Fred Howard replaces Bobby Mack; all instruments dropped

40 Long Years	Randy's Spirituals-1025
Jesus Traveled	Randy's Spirituals-1025
Morning Train	Randy's Spirituals-1025
Talking about Jesus	Randy's Spirituals-1025

I,m a Pilgrim	Randy's Spirituals-1025
Swing Down (1)	Randy's Spirituals-1025
Woman at the Well	Randy's Spirituals-1025
You Better Run (1)	Randy's Spirituals-1025
Go Down Moses	Randy's Spirituals-1025

Memphis, circa 1975

You'd Better Run (1)	Gospel Train LP

Memphis, circa 1976
Unknown personnel, presumably similar to above

6-2276-A	America	Gospel Express
6-2276-B	Rest for the Weary	Gospel Express

Memphis, circa 1978
Percy Cole replaces Fred Howard (tenor); add Melvin Mosley (tenor and possibly lead on some selections) and Glenn Carr (drums)

Liar	ABEC ALP 7005
This Is a Mean Old World	ABEC ALP 7005
'Twill the Glory	ABEC ALP 7005
Lord, Count on Me	ABEC ALP 7005
See What the End Gonna Be	ABEC ALP 7005
My Friend	ABEC ALP 7005
I Thank You Lord	ABEC ALP 7005
Who Made the Pattern?	ABEC ALP 7005
There Is No God Like Thee	ABEC ALP 7005
Why?	ABEC ALP 7005

Memphis, May 3, 1983
Jimmie Allen replaces Fred Howard (lead-8); Jack Stepter replaces Earl Malone (lead-9); add Melvin Mosley (tenor and lead-10); Brown Berry dropped

Just to Behold His Face	High Water 1002

Hubert Crawford replaces William Dixon

Swing Down, Chariot (1)	High Water 1002

Memphis, Mar. 16, 1984
Add Clifford Jackson (drums, Earl Malone, Hubert Crawford (lead-11 and
bass guitar-f), and Brown Berry

I Believe in God (10 and f)	High Water 1005
Talking about a Child That)	High Water 1005
Do Love Jesus (9	
I John Saw (10)	High Water 1005

Memphis, Mar. 21, 1984

We Are the Spirit of Memphis	High Water 1005
Quartet (10)	
Only Jesus (11)	High Water 1005
Jesus Traveled (3, 10, and f)	High Water 1005
Go, Get the Water (8)	High Water 1005
Singing Won't Be in Vain (10)	High Water 1005
Walking with Jesus (10)	High Water 1005

Memphis, July 2, 1984

Two Little Fishes and Five Loaves	High Water 1005
of Bread (10)	
The Lord Loves Me (11)	High Water 1005
If It Ain't One Thing, It's Another	High Water 1005
(9 and f)	

Sunset Travelers

Sammy Lee Dortch (lead-1), McKinney Jones (guitar and lead-2),
Sylvester Ward (tenor), Grover Blaker (baritone), Leon Lumpkin
(baritone), Robert Lewis (bass), and Joe Duke (drums)
Houston, Jan. 20, 1953

ACA2385	Wish I Was in Heaven Sitting Down (1)	Duke 204
ACA2387	I Am Building a Home (1)	Duke 204
ACA2389	My Number Will Be Changed (2)	Duke 201
ACA2390	Yes, Yes I've Done My Duty (1 and 2)	Duke 201

Memphis, May 16, 1957
O. V. Wright replaces Sammy Lee Dortch and McKinney Jones; Junior
Thompson replaces Robert Lewis; add Tommy Tucker (tenor) and
Sylvester McKinney (guitar)

Sit Down and Rest a Little While	Pea-Vine PLP
	9051 and
	Rounder 2063

Probably Houston, circa 1963
O. V. Wright (lead-1), unknown guitar and drums (2)

Lazarus (1)	Peacock 1816
Move These Things	Peacock 1816

FR8045	Couldn't Hear Nobody Pray (2)	Peacock 1848
FR8046	You Are Blessed (1 and 2)	Peacock 1848
UV8181	Nobody Knows (the trouble I see) (1 and 2)	Peacock 1888
UV8182	Glory Is Coming (1 and 2)	Peacock 1888
	Blind Bartemaeus [sic] (1)	Peacock 3014
	There's a Change in Me	Peacock 3014

Houston, circa 1964

Add Johnny Frierson (tenor), Robert Lewis (bass), Rev. Jeff Brown (lead-3), Daniel Scott (vocals), with Johnny Frierson (guitar), unknown organ, bass, and drums, unknown piano (4) replaces organ

UV8302	On Jesus' Program (1)	Peacock PLP122, 3039
UV8303	Another Day Lost (1 and 2)	Peacock PLP122, 3089
UV8382	Wonderful Jesus (2 and 3)	Peacock PLP122, 3074
UV8383	Hide Me in Your Bosom (4)	Peacock PLP122, 3074
	I Made It Over (4)	Peacock PLP122
	Looking for a Better Place (4)	Peacock PLP122
	What Do You Think About Jesus (4)	Peacock PLP122
	Have You Ever Been Touched	Peacock PLP122
	When Jesus Comes	Peacock PLP122
	My Trouble Is Hard (4)	Peacock PLP122
	You'll Never Know -1	—
	Ain't That Good News	—

Probably Houston, circa 1968

O. V. Wright is lead on the first two tracks only and may not be present on the rest of PLP122; an alternate take of UV8302 is used on PLP122; UV8303 as "Another Day" is on Peacock 3039; and UV8383 as "Hide Me" is on Peacock 3074.

Presumably as above

| | Victory | Peacock 3141 |
| | I Won't Be Back | Peacock 3141 |

Selected Gospel Quartet Audiography

These recordings contain some of the best performances by African-American sacred quartets ever to be captured by microphones and released to the general public. With the exception of the releases on Gospel Jubilee, which were issued as long-play albums only, most of them are available as compact discs or on cassette, and nearly all of them were "in print" as of January 1994. Most of these releases consist of commercial recordings that were first issued on 78-rpm discs in the 1920s through the 1950s, and have been gathered together, reformatted, and reissued for a contemporary (and largely white) audience. These are noted with an "R" (for reissue). A handful of the following releases are more recent recordings, which are marked with a "C" (for contemporary). They all contain liner notes, though some also include more extensive, separately printed booklets with photographs.

Individuals or Groups

Broadnax, Willmer. "So Many Years." Gospel Jubilee RF-1403. (R)
Charioteers. "Jesus Is a Rock in the Weary Land." Gospel Jubilee 1407. (R)
Dixie Hummingbirds. "Dixie Hummingbirds." Gospel Heritage HT 318. (R)
———. "In the Storm Too Long." Gospel Jubilee 1405. (R)
Dixieaires. "Dixieaires: Let Me Fly." Gospel Heritage HT 317. (R)
Fairfield Four. "The Harmonizing Four" and "God Will Take Care of You." Vee-Jay NVG2-604. (R)
———. "Standing in the Safety Zone." Warner 9 26945-2. (C)
———. "Standing on the Rock." Ace CDCHD 449. (R)
Five Blind Boys of Alabama. "Deep River." Elektra Nonesuch 61441-2. (C)
———. "The Five Blind Boys of Alabama." Gospel Heritage HT 315. (R)

———. "Oh Lord, Stand By Me" and "Marching Up to Zion." Ace CDCDH 341. (R)

———. "The Sermon." Ace CDCHD 479. (R)

Five Blind Boys of Mississippi. "The Great Lost Blind Boys Album." Vee-Jay NVG2-601. (R)

———. "The Original Blind Boys of Mississippi." Vee Jay D1-74785. (R)

———. "You Done What the Doctor Couldn't Do." Gospel Jubilee RF 1402. (R)

Four Eagle Gospel Singers. "Traditional Gospel Quartet Singing from Alabama." Global Village Cassette C 227. (C)

The Four Interns. "I'm Troubled." Gospel Jubilee RF-1400. (R)

Golden Gate Quartet. "Swing Down, Chariot." CBS/Sony. (R)

———. "Travelin' Shoes." RCA 66063-2. (R)

Gospel Christian Singers of Charlotte, North Carolina. "A Capella Since 1929." Global Village C212. (C)

Gospel Harmonettes. "Gospel Harmonettes of Demopolis." Global Village.

Harmonizing Four (of Richmond). "The Harmonizing Four" and "God Will Take Care of You." Vee-Jay NVG2-604. (R)

Heavenly Gospel Singers. "Heavenly Gospel Singers." Heritage HT 305. (R)

Highway QCs. "The Highway QC's." Vee Jay D1-24800. (R)

———. "Jesus Is Waiting." Vee Jay NVG2-603. (R)

Norfolk Jubilee Quartet. "Norfolk Jubilee Quartet 1927–1938." Heritage HT 310. (R)

Paramount Singers. "Work and Pray On." Arhoolie CD 382. (C)

Pilgrim Travelers. "The Best Of." ACE CDCHD 342. (R)

———. "Stand Up and Testify! 14 Songs of Soul and Inspiration from Gospel's Heavenly Stars." Solid Smoke 8034. (R)

———. "Walking Rhythm." Specialty SPCD 7030-2. (R)

Radio Four. "There's Gonna Be Joy." Ace CDCHD 448. (R)

Soul Stirrers. "Heaven Is My Home." Specialty CDCHD 478. (R)

———. "In the Beginning." Ace CHD 280. (R)

———. "Jesus Gave Me Water." Specialty SPCD 7031-2. (R)

Southern Sons. "Deep South Gospel." Alligator ALCD 2802. (R)

———. "When They Ring Them Golden Bells." Gospel Jubilee 1406. (R)

Spirit of Memphis. "When Mother's Gone." Gospel Jubilee 1404. (R)

Swan Silvertones. "Heavenly Light." Ace CDCHD 482. (R)

———. "My Rock"/"Love Lifted Me." Ace CDCHD 340. (R)

———. "Pray for Me"/"Let's Go to Church Together." Vee-Jay NVG2-602. (R)

Trumpeteers. "Milky White Way." Gospel Jubilee 1401. (R)

Zion Harmonizers. "You Don't Have to Get in Trouble." Flying Fish 002. (C)

Anthologies

"A Cappella Gospel Singing." Folklyric Records 9045. (R)

"All of My Appointed Time: Forty Years of A Cappella Gospel." Stash St
114. (R)

"The Assassination." Zu-Zazz ZCD 2019. (R)

"Atlanta Gospel." Gospel Heritage HT 312. (R)

"Amazing Grace—Gotham Gospel." Krazy Kat KK 836. (R)

"Birmingham Quartet Anthology: Jefferson County Alabama (1926–1956)."
Clanka Lanka CL 144, 001. (R)

"Bless My Bones: Memphis Gospel Radio—1950s." Rounder 6032. (R)

"Cleveland Gospel." Gospel Heritage HT 316. (R)

"Earliest Negro Vocal Quartets (1894–1928)." Document-5061. (R)

"The Early Negro Quartets Vol. 1 (1902–1928)." Document DLP 583. (R)

"Fathers and Sons." Spirit Feel 1001. (R)

"The Golden Age of Gospel Singing." Folklyric 9046. (R)

"Gotham Gospel Vol. One." Krazy Kat KK 812. (R)

"Gotham Gospel Vol. Two." Krazy Kat KK 825. (R)

"I Hear Music in the Air." RCA 2099-2-R. (R)

"Newark Gospel Quartets." Gospel Heritage HT 324. (R)

"New Orleans Gospel Quartets, 1947–1956." Heritage HT 306. (R)

"New York Grassroots Gospel—The Sacred Black Quartet Tradition."
Global Village Music GVM-206. (C)

"Religious Recordings from Black New Orleans 1924–1931." 504 LP 20. (R)

"San Francisco Bay Gospel." Gospel Heritage HT 314. (R)

Sources and Resources

This book is largely shaped by interviews and oral histories conducted with quartet singers and other members of the Memphis quartet community. Of secondary importance to these primary sources is the slim corpus of written material related to black American gospel quartets, most of which has been published by Lynn Abbott, Ray Funk, and Doug Seroff. None of these researchers has any academic affiliations or advanced scholarly training in folklore, ethnomusicology, anthropology, or oral history, which is not unusual in the field of American vernacular music. A strong orientation toward historical, biographical, and discographical information places them in the mainstream of writers who have contributed significantly to our knowledge and understanding of blues, rock 'n' roll, and jazz.

These researchers have written largely for popular and "fan" journals such as *Whiskey, Women and . . . , Goldmine,* and *Blues Unlimited,* or brochure notes for long-playing records. Such "amateur" journal articles and "commercial" album productions might discourage the less adventuresome academic scholars from taking their work seriously. However, their publications generally include substantial, groundbreaking research taken from a large body of previously unexplored primary material gleaned from newspaper files, interviews, photographs, college yearbooks, and archives. And their work is finally gaining some of the recognition it deserves. Two of Seroff's brochure notes, "Birmingham Quartet Anthology: Jefferson County, Alabama (1926–1953)" and "The Human Orchestra," were nominated for Grammy Awards in 1982 and 1985, respectively. The most intensive, least recognized single work is Abbott's monograph on New Orleans's Siprocco Singers, published by the National Park Service. Most recently Ray Funk had been annotating and producing a well-received, groundbreaking series of gospel quartet anthologies for an English label, Heritage.

Viv Broughton's 1985 book, *Black Gospel: An Illustrated History of the Gospel Sound,* nicely complements Tony Heilbut's groundbreaking 1971 study, *The Gospel Sound: Good News and Bad Times.* Both offer a popular history of the genre and contain many references and substantial information related to quartets. One major drawback of their work is an obsessive orientation toward the most commercially successful quartets, which badly understates the role of the nonprofessional community groups. Furthermore, neither author footnotes specific references and quotes, an annoying limitation endemic to books aimed at a mass audience.

Three academic writers—George Ricks, Charles Cobb, and Kerill Rubman—have also discussed some aspect of this genre. Ricks's transcription and analyses of several quartet selections appeared in his 1958 dissertation, *Some Aspects of the Religious Music of the United States Negro: An Ethnomusicological Study with Special Emphasis on the Gospel Tradition.* His research is noteworthy for its quality and because it is the first book-length study by a black music scholar to critically examine contemporary Afro-American religious music.

In 1974 Charles Cobb completed a master's thesis in music, "A Theoretical Analysis of Black American Quartet Gospel Music," which notates the harmonic progressions found on commercial recordings of five popular quartets from the 1950s—the Dixie Hummingbirds, the Mighty Clouds of Joy, the Sensational Nightingales, the Soul Stirrers, and the Swan Silvertone Singers. Despite Cobb's excessive thoroughness—nearly 600 pages of analysis are included—his work is of minor importance: his principal conclusion is that the progressions used by these performers are highly repetitive.

Kerill Rubman's 1980 folklore master's thesis, "From 'Jubilee' to 'Gospel' in Black Male Quartet Singing," is a historical survey covering the years 1880 to 1960. Its simultaneous value and limitation lies in the scope of the research, which is almost too broad. But the real strengths of this work are the interviews Rubman conducted with several important quartet singers and her ability to encapsulate large amounts of information.

Even with these publications, a paucity of primary and secondary information haunts this book, particulary in chapter 1. The research available today makes it impossible to construct an accurate, comprehensive historical survey of Afro-American gospel quartets. A massive, complex, and challenging task awaits anyone attempting such a study, though Rubman and Seroff have made a strong start.

A notable lack of primary sources also hampered my research in Memphis and is typified by the information gathered from the local black-oriented newspapers—the *Memphis World* and the *Tri-State Defender*. I examined the available issues of these papers from 1931, when the *Memphis World* began publication, until 1960, the dusk of the quartets' popularity. It was a fruitful yet frustrating search that yielded many minor facts, some program announcements, and a few grainy photographs. I also discovered, much to my astonishment, that no library or archive in the United States owns a complete run of the *Memphis World* and that very few issues from 1931 through 1943 have been preserved. Because the *Tri-State Defender* did not begin its weekly publication until 1951, a critical information gap exists.

The lack of printed sources within the black community's press makes it impossible, for instance, to pinpoint specific information regarding the broadcasting activity of quartets during the 1930s. Radio station logs from this period were disposed of decades ago, and the two daily newspapers, the *Commercial Appeal* and the *Press Scimitar*, did not carry regular radio listings for black groups. For that matter, neither of the white newspapers published very many stories about black religious music.

Nor is the recording activity of local quartets easy to document, particularly in recent years when the groups tended to work with small, Memphis-based companies. Style Wooten's Designer label and the Fernwood Record Company are almost impossible to detail because they are so ephemeral. Such labels issued relatively few discs and operated from as many as three different addresses over a five-year period. None of these companies kept accurate files or logs for their sessions, which means that compiling a comprehensive discography of Memphis quartets is a task that lies somewhere between an inexact science and detective work.

Photographs proved to be one helpful primary source. I located nearly one hundred prints that represent a visual portrait of Memphis's black gospel quartets from 1937 to the present. These photographs came primarily from individuals—most important were those from Mrs. Essie Wade, Cleo Satterfield, Jack Franklin, and Jethroe Bledsoe. Photographs, along with other related paper material such as posters, handbills, and programs, were useful in piecing together the history of Memphis quartets because they provided a visual, tangible link to the past.

But the paramount sources for primary information were still the personal experiences and life stories of the singers, which were supplemented by information gleaned from written sources like the city directory and newspaper accounts. The sources described in this essay underscore the research limitations unique to this study and help to explain how *"Happy in the Service of the Lord"* was shaped and why certain historical, cultural, and discographical facets of quartet singing are not examined as thoroughly as they deserve to be.

Interviews

Except for the interviews with Grover Blake (February 1, 1981), Earl Malone (August 5, 1979), Nathanial Peck (April 28, 1981), Nina Jai Daugherty (May 7 and 12, 1981), and Julia Anderson Todd and Tommie Todd (February 1, 1981), which were conducted by Doug Seroff; with Earl Malone (October 11, 1980), which was conducted by Doug Seroff and Brenda MacCallum; with Jethroe Bledsoe (January 31, 1981), Nathanial Peck (January 31, 1981), and Mary L. Thomas and Doris Jean Gary (February 3, 1983), which were conducted by Doug Seroff and Kip Lornell; and with Jack Miller (June 6, 1979), which was conducted by David Evans, all of the following interviews were conducted by Kip Lornell in Memphis, Tennessee. Transcripts and copies of these taped interviews are deposited at the Mississippi Valley Collection, Brister Library, Memphis State University.

Anderson, Clara, April 18, 1982

Beans, Etherlene, July 3, 1982

Blake, Grover, July 10, 1982

Bledsoe, Jethroe, January 31, 1981

Bledsoe, Jethroe and Shirley, May 21, 1982

Clark, David, February 25, 1982 (Jackson, Mississippi)

Darling, James, July 21, 1982; August 2, 1983

Daugherty, Nina Jai, May 7 and 12, 1981; August 4, 1982

Davis, Mary, May 10, 1982

Franklin, Jack, May 21, 1980; May 31, 1981

Gaines, Haywood, June 24, 1982

Gary, Doris Jean, February 3, 1983

Gordon, Willie, April 14, 1981

Harvey, James, June 19, 1982

Jones, Elijah, October 1979

Kelley, Andrew, May 9, 1982

Leland, Flozell, June 14, 1982

Malone, Earl, August 5, 1979; October 11, 1980

Miller, Frank, August 8, 1982
Miller, Jack, June 6, 1979; February 1980
Moody, Leon, February 8, 1981
Moore, Ernest, May 31, 1982
Moore, Huddie, February 2, 1983
Neal, Willie, April 14, 1981
Nelson, Ford, June 2, 1981
Peck, Nathanial, January 31, 1981; April 28, 1981
Readers, Julius, May 28, 1982
Rodgers, Will, June 9, 1982
Rooks, George, April 27, 1982
Royston, Robert, April 21, 1982
Ruffin, Elijah, March 2, 1981

Satterfield, Cleo, June 7, 1982
Satterfield, Louis, May 29, 1982
Savage, Avery, March 22, 1982
Shells, James, May 5, 1982
Thomas, Mary, February 3, 1983
Todd, Julia and Tommie, February 1, 1981
Todd, Tommie, August 11, 1982
Wade, Theo, October 1979
Walton, Eugene, March 1980; February 2, 1982
Wiley, Floyd, March 15, 1982
Winfield, Harry, July 7, 1982
Wooten, Style, July 17, 1982

Bibliography

Abbott, Lynn. "Black Gospel & Barbershop Quartets," *American Music,* 10 (Fall 1992), pp. 289–326.

———. Liner notes, New Orleans Gospel Quartets 1947–1956, Heritage HT 306.

———. "The New Orleans Humming Four," *Whiskey, Women, and . . . ,* 13 (1984), pp. 4–8.

———. "The Soproco Spiritual Singers: A New Orleans Quartet Family Tree" (New Orleans: National Park Service, 1983).

Allen, Raymond. "Old-Time Music and the Urban Folk Revival" (M.A. thesis, Western Kentucky University, 1980).

———. "Old-Time Music and the Urban Folk Revival," *New York Folklore Quarterly,* 7 (1981), pp. 65–81.

———. *"Singing in the Spirit": African-American Sacred Quartets in New York City*. Philadelphia: University of Pennsylvania Press, 1992.

———. "'Singing in the Spirit': An Ethnography of Gospel Performance in New York City's African American Church Community" (Ph.D. dissertation, University of Pennsylvania, 1987).

Allen, William Charles Ware, and Lucy McKim Garrison. *Slaves Songs of the United States*. New York: Oak Publications, 1965 (originally published in 1867).

Baker, Barbara Wesley. "Black Gospel Music Styles, 1942–1975: Analysis and Interpretation for Music Education" (Ph.D. dissertation, University of Maryland, 1978).

Bechtol, Paul. "Migration and Economic Opportunities in Tennessee Counties" (Ph.D. dissertation, Vanderbilt University, 1962).

Ben-Amos, Dan. "Towards a Definition of Folklore in Context," *Journal of American Folklore,* 84 (1971), pp. 3–15.

Boyd, Joe Dan. "Judge Jackson: Black Giant of White Spirituals," *Mississippi Folklore Register,* 4 (1970), pp. 7-11.

Boyer, Horace. "An Analysis of Black Church Music with Examples Drawn from Services in Rochester, New York" (Ph.D. dissertation, University of Rochester, Eastman School of Music, 1973).

———. "Charles Albert Tindley: Progenitor of Afro-American Gospel Music," *The Black Perspective in Music,* 11 (no. 2, 1981), pp. 103-33.

———. "A Comparative Analysis of Traditional and Contemporary Gospel Music," in *More Than Dancing: Essays on Afro-American Music and Musicians,* ed. Irene Jackson. Westport, Conn.: Greenwood Press, 1985, pp. 127-47.

———. "Contemporary Gospel," *The Black Perspective in Music,* 7 (no. 1, 1979), pp. 5-59.

———. "Gospel Music," *Music Educators Journal,* 64 (1978), pp. 34-43.

———. "The Gospel Song: A Historical and Analytical Survey" (M.A. thesis, University of Rochester, Eastman School of Music, 1964.)

Bremer, Frederika. *The Homes of the New World: Impressions of America.* New York: Harper and Brothers, 1853. Quoted in Dena Epstein, *Sinful Tunes and Spirituals.* Urbana: University of Illinois Press, 1977, p. 164.

Broughton, Viv. *Black Gospel: An illustrated History of the Gospel Sound.* Dorset, England: Blandford Press, 1985.

Buchanan, Samuel Carroll. "A Critical Analysis of Style in Four Black Jubilee Quartets in the United States" (Ph.D. dissertation, New York University, 1987).

Burnim, Mellonee. "The Black Gospel Music Tradition: A Complex of Ideology, Aesthetic, and Behavior," in *More Than Dancing: Essays on Afro-American Music and Musicians,* ed. Irene Jackson. Westport, Conn.: Greenwood Press, 1985, pp. 148-69.

———. "The Black Gospel Music Tradition: A Symbol of Ethnicity" (Ph.D. dissertation, Indiana University, 1980).

———. "Cultural Bearer and Tradition Bearer: An Ethnomusicologist's Research on Gospel Music," *Ethnomusicology,* 29 (Fall 1985), pp. 432-47.

———. "Functional Dimensions of Gospel Music Performance," *Western Journal of Black Studies,* 12 (no. 2, 1988) pp. 112-21.

———. "The Performance of Black Gospel Music as Transformation," *Concilium: International Review of Theology,* 2 (March/April 1989) pp. 52-61.

Byrd, Walter. "The Shape-Note Singing Convention as a Musical Institution in Alabama" (M.A. thesis, University of Alabama, 1962).

Cantor, Louis. *Wheelin' on Beale.* New York City, Pharos Books, 1992.

Carney, George O., ed. *The Sounds of People and Places: Readings in the Geography of American Folk and Popular Music.* 3rd ed. Lanham, Md.: Rowman & Littlefield, 1994.

Cobb, Charles. "A Theoretical Analysis of Black American Quartet Gospel Music" (M.A. thesis, University of Wisconsin, 1974).

Courlander, Harold. *Negro Music U.S.A.* New York: Columbia University Press, 1963.

Dargin, William. "Congregational Gospel" (Ph.D. dissertation, Wesleyan University, 1983).

Davis, George, and Fred Donaldson. *Blacks in the United States: A Geographic Perspective.* Boston: Houghton Mifflin, 1975.

Davis, Hank. "Sun's Jones Brothers," *Whiskey, Women, and . . . ,* 16 (Spring 1987), pp. 16, 17.

Densmore, Frances. *Chippewa Music.* Washington, D.C.: Smithsonian Institution, 1910.

———. *Nootka and Quileute Music.* Washington, D.C.: Smithsonian Institution, 1939.

Dje Dje, Jacqueline. *American Black Spiritual and Gospel Songs from Southeast Georgia: A Comparative Study.* Los Angeles: University of California Center for Afro-American Studies, 1978.

———. "Change and Differentiation: The Adoption of Black Gospel Music in the Catholic Church," *Ethnomusicology,* 30 (Spring/Summer 1986), pp. 223-52.

Dorson, Richard. *Folklore and Folklife.* Chicago: University of Chicago Press, 1972.

Dupree, Sherry, and Herbert C. *African American Good News (Gospel) Music.* Washington, D.C.: Middle Atlantic Regional Press, 1992.

Dyen, Doris. "The Role of Black Shape-Note Music in the Musical Culture of Black Communities in Southeast Alabama" (Ph.D. dissertation, University of Illinois, 1977).

Escott, Colin, with Martin Hawkins. *Good Rockin' Tonight: Sun Records and the Birth of Rock 'N' Roll.* New York. St. Martins Press, 1991.

Evans, David. *Big Road Blues: Tradition and Creativity in the Folk Blues.* Berkeley: University of California Press, 1982.

———. Liner notes, Let's Get Loose, New World Records NW 290.

———. "The Roots of Afro-American Gospel Music," *Jazzforschung,* 8 (1976), pp. 119-35.

Feintuck, Burt. "A Noncommercial Black Gospel Group in Context: We Live the Life We Sing About," *Black Music Research Journal,* 1 (1980) pp. 37-50.

Ferris, William, *Blues from the Delta.* New York: Doubleday, 1979.

Foreman, Ronald. "Jazz and Race Records, 1920-1932" (Ph.D. dissertation, University of Illinois, 1968).

Foster, George. "What Is Folk Culture?" *American Anthropologist,* 55 (1953), pp. 159-73.

Franklin, Marion Joseph. "The Relationship of Black Preaching to Black Gospel Music" (Ph.D. dissertation, Drew University, 1982).

Funk, Ray. "The Imperial Quintet," *Blues and Rhythm—The Gospel Truth,* 9 (1985), pp. 4, 5.

———. Liner notes, "A Capella Gospel Singing," Folklyric Records 9045.

———. Liner notes, "Atlanta Gospel," Heritage HT 312.

———. Liner notes, "Cleveland Gospel," Heritage HT 316.

———. Liner notes, "Detroit Gospel," Heritage HT 311.

———. Liner notes, "Dixieaires: Let Me Fly," Heritage HT 317.

———. Liner notes, "The Five Blind Boys of Alabama," Heritage HT 315.

———. Liner notes, "Get Right with the Swan Silvertones," Rhino Records.

———. Liner notes, "Golden Age of Gospel Singing," Folklyric Records 9046.

———. Liner notes, "Little Axe: So Many Years," Gospel Jubilee Records 1403.

———. Liner notes, "Norfolk Jubilee Quartet 1927/1938," Heritage HT 310.

———. Liner notes, "The Pilgrim Travelers," Solid Smoke Records 8034.

Gardner, Judith, and Richard McMann. "Culture, Community, and Identity: Working Definition," in *Culture, Community, and Identity,* ed. Judith Garner and Richard McMann. Detroit: Wayne State University Press, 1976, pp. 11-12.

Godrich, John, and Robert M. W. Dixon. *Blues and Gospel Records 1902-1943,* 3d ed. Essex, England: Storyville Publications, 1982.

Grendysa, Pete. "The Golden Gate Quartet," *Record Exchanger,* 5 (1976), pp. 5-9.

———. "Harry Douglas and the Deep River Boys," *Goldmine,* July 1979, pp. 6-11.

———. "Lee Gaines—Singing Low for the Delta Rhythm Boys," *Goldmine,* March 1979, pp. 10-23.

Harris, Michael W. *The Rise of Gospel Blues: The Music of Thomas Andrew Dorsey in the Urban Church.* New York: Oxford University Press, 1992.

Hayes, Cedric, and Robert Laughton. *Gospel Records, 1943-1969: A Black Music Discography.* London: Record Information Services, 1992.

Heilbut, Tony. *The Gospel Sound: Good News and Bad Times,* 2d ed. New York: Simon and Schuster, 1985.

Herzog, George. "The Yuman Music Style," *Journal of American Folklore,* 41 (1928), pp. 183-231.

Hood, Mantle. *The Ethnomusicologist,* 2d ed. Kent, Ohio: Kent State University Press, 1984.

Jackson, Irene V. "Afro-American Gospel Music and Its Social Settings with Special Attention to Roberta Martin" (Ph.D. dissertation, Wesleyan University, 1974).

——. *Afro-American Religious Music: A Bibliography and a Catalogue of Gospel Music.* Westport, Conn.: Greenwood Press, 1979.

——., ed. *More Than Dancing: Essays on Afro-American Music and Musicians.* Westport, Conn.: Greenwood Press, 1985.

Jackson, Joyce. "The Performing Black Sacred Quartet: An Expression of Cultural Values and Aesthetics" (Ph.D. Dissertation, Indiana University, 1988).

Johnson, James Weldon. "The Origins of the 'Barber Chord,'" *The Mentor,* February 1929, p. 53.

Jones, A. M. *Studies in African Music.* London: Oxford University Press, 1959.

Jones, Ralph H. *Charles Albert Tindley: Prince of Preachers.* Nashville: Abingdon Press, 1982.

Kubik, Gerhard. *The Kachamba Brothers Band: A Study of Neo-Traditional Music in Malawi.* Manchester, England: University of Manchester Press, 1974.

Levine, Lawrence. *Black Culture and Black Consciousness.* New York: Oxford University Press, 1977.

Lomax, Alan. *Cantometrics.* Berkeley: University of California Press, 1976.

——. *Folk Song Style and Culture.* Washington, D.C.: American Association for the Advancement of Science, 1968.

Lornell, Kip. "Afro-American Gospel Quartets: An Annotated Bibliography and LP Discography of Pre-War Recordings," *John Edwards Memorial Foundation Quarterly,* 61 (1981), pp. 19–24.

——. "Banjos and Blues," in *Arts in Earnest: North Carolina Folklife,* ed. Daniel W. Patterson and Charles G. Zug III. Durham, N.C.: Duke University Press, 1990.

——. Brochure notes, Happy in the Service of the Lord: Memphis Quartet Heritage—The 1980s, High Water Records 1002.

——. Brochure notes, Tidewater Blues, Blue Ridge Institute Records BRI 006, p. 6.

——. "The Geography of American Music: Diffusion, Migration, and Sense of Place," *Current Musicology,* 37/8 (1984), pp. 127–35.

——. "Spatial Perspectives on the Field Recording of Traditional American Music: A Case Study from Tennessee in 1928," in *The Sounds of People and Places: Readings in the Geography of American Folk and Popular Music,* ed. George Carney. Lanham, MD: Rowman & Littlefield, 1994, pp. 128-37.

Lovell, John. *Black Song: The Forge and the Flame*. New York: Macmillan, 1972.

Mapson, Jesse Wendell. "Some Guidelines for the Use of Music in the Black Church" (Ph.D. dissertation, Eastern Baptist Theological Seminary, 1983).

Marks, Morton. "Uncovering Ritual Structure in Afro-American Music," in *Religious Movements in Contemporary America,* ed. Irving Zaretsky and Mark Leone. Princeton, N.J.: Princeton University Press, 1974, pp. 60-134.

Marsh, J. B. T. *The Story of the Jubilee Singers*. Cleveland: Cleveland Printing and Publishing, n.d.

Martin, Deac. *Book of Musical America*. New York: Prentice-Hall, 1970.

———. "The Evolution of Barbershop Harmony," *Music Journal Annual,* 23 (1965), pp. 24, 106.

Martinsdale, Donald. *Social Life and Cultural Change*. New York: Van Nostrand, 1962.

Maultsby, Portia. *Afro-American Religious Music: A Study in Musical Diversity*. Springfield, Ohio: The Hymn Society of America—Wittenberg University, 1986.

———. Review of Jubilee to Gospel: A Selection of Commercially Recorded Black Religious Music, 1921-1953, JEMF-108, in *Ethnomusicology,* 27 (1983), pp. 162-63.

———. "The Use and Performance of Hymnody, Spirituals, and Gospels in the Black Church," *The Journal of Interdenominational Theological Center,* 19 (Fall 1986/Spring 1987), pp. 141-59.

McCallum, Brenda, and Ray Funk. Brochure notes, *Birmingham Boys— Jubilee Quartets from Jefferson County, Alabama,* Alabama Traditions. LP 101.

Merriam, Alan. "African Music," in *Continuity and Change in African Cultures,* ed. William Bascom and Melville Herskovits. Chicago: University of Chicago Press, 1959, pp. 49-86.

———. *The Anthropology of Music*. Evanston, Ill.: Northwestern University Press, 1966.

———., and Raymond Mack. "The Jazz Community," *Social Forces,* 38 (1960), pp. 200-219.

Moonoogian, George, and Roger Meeden. "Duke Records—The Early Years: An Interview with David J. Mattis," *Whiskey, Women and . . . ,* 14 (June 1983), pp. 14-18.

Oliver, Paul. "Black Gospel Music," in *New Grove Dictionary of Music and Musicians,* vol. 7, ed. Stanley Sadie. London: Macmillan, 1980, pp. 254-59.

———. *Story of the Blues*. Philadelphia: Chilton Book, 1969.

Raichelson, Richard. "Black Religious Folksong: A Study in Generic and Social Change" (Ph.D. dissertation, University of Pennsylvania, 1975).

Reagon, Bernice Johnson, ed. *We'll Understand It By and By: Pioneering African American Gospel Composers.* Washington, D.C.: Smithsonian Institution Press, 1992.

Redd, Lawrence. *Rock Is Rhythm and Blues.* East Lansing: Michigan State University Press, 1974.

Ricks, George. *Some Aspects of the Religious Music of the United States Negro: An Ethnomusicological Study with Special Emphasis on the Gospel Tradition.* New York: Arno Press, 1970.

Riis, Thomas. "Black Musical Theater in New York, 1890-1915" (Ph.D. dissertation, University of Michigan, 1981).

Roberts, Helen. *Musical Areas in Aboriginal North America.* New Haven: Yale University Publications in Anthropology, 1936.

Rubman, Kerill. "From 'Jubilee' to 'Gospel' in Black Male Quartet Singing" (M.A. thesis, University of North Carolina, 1980).

Rust, Brian. *Jazz Records 1897-1942.* New Rochelle, N.Y.: Arlington House, 1978.

Sachs, Curt. *Geist und Werden der Musikinstrumente.* Berlin: J. Ard, 1929.

Schaefer, William, and Johannes Reidel. *The Art of Ragtime.* Baton Rouge: Louisiana State University Press, 1973.

Seroff, Doug. Brochure notes, "Birmingham Quartet Anthology" (Clanka Lanka Records CL 144, 1980).

———. Brochure notes, "Bless My Bones": Memphis Gospel Radio—The 1950s, Pea-Vine PLP 9051.

———. "Gospel Arts Day," Nashville: Fisk University, 1988.

———. "Gospel Arts Day," Nashville: Fisk University, 1989.

———. "On the Battlefield," in *Repercussions,* ed. Geoffrey Haydon and Dennis Marks. London: Century Publishing, 1985, pp. 30-54.

———. "Polk Miller and the Old South Quartette," *John Edwards Memorial Foundation Quarterly,* 18 (1982), pp. 147-50.

———. "Sing Me That Song Again: An Interview with Lewis Herring," *Blues Unlimited,* 139 (1980), pp. 24-26.

Simond, Ike. *Old Slack's Reminiscences and Pocket History of the Colored Profession from 1865 to 1891.* Chicago: by the author, 1891.

Southern, Eileen. "Lucie Eddie Campbell," in *Biographical Dictionary of Afro-American and African Music.* Westport, Conn.: Greenwood Press, 1982, p. 51.

———. *The Music of Black America,* 2d ed. New York: W. W. Norton, 1983.

———. "W. Herbert Brewster," in *Biographical Dictionary of Afro-American and African Music*. Westport, Conn.: Greenwood Press, 1982, p. 47.

Schwerin, Jules. *Got to Tell It—Mahalia Jackson, Queen of Gospel*. New York: Oxford University Press, 1992.

Stebbins, Robert. "The Jazz Community: The Sociology of a Musical Sub-Culture" (Ph.D. dissertation, University of Minnesota, 1964).

———. "A Theory of the Jazz Community," in *American Music: From Storyville to Woodstock,* ed. Charles Nanry. New Brunswick, N.J.: Transactional Books, 1972, pp. 115–34.

Tallmadge, William. Brochure notes, Jubilee to Gospel: A Selection of Commercially Recorded Black Religious Music 1921–1953, JEMF-108.

Titon, Jeff. *Downhome Blues Lyrics*. Boston: G. K. Hall, 1982.

———. *Early Downhome Blues: A Musical and Cultural Analysis*. Urbana: University of Illinois Press, 1977.

Toll, Robert. *Blacking Up: The Minstrel Show in Nineteenth-Century America*. New York: Oxford University Press, 1974.

Tyler, Mary Ann Lancaster. "The Music of Charles Henry Pace and Its Relationship to the Afro-American Church Experience" (Ph.D. dissertation, University of Pittsburgh, 1980).

Walker, Wyatt Tee. "Somebody's Calling My Name": *Black Sacred Music and Social Change*. Valley Forge, Pa.: Judson Press, 1979.

Williams-Jones, Pearl. "Afro-American Gospel Music: A Crystallization of the Black Aesthetic," *Ethnomusicology,* 19 (September 1975), pp. 373–85.

Wittke, Carl. *Tambo and Bones*. Durham, N.C.: Duke University Press, 1930.

Work, John. "Plantation Meistersinger," *Musical Quarterly,* 39 (1941), pp. 41–49.

Index

Abbott, Lynn, xi, xvii, xix, 7, 9, 15–16, 29
African-American flexible sense of time, 159–62
Alabama and Georgia Quartet, 37
Allen, Ray, xi, xvii, 148, 151, 156–57, 162
Anderson, Clara: acknowledging help, xix; early career, 52, 61, 118; performance practices, 156–57; performing with sister, 110, 120; theme song, 150; training quartets, 122; travel for performance, 85
Anderson, Queen C., 74, 143, 145, 181
anniversary programs, 158–59
Apollo Records, 35, 168
ARC (American Record Corporation), 168
Atlantic Records, 168
"The Atomic Telephone," 171

barbershops, 1, 9–10
Beale Street Jug Band, 89
Beans, Etherlene, xvii, 114, 118, 121, 135, 152, 158
Bells of Joy, 86
Benton, Brook, 35
Berlin Philharmonic, 159
Birmingham Jubilee Singers, xiv, 16, 18
Black Swan Records, 15
Blake, Grover, 64, 65, 85–86, 172
Bledsoe, Jethroe: Shirley Bledsoe, 110; broadcasting, 64; death of,

xvi; decline of professional quartets, 73–74; early career, 52; height of popularity, 170; packaged programs, 65; singing techniques, 69, 127; travel for performance, 62, 87
"Blessed are the Dead," 68
"Blind Bartimus," 149
Blues and Gospel Records 1902–1943, xi, 198
Blues & Rhythm: The Gospel Truth, xi, xiv
Boone, Pat, 139
Boyer, Horace, 145, 146
Bradford, Alex, 28, 30
Bremer, Frederika, 8
Brewster, W. Herbert: compositions, xi, 22, 66–68, 147, 190; conservative forces, 135; death of, xvi; East Trigg Baptist
Brewster, W. Herbert: compositions,Church, 142–43; essay about, xiii; gospel blues, 146; groups named after, 74, 90; passion plays, 140–41; symposium about, 197; themes, 144–46; WDIA, 181
Brewster Ensemble, 142
Brewster Singers, 74, 90, 182
Brewsteraires, 66, 90–91, 112, 142, 151, 171, 181
Broadnax, Willmer (Little Ax), 62, 170
Buchannan, Samuel, xi
Buffalo Booking Agency, 86, 173

Burnim, Mellonee, 159
Busyline Soft Singers, 46, 61, 110, 119

Cafe Society, 23
"Camp Meeting on the Air," 181
Campbell, Lucie: compositions, xi, 22, 66–67, 145–46; essay about, xiii; , 66–67; group named after, 142; life of, 138–40; national recognition, 190; themes, 143–44, 150, 152–53; symposium about, 197
Campbellaires, 85, 142
Capitol Records, 26
Cheeks, Julius, 28, 34
Chicago Defender, 85
"Chickasaw Train," 136
Christian Harmonizers, 89
Chudd, Lew, 35
City Quartette Union, 111–15, 125, 126
Clara Ward Singers, 74, 139, 143
Clark, Dave, 174–75
Columbia Records, 16, 18, 19, 21, 166–68
"Come, Lord Jesus, Abide with Me," 138
"Come on, Don't You Want to Go?," 49
Contests, 129–31
Cook, Will Marion, 3
Cooke, Sam, 33, 174

Darling, Elizabeth, 52, 110
Darling, James: City Quartette Union, 111; Elizabeth Darling, 110; death of, xx; early professional bookings, 50; Spirit of Memphis, 45, 62–63, 183; Southern Wonders, 69
Daugherty, Nina Jai, 142, 143, 182
Davis, Mary, 84, 135
De Luxe Records, 63, 169–70
Decca Records, 14
Designer Records, 75
"Diminuendo and Crescendo in Blue," 159
Dinwiddie Colored Quartet, 11–12, 19, 189
Dixie Hummingbirds: performance style, 160; professional status, 37, 71, 125; recordings by, 180; touring, 30, 64–65, 158; Ira Tucker, 28

Dixie Nightingales: Goodwill Revue, 151; origins, 110, 123; professional status, 70; radio broadcasts, 84–85, 184; recording, 176; regional orientation, 89
Dixie Wonders, 74–75, 89
Dorsey, Thomas A.: book about, xiii–xiv; compositions, 22, 24, 139, 142, 190; gospel blues, 146; influence of, 153; National Convention of Gospel Choirs and Choruses, 111; popularity, 66
Dortch, Sammie, 69
Dranes, Arizona, 147
drive section (performance), 148
Duke Records, 35, 65, 166, 171–78

Excelsior Quartet, 14

Fairfield Four, 25, 30, 65
Famous Blue Jay Singers: early professional status, 22, 24, 50–51; National Quartet Convention, 114; performance style, 33; Silas Steele, 29, 62
Fisk Jubilee Quartet, 12
Fisk University (Nashville, Tenneessee), 4, 36
Fisk University Jubilee Singers, xi, 4–7, 134, 197
Five Blind Boys of Alabama, 29, 32, 33, 37
Five Blind Boys of Mississippi, 18, 86, 125
Foster, R. C., 18
Fountain, Clarence, 32
Four Kings of Harmony, 89
Franklin, Jack, 52, 63, 85–86, 157, 172–73
Frost, "Doctor," 111, 114, 126
Funk, Ray, xi, xix, 17

Gableaires, 70
Gaines, Haywood, 43
Gary, Doris Jean, 52, 71, 111
Gennett Records, 15
Gluck, Christoph Willibald, 134
"God's Chariot," 175
Golden Gate Quartet: KWAM, 180; Middle Atlantic States, 27; Norfolk, 14, 17; performing in Memphis, 50; performance style, 22–23, 68; popularity of, 23–25;

recording, 168; repertoire, 144; research about, xi; white audiences, 189
Golden Stars, 52, 61, 82, 85, 110, 120
Goodwill Revue (WDIA), 150–51, 184
gospel blues form, 146
Gospel Harmonettes, xv
Gospel Records, 1943–1969: A Black Music Discography, xii
"Gospel Writer Boys Are We," 48
Gospel Writer Junior Boys, 110
Gospel Writers, 188; building churches, 150; bylaws, 116; celestial song title, 91; disbanding in 1950s, 123; expanding audience, 52; performance style, 148, 155, 161; performing in the 1980s, 47–49, 75, 132
Greenwich, Sonny, 146

Hallelujah Records, 63, 169
Hampton Institute Quartette, 6, 10–11, 35, 189
Hampton Roads (Virginia Tidewater), 13–15, 17, 42, 129
Hampton University, 6, 8, 197
The Harmonizers: celestial song title, 91; Hershell McDonald, 152; performance style, 159–60; repertoire, 47–48; singing style, 49; travel for performance, 84
Harmonizing Four of Richmond, 30, 37, 48, 65
Harmony Four, 44
Harps of Melody: Clara Anderson, 111; broadcasting, 179; bylaws, 116–17; celestial song title, 91; longevity, 188; lyrical themes, 149–50; musical ministry, 72, 74; performance location, 82; performance style, 48–49, 156–57; performing in the 1980s, 47; recording, 176; training, 120
Michael Harris, xiii, xiv
Harris, Robert, 62
Harvey, James, 46, 52, 63, 118, 122
Hayes, Roland, 8
"He Understands; He'll Say 'Well Done,'" 153
"He's Worthy," 147, 153, 155
Heavenly Gospel Singers, xiv, 25, 168
"Heavenly Sunshine," 138, 152

"Hide Me in Thy Bosom," xiii
High Water Records, 47–48, 153, 177
Highway QC's, 35, 65
"Highway to Heaven," 91
Hinton, Joe, 173
Hollywood Specials, 42
Holy Ghost Spirituals, 91, 137, 147, 150
holy spirit (in performances), 153–56
"Home in the Sky," 91
Humming Four Quartet of New Orleans, 16

"I am Bound for the Promised Land," 91
"I am Happy in the Service of the Lord," 63, 67, 169–70
I.C. Glee Club Quartet: formation, 42–44; geographical orientation, 90–91; musical style, 47–48, 67, 136; radio broadcasts, 84, 178; recording, 118, 167
"I Feel Something Drawing Me On," 153
"I Need Thee," 47
"I Shall Not Be Moved," 47
"I'll Fly Away," 49
"I'm Climbing Higher and Higher," 144
"I'm Going Home on the Chickasaw Train," 47
"I'm Leaning on the Everlasting Arms," 47, 49
"I'm on My Way to the Kingdom Land," 23
Imperial Records, 36
"In the Upper Room with My Lord," 152

Jackson, Irene V., xiii
Jackson, Joyce, xi, 136, 152, 157, 159–60
Jackson, Mahalia, 28, 34, 68, 74, 143
Jefferson County, Alabama, 15–18, 42, 52
Jeter, Claude, 32, 34
Johnson, James Weldon, 9, 141
Johnson, Willie, 14, 22, 68
Jolly Sunshine Boosters Club Quartet, 61, 84, 118, 121
Jones, Elijah: contests, 129–31; Gospel Writer Junior Boys, 110; Gospel Writers, 46–49, 75, 162; training, 118–19, 121–22, 156

Jones Brothers Quartet, 70
Jordan Wonders, 71, 87, 148
Jubilee Hummingbirds, 70, 74–75
Juke Blues, xiv
"Just to Behold His Face," 67, 144

King Records, 26, 170
"The King's Highway," 138, 143
KWAM, 185
KWEM, 126, 177–81

Larks, 35
Little Ax. *See* Broadnax
"The Lord is My Shepherd," 138
"Lord Jesus," 69, 72, 170
Loudin, Frederick J., 5

Majestic Soft Singers, 72, 84, 112–13
Malone, Earl: early career, 52; mentor, 132; popular music, 173; recording, 169, 171; singing style, 68; Silas Steele, 72; thanks to, xix
Martin, Roberta, xiii, 30, 139
Martin, Sallie, 142
Mason's Temple: performance venue (post–WW II), 65, 73, 124, 143, 166, 190; recording in, 72, 170; song battles, 130
Mattis, David, 175–76
Maultsby, Portia, xiii
May, Brother Joe, 30
McDonald, Hershell, 152
"Meet Me in Gloryland," 49
Memphis World, 65
Middle Baptist Quartet, 46, 90, 122, 188
"Milky White Way," 91
Miller, Gus, 44–46, 118–19, 121–22, 131
Miller, Jack, 44, 46, 120
Mills Brothers, 10
minstrel shows, 1–3
Mitchell's Christian Singers, xi, 25, 168
Moody, Leon, 121, 127
Moore, Huddie, 114, 118, 172, 151, 177
Morris, Kenneth, xiii, 22, 139, 142
Mount Olive Wonders, 42, 44
"Move On Up a Little Higher," 67, 141, 143–44
"My Life is in His Hands," 63
"My Lord is Writing," 49
"My Lord's Gonna Move This Wicked Race," 20

Nashboro Records, 176
National Quartet Convention, 82, 114–15
Neal, Willie, 110, 125, 144, 155
Nelson, Ford, 158, 182–83
"New Born Soul," 49, 148, 161
"Ninety-Nine and a Half Won't Do," 137, 150
Norfolk Journal and Guide, 6
Norfolk Jubilee/Jazz Quartet, xi, xiv, xv, 13–15, 18, 20, 169
North Memphis Singing Union, 112

OKeh Records, 14–15, 19, 21, 42, 90, 147, 167
"Old Landmark," 67, 135, 147
"Old Time Religion," 48
"On the Battlefield for my Lord," 66
Orange Mound Specials, 81–82, 89
Original Tennesseans, 4
"Our God is Able," 144

"Packing Up," 144
"Panama to Chi," 47, 178
Paramount Records, 14, 19–21
Pattersonaires: Reverend Brewster, 143, 155; community base, 132; Willie Gordan, 111; gospel meter, 68; naming of, 84, 90; recording, 153; vamps, 146
"Peace in the Valley," 47, 66
Peacock Records, 26, 33, 35, 69, 86, 166, 171–78
Pentecostal church (influence upon performance style), 147, 154, 190
Perkins, Frank, 71
Phillips, Sam, 168, 171
Philwood Records, 75
Pilgrim Travelers: Memphis performances, 50; New Orleans performance, 27, 33; performance style, 158; professional touring, 29–30, 65; Lou Rawls, 35; recordings of, xv
Pilgrim Spirituals, 85, 89
Polk Miller's Old South Quartette, 12
Porterfield, Gilbert, 16–17
"Precious Lord," 66

"A Quartette Rehearsal," 11–12

radio broadcasting, 20–21
Rainey, Gertrude "Ma," 3
Rawls, Lou, 35

Readers, Julius, 69–71, 87, 130
Reed, Robert, 52, 68, 161, 169
Regis Records, 26
Rejoice!, xiv
"Riding on the Seminole Train," 47, 49
The Rise of Gospel Blues: The Music of Thomas Andrew Dorsey in the Urban Church, xiii
Robey, Don, 35, 65, 171–78
"Roll, Jordan, Roll," 12, 48–49, 137, 141
"Rollin' Through an Unfriendly Land," 19, 48
Rooks, George: Elijah Jones, 48, 119, 156; "new" Gospel Writers, 75; performance style, 148, 161–62; thanks to, xix
Royal Harmony Four: community-based group, 61; early group sound, 47; longevity, 37, 44–45, 74; performance context, 124; recording, 176
Rubman, Kerrill, 13
Ruffin, Elijah: death of, xvi; early days, 79; Harmonizers, 75; performance style, 137; thanks to, xix; trainer, 48, 118–19, 122, 159
Ruth, Thurmon, 13, 30

sacred plays, 139–41
Satterfield, Cleo, 110, 113
Satterfield, Louis, 110
Savage, Avery, 78–79
Savoy Records, 26
"Search Me, Lord," xiii
Selah Jubilee Singers, xi, 13, 25–26, 30
Sensational Nightingales, 28, 30, 34, 65
sermonettes, 157, 161
Seroff, Doug, xi, 5, 7, 31, 110, 181, 184
shape note singing, 10
Silver Leaf Quartette of Norfolk, 14, 20, 36
"Sing and Make Melody unto the Lord," 49, 150, 157
"Singing in the Spirit—African American Sacred Quartets in New York, xii
"Sleep on, Mother," 14
"Something Within," 138
Songbirds of the South: beginnings, 52, 123; Doris Jean Gary, 111; geographical orientation, 89; ra-
dio broadcasting, 84, 183–85; travel for performance, 71
Sons of Jehovah, 68, 70, 85, 89, 151, 176
Soul Stirrers: National Quartet Convention, 114; national recognition, xv, 22, 30; performance practices, 160; performing in Memphis, 50; physical movement, 24, 65; professional status, 37; Sam Cooke, 33
South Memphis Singing Union, 112
Southern Bells, 89
Southern Harmony Boys, 89
Southern Jubilees: geographical orientation, 89; KWAM, 179; professional status, 74; recording, 171; travel for performance, 81; Floyd Wiley, 157
Southern Wonders: cross-over, 172–73; disbanding, 74; Jack Franklin, 157; James Harvey, 52; Pet Milk Company, 182; professional status, 63–69; travel patterns, 85–86, 89; WDIA, 184
Specialty Records, 33
Spencer, Jon Michael, xiv
Spirit of Memphis Quartette: Jet Bledsoe, 127; celestial song title, 91; early career, 42, 45–46; Joe Hinton, 35; live recording, 72; Earl Malone, 132; physical movement, 85, 97, 89; professional status, 30, 37, 51–52, 61–69, 85, 87, 89, 125
Spiritual Four, 177
Spiritual Pilgrims, 71, 82, 87, 112, 113
Spiritual Travelers, 69–70, 85
Standard Negro Quartete of Chicago, 12, 19
"Steal Away," 48
Steele, Silas: Famous Blue Jay Singers, 24, 28; joining Spirit of Memphis, 62; lead singing, 69, 72, 127, 170; performance style, 154, 157–58, 161
Sterling Jubilees, 37
Sun Records, 168, 171
Sunset Travelers: celestial song title, 91; professional status, 64; recording, 65–66, 172; travel for performance, 85–86; WDIA, 184; O. V. Wright, 173

"Surely, God is Able," 67–68, 143
Swan Silvertone Singers, 26, 28, 32, 34, 65, 170
"Swing Down, Chariot," 67–68, 147
switch leading, 24

"Take My Hand, Precious Lord," xiii
"Take Your Burden to the Lord," 66
Taylor, Little Johnny, 35
Tharpe, Sister Rosetta, 28, 68
themes in gospel compositions, 141–45
Theomusicology: A Journal of Black Sacred Music, xiv
Tindley, Rev. C. Albert, xiii, 145, 190
Todd, Tommie, xvii, 127, 150, 152
"Touch Me, Lord Jesus," 152
training of quartets, 118–23
"Trampin'," 48
"Travelin' Shoes," 68
Tri-State Defender, 65, 184
Trumpeteers, 29, 180
Tucker, Ira, 28

United Singing Union, 112, 113, 115, 125
"Up Above My Head, I Hear Music in the Air," 48, 155

vamp (harmonic), 146
Veteran Jubilees, 162
Victor Records, 16, 19, 90, 166, 168
Vocalion Records, 16

Wade, Theo, 44, 51, 126, 182
"Wade in the Water," 48
Wafford, Lillian, 112–13
Walton, "Cousin" Eugene, 126, 174, 179–80

Ward, Clara, 143
Ward Singers, 30
WDIA: Rev. Brewster, 142; 50,000 watts, 64; "Goodwill Revue," 150; history of, 177–79; David Mattis, 175; Ford Nelson, 158; Sunday performances, 75, 166; Theo Wade, 126, 181–85
Weaver, R. L., 63, 69
Welk, Lawrence, 139
We'll Understand It Better By and By, xii, xiii
WEVL, 185
WHBQ, 178
Whilfarht, Whoopie John, 30
Wiley, Floyd, 81–82, 110, 115, 157
Williams, Bert, 3
Willing Four Soft Singers, 74, 89, 114, 118, 152
Wills, Bob and the Texas Playboys, 30
WIS, 23
"Wish I Was in Heaven Sitting Down," 66, 68, 91
WLAC, 25
WLOK, 178, 185
WMC, 178
WMPS, 178
Wooten, Style, 176–77
WPTF, 26
WREC, 178
WREG-TV, 75
Wright, O. V., 35, 69, 173
WSMS, 185

"You May Talk About Jerusalem Morning," 12

Zion Hill Spirituals, 78–79, 81, 82

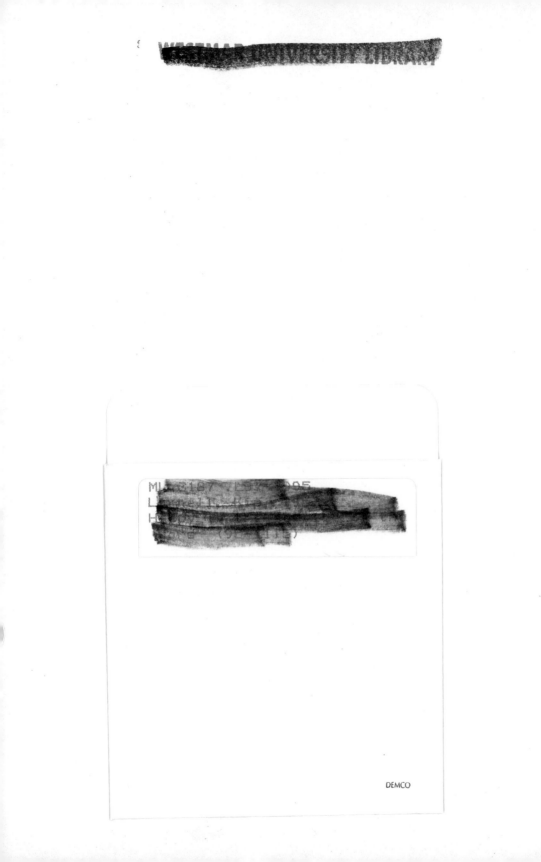